YORKSHIRE HERITAGE

HARRY J. SCOTT

Yorkshire Heritage

Illustrated and with map

ROBERT HALE · LONDON

© *Harry J. Scott* 1970
First published in Great Britain 1970
Reprinted with amendments 1973

ISBN 0 7091 1621 7

Robert Hale & Company
63 Old Brompton Road
London S.W.7

Printed in Great Britain by
Redwood Press Limited
Trowbridge, Wiltshire

Contents

ACKNOWLEDGEMENTS

The author is indebted to the following for the photographic illustrations: Mr John Edenbrow of Leeds, for numbers 1, 2, 4, 5, 10, 14, 16, 17, 18, 19, 20, 21, 22, 23, 26, 27, 28, 29, 30, 31, 32; Mr W. R. Mitchell of Settle, for 3, 6, 7, 8, 13, 15, 24, 25, 33; Mr L. Jackson of Heswall, for 9. Numbers 11 and 12 are from Walker's *Costumes of Yorkshire* (1814), and numbers 34 and 36 are by courtesy of Leeds Public Library.

Illustrations

By Way of Preamble

One need not travel far in Yorkshire to become aware of the richness of the county's heritage. For thirty years I lived in a small village in the Yorkshire Dales. The stone walls of my home were four feet thick and at some time long past had been part of a farm building, probably the 'house place'. On the walls outside were ancient lamp brackets which once probably lighted the way to the stables. Leading out of one room was a rounded arch cut in the thickness of what had been an outside wall, and this led into a large drawing room containing a fireplace of Dent 'marble', the black, fossil-veined limestone first worked in Dentdale in the seventeenth century. All the lower floors of the house were of slate, and in the garden was a large water-tank built of immense slabs of slate quarried in Ribblesdale.

The village itself dated back to Anglian times. Its first settlers may have given the name Clapdale to the narrow limestone rift carrying the mountain stream on which the village stands, and then Clapham to their first settlement upon it, for it all derived from the Middle English 'clappe', meaning 'noise'. It is still a noisy beck in flood time. On a hillside just outside the village are the remains of early 'lynchets' – terraced strips of land which was the earliest form of organised cultivation and continued into medieval times. After the Angles had settled and made it their 'ham' or homestead, Norse invaders reached these parts and a couple of miles to the east of Clapham established their 'wick' or farmstead, which they called East-wick, now the village of Austwick.

If this were not heritage enough we could go further back to Romano-British times when the Romans left this country to the mercy of all comers and the natives had no strong arm to

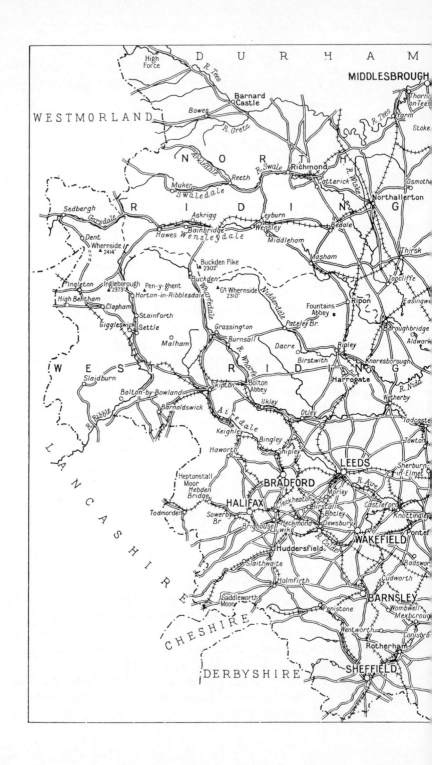

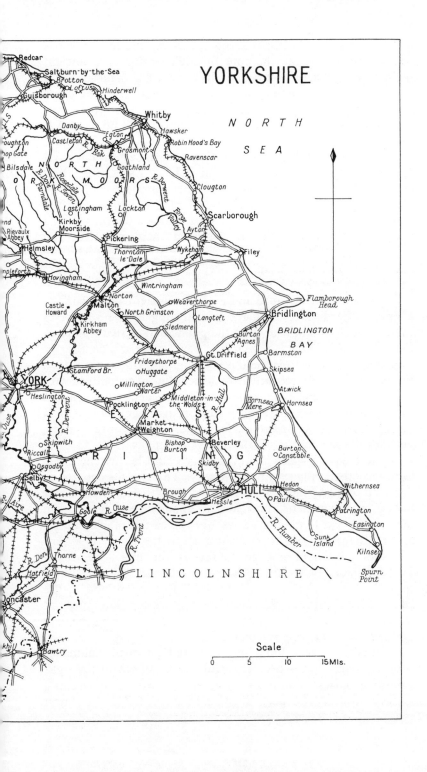

YORKSHIRE

defend them. Many sought refuge in caves, and in the woods behind the village at the foot of Ingleborough are ancient shelter caves where excavations have revealed signs of early habitation. A later name of Foxholes suggests that the caves had other residents later. On Ingleborough itself there was probably a Roman signal station and on its slopes are Iron Age sites.

A village church has existed in Clapham since Norman days, and its present tower was built when Henry I was king. High on the fells which form a background to the place is Clapdale Hall, the home at one time of the Claphams, who owned the manor. When I first went to live in the village old inhabitants told me of regular fairs they remembered when every street (up to my own front door) had its sheep and cattle pens, and buyers and sellers gathered from all over the country. The market charter dated back to 1201.

There was much, much more of this ancient patchwork of history to be discovered. Caves penetrating into the heart of Ingleborough and now open to the public had existed unknown for thousands of years. When they were explored a century or so ago they revealed marvellous stalagmitic formations. An old toll bar house, only recently demolished, linked the village with the days of the first turnpike road. Almost every cottage garden today has in it descendants of plants brought back from travels in the East by Reginald Farrer, whose rock garden in the grounds of Ingleborough Hall was world famous.

What I have written of this village could be matched in a hundred other villages in the county. There is history at the doorstep of all of them, and when you add the contribution of historic cities, ancient industries, an abundance of rivers from mountain becks to great seaways, abbeys, castles, noble houses, and the long line of the Yorkshire coast, the legacy is almost boundless. I would not go so far as the man – he was a Yorkshireman, of course – who once told me, "When you've seen Yorkshire you've seen England." But if you add to the legacy I have outlined Yorkshire sport, Yorkshire humour, and those three Yorkshire products of cloth, coal and steel, he may not have been far from the truth.

"Yorkshire", said John Speed the tailor turned mapmaker 350 years ago, "presents delightful varieties both to the sight and other senses," and in so saying he summed up the essential feature of what the poet Michael Drayton called the "most renowned of shires". One cannot journey about this county of over 6,000 square miles – almost as large as Wales – bounded so completely by the Tees in the north, by 120 miles of coastline in the east, by the Humber and Don in the south, and the Pennine barrier on the west – without being aware of its infinite variety, whether of natural features or of the handiwork of man.

Yorkshire folk for the most part take this for granted. To them this is a broad land of broad acres intended by nature to be more than a county, rather a world to itself with a broad diversity which becomes almost self-sufficiency in the essentials of a good life not shared by less-favoured counties. Many a Yorkshire exile has boasted in far lands of the manifold richness of his home territory: sheep on the hills and an abundance of minerals beneath the ground, rich farms on the plains and wolds and a multitude of manufactories in the industrial valleys, the age-old industry of bringing fish from the sea and the modern production of chemicals along the river estuaries. All this against a background of ancient abbeys and castles, lonely fells and remote moors and dales, historic architecture side by side with new universities and modern housing estates. It is a county of which to be proud. Yet it must be admitted that there are moments when one wonders if Yorkshire folk at home, for all their aggressive loyalty, are not insensitive of the riches which are their heritage. So much is ignored or forgotten in these days when we speed through our land more concerned with miles per gallon than the panorama of the landscape.

This is not an inanimate unchanging county with a fixed pattern of set ways, moulded only by its stony structure, its climate, or even by government decree. There is some other quality which breaks through and provides a living thread. It can be found in the fascination of map-reading, in the thrill of every historical event, in the quickening of the imagination in every human encounter. Just as every journey along a modern Yorkshire motorway can bring its reminder of the coach road which preceded it, of the Roman road which underlies it, of the cart track, the footpath and the sheep track which came before, so a pile of ruins in a field, a maypole on a village green, an ancient ceremony still observed, a craftsman's way with the tools of his trade, are all part of the human heritage which underlies it all and in which Yorkshire is so richly diverse.

Amid all this vast diversity of Yorkshire a striking thing is its unity. History, through the Scandinavian settlement, gave it the unusual pattern of division into three Ridings, originally Thirdings – North, East and West – each now with its county council, its lord lieutenant, magistrates and until recently its own constabulary. There are twenty-six wapentakes, again a Scandinavian legacy, still having a minor administrative application. There are seven cities, over twenty municipal boroughs and many urban and rural district councils, as well as parish councils and meetings. Yet, despite its area, its vast population and its complicated pattern of local government, its people never forget they are 'Yorkshire', which is something which confers on them a certain virtue, if not always an obligation.

It was a dream of Sir Bernard Kenyon, for over a quarter of a century Clerk to the West Riding County Council, that the Royal Commission on Local Government would propose "one Yorkshire", as a single organ of government for the county. "I should like to see established a first-tier unit of local government covering the whole of the geographical county of Yorkshire," he said, "for this would provide for future developments based on a defined area whose roots go deep into the history of England."

There are many ways of looking at this county. Topographically we would begin with the stripling rivers and the famous dales down which they run, plunging over falls and through potholes in their exciting youth before achieving their middle-age spread and becoming sedate and portly streams, often dirtied by their touch with commerce. Or if this were a history of the county we would begin in the Stone Age, with its flint implements, its lake dwellings and its first steps in agriculture, and proceed along that broadening way of kings and kingdoms, of castles and battles, of plottings and achievements which might end, for the moment, with the early warning station of the Radar Age, whose monstrous evidence with its spheres and its masts stand today on the Fylingdale moors within sight of the Stone Age burial mounds. Or we could journey through the industrial progress of Yorkshire from its open fields and wool-producing sheep, its mines, its mills and its factories, to the vast chemical complexes which mark the Technological Age. The subject matter is rich and ample as befits the largest county and has already attracted writers of mighty tomes and miniscule guide books. And I have already added to them. This is none of these. Rather it is a notebook of some of those human aspects of that rich heritage wherein personalities and people loom large amid places and things, in which their passions and humours, their customs and manners, their oddities of character and of speech, can be gathered up before they and their meaning have been forgotten. Against the background of their scenery, their homes and their industry, I would rediscover their ghosts and their realities, their aspirations and their achievements, and some of those tangible survivals of the past which are part of the fabric of Yorkshire today. Free from the shackles of ordered topography or the stern sequence of history we may roam at will over the nearly 4 million acres which in their variety constitute the county.

Yet I would add a warning. In this book we are looking at the background of Yorkshire as it has been built up over the centuries. But even as I write the pattern is changing again. It is becoming more complex as it becomes more mechanical, more uniform as the old distinctions between town and country and class and class vanish, more subtopian as the green fields and coloured moors give way to brick and stone and concrete. The old Yorkshire speech remains, but that which is spoken about is different from what it was thirty years ago. Outwardly the appearance of people is largely unchanged in town and country but their attitude to life is moulded more by external influences and less by inner conviction.

The rural Yorkshireman's 'shop talk' is still about the land, farming and the weather, but that land is no longer kept in good heart by the old method of muck-spreading by hand; it is done by mechanical spreaders. The old ways of haytime and harvest are transformed by machinery. Milking is an electrically performed task, the product is pasteurized, the dairy output is collected by road tankers. When I recently asked an old dalesman in my village what the weather was going to be he replied, "Nay, Ah can't tell thee. Ah haven't heard t'wireless yet." Down the road as I left him were newly-erected posts defining the course of a new by-pass that will avoid the old hump-backed bridge over the stream. What was once the cultivated garden of the 'great house' is now converted into a car park.

In one sense it is not new. It has all happened before. The term 'carucate' was once a unit of valuation, based on the area which could be ploughed by a team of eight oxen in a year, probably about 120 acres on easy arable land, but only a hundred acres of rough stony land. It was often estimated, of course, for the unit was used for land which was never ploughed. A sub-division of the 'carucate' was a 'bovate', which was the area one ox of the team of eight could have ploughed and was sometimes called an 'oxgang'. Besides being a unit of valuation it was a measure applied by a farmer to his land. Then, as oxen gave way to horses, a man would regard his ploughland as a one-horse or two-horse field and measure his needs accordingly. Now he thinks in terms of what a tractor can do in a fraction of the time, and it may well be that a tractor or other propelled machine will become an accepted standard of measurement.

The farm man appears to be much like his predecessors down the years, save that he may now wear overalls instead of an ancient coat or a smock. But that change of garb is significant. He has become a highly-skilled mechanic with probably more knowledge of machinery and plant, diesel engines and motorised equipment than his counterpart in the factory. His wife has a home with a washing machine, an electric cooker, a vacuum cleaner, and probably an electric hair-dryer. The ancient 'side boiler' may still be built into the fireplace of her cottage, but she is in rebellion if she has not a supply of constant hot water from another source.

In the industrial areas, too, there are mills with creches staffed by nurses, pit-head baths for miners, air-conditioned workrooms, houses with every 'mod-con', sophisticated clubs offering London 'stars' in stage shows, bingo sessions both afternoon and evening, and, for the more ambitious, regular classes and courses offering every subject from housecraft to art. Local lore and traditional customs are forgotten in the new world introduced by televsion.

Even the ancient broad acres themselves are undergoing change. The motor age is bringing more tourism and more traffic to the remotest moors and dales, with a demand for more and wider roads where once were quiet stone-walled lanes and green tracks. A vast increase in quarrying for limestone and roadstone, with its accompaniment of heavy traffic, smoke and dust is scarring the landscape. Many who once worked on the farms now look to the quarries for employment, while new labour is brought in from the urban areas. Cities and towns are

CONTRASTS: *1, Blackstone Edge*

being redesigned and rebuilt so that historic properties are vanishing almost overnight to be replaced by giant office buildings, monstrous blocks of flats and miles of new motorways.

What, then, will be the outcome? Will this heritage of Yorkshire crumble away to leave only a mechanised region indistinguishable in a general uniformity of pattern, with our history a shadow play, exciting at times but insubstantial. Or will that living thread to which I have referred continue unbroken? Thin though it may seem, like a fisherman's line which can bring to land a mighty weight. I have hope that the human thread which has run through all Yorkshire history will hold for many generations yet to give this county a distinctive character and place, for, as George Orwell said of England when he wrote in the dark days of 1941, it is "an everlasting animal, stretching into the future and the past, and, like all living things, having the power to change out of recognition and yet remain the same".

CONTRASTS: *2, Docks at Hull*

1
Ways In

A car drew up at the kerbside of a Yorkshire village and the driver called to an elderly farmer.

"Am I right for York?" he asked.

"Nay," said the farmer. "You're as wrong as you could be and, what's more, if I were you I wouldn't start from here."

Many beckoning corners of Britain are not easy to reach. The bracing north-east corner of Scotland is one and the delightful south-west corner that is Galloway is another; the first because of its distance from the south and the other because the traveller will not make the required left-hand turn at Gretna Green but goes straight on to the Highlands. Similarly, the sky-dominated landscape of East Anglia is unknown to many North Country folk because of its inaccessibility which recent railway policy has not improved. The English Lake District was for long hard of entry until a new motorway brought tens of thousands hurrying to its delights.

It is the good fortune of Yorkshire that it has many doorsteps, at all points of the compass, as befits its vast extent. And most of them are historic ways in. You may enter it from the south through Bawtry and on to Doncaster, as so many coach travellers and wayfarers did in the old days – being careful as you do so not to emulate the saddler of Bawtry who was hanged for leaving his liquor. A story of last century tells why. It relates that outside York, there was formerly a hostelry called the 'Gallows House' at which the cart carrying the condemned to execution always stopped to enable him to have a final drink. A saddler from Bawtry was making this last 'journey', but the rash and precipitate saddler, under sentence and on his road to the fatal tree, refused this little regale and hastened on to the place of execution, where, very soon after he was 'turn'd off', a reprieve arrived. Had he stopped, as was usual, at the Gallows House, the time consumed there would have been the means of saving his life. So the saddler of Bawtry became a warning against impatience.

In these days you may pass impatiently into Yorkshire along the Great North Road and scarcely notice Bawtry, yet this was once the county's front door, at which royal visitors were received in state. When Henry VIII visited Yorkshire after the Pilgrimage of Grace he was met at Bawtry by "200 gentlemen of the county in velvet and 4000 tall yeomen and serving men well-horsed". It was a stopping place for kings, pilgrims and armies alike, a market for commerce in and out of the county and a notable haunt of highwaymen who were reputed to be in league with all the ostlers in the town.

Evidence of the historic importance of this corner of Yorkshire can be seen nearby in the early Norman mount-and-bailey castle at Tickhill and the beautifully sited Cistercian abbey of Roche. Tickhill, under its earlier name of Blyth, was one of the first castles to be founded in Yorkshire by the Conqueror to consolidate his power, and it was vested in Roger de Busli who probably completed its building. An old drawing in the Records of the Duchy of Lancaster show it to be an impressive edifice with tower, walls, gatehouse, moat and drawbridge – a small boy's idea of a castle – but this was a later version after the original structure had been largely demolished in the Civil War. Only fragments of the Norman building remain. Of no less interest to the small boy is that this is reputed to be one of the five places in England where royal jousting tournaments were held. Roche Abbey was founded by the Cistercians in 1147 in a narrow valley where wandering monks discovered a natural crucifix in the rocks, hence its name. Destruction at the dissolution of the monasteries was more thorough here than usual, for even the choir stalls were burned to melt the lead from the roof.

When that lively seventeenth-century traveller, Miss Celia Fiennes, came this way she did not feel she was really into the county until she reached Doncaster, nine miles beyond Bawtry. "Here", she wrote, "Yorkshire beginns and here the Musick wellcom'd us into Yorkshire."

Our next threshold is what might be called the 'business entrance', linking industrial Lancashire and industrial Yorkshire. This enters over Blackstone Edge between Rochdale and

Halifax and is old enough in time to have begun as a packhorse track climbing grimly to the bleak 1,475-foot crossing. Over it in pony-borne loads must have been carried goods from both sides of the Pennines during many centuries, and the old track can still be seen. Then it changed to a new route as a coach road, faster but still hazardous for both horses and vehicles. Finally it has become a modern A58 highway with easier gradients and speedier traffic, to round off the evolution of this bleak entry. In recent years there has been considerable controversy over whether or not there was also a Roman road across this desolate moorland – a paved causeway of Roman type exists but other evidence is lacking, although flint implements of a much earlier time have been found on these hills.

It was of a similar edge not far away that the late C. E. Montague wrote of "the moorland slopes sinewy and knotty with the twisted and notched roots that are still left of the chase where Garth and Wamba talked together when Yorkshire was still roamed by droves of swine". A less romantic description was that of Taylor, the water poet in the reign of James I, who wrote: "I rode over such ways as were past comparison or amendment, for when I went over a lofty mountain called Blackstone Edge, I thought myself in the land of break-neck, it was so very steep and tedious." Even Daniel Defoe, making a journey from Rochdale to Halifax many years later, was dismayed when in the midst of a blinding snowstorm during the ascent there came "a surprising clap of thunder, the first that ever I heard in a storm of snow or, I hope, ever shall". Much travelled though he was, he wrote in his *Tour Through Great Britain*: "From Blackstone Edge to Halifax is eight miles; and all the way, except from Sowerby to Halifax, is this up hill and down; so that, I suppose, we mounted up to the clouds and descended to the water level about eight times in that little part of the journey."

Nowhere else, not even on the high fells of the west, do you get such a vivid sense of the Pennines as 'the backbone of England' as on this bleak edge which separates the two sides of the country. It really is a spine. The crossing today, with all the advantages of modern road works and high-powered cars, can still be an unpleasant ordeal in winter.

Should you wilt at the thought of so much bleakness, there is another entrance from Lancashire and the south-west through Gisburn and Skipton – which sometimes calls itself 'the gateway to the Dales'. So much a border village is Gisburn that, although actually in Yorkshire, it is administered from the rural district office in Lancashire's Clitheroe. I once counted nearly a dozen hotels, cafes and other places of refreshment and restoration for the weary motorist in the single street of this village of less than 400 people. Travellers have long been entering this way, and many of the hotels still have stable accommodation, now usually converted into garages but in one case at least still maintained for housing hunters owned by the Pendle Forest Harriers.

Horses bred in the district, and the regular market for farm stock, provide a strong agricultural and sporting atmosphere, perhaps not unexpected when you remember that this was once part of a very considerable estate owned by the Lords Ribblesdale of Gisburn Park. The first of those lords is reputed to have planted over a million oak trees in this stretch of the Ribble valley, another maintained stags for hunting, and the fourth and last used always to carry his stirrup leathers in his bag when he travelled, being too keen a horseman to risk borrowed leathers. King Edward nick-named this last owner of Gisburn 'The Ancestor' because of his dignified appearance, but alas he was the end of his line. At one time white cattle, like those which can be seen at Chillingham in Northumberland, were reared in Gisburn Park. I believe that the only difference between the two herds was that the Gisburn cattle were hornless. The last of them were killed off about a hundred years ago.

Close by is the great hill of Pendle, visible from deep into Lancashire as well as from the remote western hills of Yorkshire. It has looked down during long years of history on armies marching and counter-marching at its foot, on conflicts between Puritans and Papists, and on a rather doleful period when Pendle Hill was the home of much witchcraft and local characters like 'Mother Demdike' were feared and talked about in whispers. This part of the Ribble valley is still well-wooded and pastoral, and I recall many delightful journeys on what was then a naturally 'scenic railway' when the old line through Clitheroe and the baronial-style station at Gisburn linked this way into Yorkshire with Hellifield, Settle and the Dales country. Of late years there were never enough passengers to fill even the few compartments of the little train, and where there are no passengers there are no trains. The line is closed and the rails are torn up.

A way of entry into Yorkshire known to the Norsemen was by the crossing of the western Pennines. Theirs was a roundabout journey. They sailed from Norway by way of Orkney, Shetland and Northern Ireland, and came round or over the Pennines into the southern Lake District, across to the Dales and Stainmore, and down into Craven and the Calder valley. Today there are modern roads from Lancaster and from Kendal, but they still follow the line of earlier roads which linked Chester and Lancaster with York, and the Lakeland area with Keighley and the Aire valley. Some of these roads carry evidence of their turnpike days in the little well-windowed toll-houses along the roadside, although these become fewer each year.

It is still possible on this western side of Yorkshire to find evidence of that early Norse invasion, and even of the Celtic people before them. Mainly, of course, in the place names. Penyghent, Pen Hill, and the Chevin are mountain names and Wharfe, Derwent, and even Northumberland's Tyne are river names the Celts left. The Romans can show few traces apart from their roads, for this was to them a lost land of peat mosses, woodland and scrub. But the Norsemen liked these high fell lands and the valleys which divided them. There they set up their 'saetrs', where they pastured their stock, moving the cattle up the mountains in summer and into the valleys in winter. So we have Appersett, Burtersett and Countersett all within a few miles of each other today. In the Lake District and in Yorkshire are many Grisdales, from the Norse 'griss' – a pig. And if you travel to the top of Wharfedale you will come across the curiously named Yockenthwaite in a valley as romantic as its name. Here, one Eogan (an Irish name surely), had his 'thwaite' or clearing, as befits an Irish-Norse farmer.

Some of the earliest ways in on this side of the county must have had their origin in salt. It is difficult for us in these days of cold stores and refrigerators to appreciate the value of salt not merely as a condiment but as a means of preserving meat through the winter in times when stock was slaughtered in November to provide food until the spring. Salt from pans on the west coast and from salt workings in Cheshire was carried by pack-ponies across the Pennines on recognised salt-ways, many of which are now roads. They, too, have left their legacy in the place-names of Saltersgate, Salterforth, Salter Hebble and others.

Finally, Yorkshire's most northerly doorstep is at the end of that Great North Road which we came upon at Bawtry. It was at the appropriately named Scotch Corner that the roads coming in from Newcastle and Carlisle met. Here you are in an embattled corner of Yorkshire, where history lies thick upon the ground, and beneath you. A Roman road, Watling Street, ran from Scotch Corner to the fort at Greta Bridge, and the legions must often have marched this way. Their road is now under the modern highway. Nearby are the crumbling ruins of Ravensworth Castle to which Scott refers in *Rokeby*. A diversion from Rokeby itself will take you to an early Bronze Age route over Stainmore. And Dorothy Wordsworth came this way and stopped at Greta Bridge to note in her journal the beauty of the view. There is an odd link, too, with that western doorstep we have already crossed, for an ancient packhorse track named Jaggers Lane crosses the landscape here, having its northern start on the Tees and going right across country to the old port of Glasson Dock just below Lancaster.

Greta Bridge itself seems to have had a troubled existence. Leland came this way into Yorkshire in the sixteenth century and wrote of his journey: "From Egleston to Gretey Bridge of two or three arches, a two mile by pasture, corn and woode. Gretey is a village standing on Watheling Streate, and hath the name of Gretey ryver that runnith through it and by Mr. Rokeby's place goith ynto Tese." Although much money was spent on its repair, it collapsed under the stress of floods many times and for a time there was no bridge at all, only a ford which can still be seen at one side. Eventually the owner of Rokeby, Mr. J. B. S. Morritt, a High Sheriff of Yorkshire, built the present graceful single-arch bridge in 1774. It was constructed to carry the coaches of those days. It remained to carry the tanks of the last war and the heavy traffic of today.

As a sort of side entrance to this part of Yorkshire you can come in through Barnard Castle, a market town in character as well as name, with a fine large square and an ancient inn, the 'King's Head', where Charles Dickens stayed while collecting the background material for *Nicholas Nickleby*. The town itself has a finely picturesque situation on the north, or Durham, bank of the Tees, which means that it is not quite in York-shire – though this can be remedied by crossing the old bridge over the river, where you have a choice of ways to Gilling and

Scotch Corner or direct to Richmond and its castle. Either way you pass through Rokeby where lived Sir Walter Scott's friend, Mr. Morritt, and where the poet stayed and observed so much so closely that almost every cliff and stone and tree appeared in his poem:

> The cliffs
> Were now all naked, wild and grey,
> Now waving all with greenwood spray;
> Here trees to every crevice clung,
> And o'er the dell their branches hung;
> And there, all splinter'd and uneven,
> The shiver'd rocks ascend to heaven.

At Rokeby, too, you may be told the tale of the fiercest pig in the north of England. She (for it was a sow) lived in a wood between the Tees and the little river Greta, and no man could tame her, although many had been rolled in the mud or badly scarred in the attempt. One man, it was said, had been killed while attempting to capture her; but there may have been more, for an old ballad declares, of the wood.

> There were few that thither went
> That came out lyve away.

Sir Ralph of Rokeby, wearying of this beast on his land and being a man of crude humour, offered the sow to the Grey Friars of Richmond twelve miles distant – the remains of whose monastery can still be seen – if they would take it away. Three stalwart brethren came to collect the animal, dreaming doubtless of savoury additions to monastic fare, but their reception from the sow was hostile. They got a rope around her but she pulled them all round the wood, knocking them about in the process. They remembered St. Cuthbert and perhaps St. Francis of Assissi, and began reading the Scriptures to her, but presumably the sow knew no Latin. They made the sign of the Cross. The only result was to enrage the beast still further, and one of the brethren had to seek refuge in a tree. Let the ballad continue the story:

> This wicked beast that had wrought the woe
> Took the rope from the other two,
>   And then they fled all three.
> They fled away by Watling Streete,
> They had no succour but their feet,
>   It was the more pitye.

The end of the tale is disappointingly prosaic. The luckless friars brought in two knights who had fought in the Crusades, hired them (by the hour or by the piece?) to kill the Felon Sow and bring the body to the monastery, where the brethren celebrated the event:

> When they saw the Felon come
> They sange merrilye Te Deum
> The Friars every one.

One hopes they enjoyed many good breakfasts afterwards.

These, of course, are not the only ways into Yorkshire. My copy of Murray's *Handbook for Travellers in Yorkshire*, dated 1874, recommends the start of a month's walking tour in the county with the words "London to Hull by steamer", which is a far cry from the way of entry by the old coach roads, the new motorways, or the way of the modern air traveller.

Mr. Walter White, a Londoner, who visited the county nearly twenty years earlier and wrote a delightful account of his travels under the title *A Month in Yorkshire*, came this way. His vessel he described as "not a very sprightly boat but enjoys or not, as the case may be, a reputation for safety, and for sleeping-cabins narrower and more stifling than any I ever crept into. But one must not expect too much when the charge for a voyage of twenty-six hours is only six and sixpence in the chief cabin."

As county pride is not unknown among Yorkshiremen you will almost certainly be told that how you arrive matters less than the discovery that it is not exclusively a county of coal mines, mill chimneys, slag heaps and utilitarian living, and that it can offer a variety of scene, place and people unequalled south of the border. Whichever way you enter, vastness and variety are its outstanding characteristics, with a basic solidity in everything from its landscape to its people. It is, of course, an industrial county, but this industry is for the most part confined to little more than a quarter of its area, and even in the most industrialised regions and along the busiest modern highway it is possible within a brief time to climb out of the world of chimneys and humming activity to rolling hills, vast expanses of grass and heather and wide views over the broad acres. This, after all, is probably the best way to appreciate the nature of this land. 'Taking the long view' is a policy which can be followed in Yorkshire better than in most other places. Few counties have so many 'view points' and few can have such extensive views.

Within the past year or so, without deliberate design, I have found myself at a number of these prominences and have marvelled again at their variety. Ingleborough, the popular mountain of western Yorkshire, has of course remarkable skylines to offer on clear days, from the shores of Morecambe Bay to the Lakeland hills, from the Howgills to Fountains Fell, with the peaks of Whernside and Penyghent included, and to the south Pendle Hill and the Bowland Fells.

Of a different kind is the wonderful view from Roseberry Topping (which the natives used to call 'the highest hill in all Yorkshire') or from 'Cook's' in the Clevelands (named after Captain Cook). There beside the rolling ranges of the Cleveland hills is the immense panorama across the northern half of the Plain of York, from the smoke of Teeside to the foothills of the western dales. Seen at sunset this can be a breath-taking vista. Not long ago I looked across the southern part of the York Plain from the oddly-shaped hill on which Crayke Castle stands. Because of the isolation of that island height in a sea of flat lands, the extent of the view becomes even greater. There are many other such view points which those who know their Yorkshire will claim as the best. It is not easy to compete with the great sweep from Baugh Fell, whence on a clear day, I am told, can be seen the Isle of Man and the Solway Firth. Then there is Penhill in Wensleydale with its all-embracing view, and a lovely one, of the dale itself and the sweep of the York Plain as far as the Hambletons. A little-known viewpoint is Bowland Knotts, with its double view of the Lancashire valley of the Ribble on the one side and the Yorkshire Three Peaks on the other.

You need not, of course, go to the high fells for all the best views. One man I know is proud of the view from Soil Hill, a modest height six miles west of Bradford, from which there is a grand view of Airedale up to the Craven hills. He tells me there is a local legend that Soil Hill is the first point of land looked for by sailors entering Grimsby – which sounds like a tale taller than the hill itself. The West Riding heights of Queensbury can provide a fine industrial landscape, and it is said that from the hills around Halifax there was once a clear view of Blackpool Tower. But that was during a long strike when all the mill chimneys were smokeless.

One intriguing query often arises about these high points. Is there any place in Yorkshire from which the North Sea and the Irish Sea are both visible? Many claims have been made for this, and much depends upon the clearness of the atmosphere. Mickle Fell; a hill called Tan End, near Hawes; and the top of Buckden Pike in Wharfedale (from which it is said you can see Morecambe Bay and Teesmouth) are all in the running. It would be remarkable if this county could claim a genuine view of the whole breadth of England. Whether or not that is possible, these high view points are rewarding. Geography, history and even economics come alive when you can see their topographical setting spread out before you. Perhaps it would be a good thing if all our schools were built on hilltops with broad vistas instead of a blackboard.

Yorkshire, by whichever way you enter it, offers a multitude of small distinctions as well as the broad vistas. If the parish churches are as ornate and beautifully decorated as small cathedrals and the stacks in the farmyards are as big as houses, you may be certain you are in the East Riding dales. If the farmhouses are small and of whitish grey stone, like the limestone walls which run for miles uphill and down – but they all turn almost black after rain – then you are in the western Dale country. If the farmhouses are still small against the vast fellsides, but are primly white-washed, you are still in the Dale country but in Teesdale, which is different. Or the fellsides may be dark and sombre and gritty, with here and there a mill standing gaunt in a cluster of houses; it is still Dale country, but this time they are the gritstone dales on the Lancashire border. And if you move out of these rural areas of the county and come to a city where the funnels and masts of ships appear over the tops of houses and shops you are probably in the centre of Hull. Or if a dark smog hangs in the air and a metallic clanging greets you and the speech has a harder ring, you are in the south Yorkshire steel area, and not far away will be the headstocks of the south Yorkshire mines. These, like the changing landscape, are part of its bewildering variety.

Along the Roads
There can be little doubt that some of these ways into York-shire – and many that are now lost to us – were trodden in prehistoric times. They were arteries in that slow bloodstream of life which existed in this land over tens of thousands of years

and which we know only through the flakes of flint and other implements of the Stone Age, the metal tools and weapons of the Bronze and Iron Ages, and the barrows and tombs which can be found on our moorlands. So small in number must have been the population then that it is difficult to imagine that their footprints could ever have hardened into a trail. Yet the still traceable Icknield Way (certainly a pre-Roman way), the Pilgrims Way and what has been termed the Jurassic Way, which linked Yorkshire with the Severn and entered the county across the Humber, suggest that some long-established tracks existed when the Romans arrived and were taken over by their road builders, straightened and strengthened, to become military highways. The very directness of their course was an asset the Romans must have appreciated.

Evidence of prehistoric people is abundant in all three Ridings. The monolith in Rudston churchyard, the remarkable site of a settlement at Starr Carr, the so-called 'Danes Dyke' at Flamborough in the East, the cup-and-ring stones at Ilkley, stone circles and forts on the Pennines, the Devil's Arrows at Boroughbridge in the West; moorland crosses and an immense number of 'howes', burial mounds and barrows on the North Yorkshire-moors; these are the legacy of people who lived and, presumably, moved from place to place along some sort of track, even if only in small numbers and over an immense period of time. Indeed there is evidence of one such track in a stretch of green road over the Hambleton Hills, close to the White Horse of Kilburn. It is believed that this was a Neolithic ridgeway – beginning near Arthur's Seat above Edinburgh and traceable all the way to the English Channel – part of which, a little incongruously, forms a section of the Cleveland Way, the new walking route over the Yorkshire moors.

One thing the earliest dwellers in Yorkshire had in common with the Roman road builders: both were concerned to join two points by the most direct line. Neither cared for scenery as such. Roman roads were military highways to make possible the movement of troops. So far as the land allowed they followed a straight course – and this has been a useful clue in tracing Roman roads. Hills were climbed by planned zig-zags with gradients to accommodate men and horses; but on level stretches, we have been told, the method was to line men spaced well apart in a single file and dress them off as a modern company sergeant major dresses off his troops. Each man had a stake which he drove into the ground as he stood – and there was a straight way. Along that line Celtic slave labour made the road to a pattern still to be found on the Blackstone Edge way into Yorkshire and on Wheeldale Moor, near Goathland. The few instruments available to the Roman road builders compared with those used by engineers today makes us marvel at the alignment they achieved along river valleys or following the ridges of hills. It is teasing to the imagination to pause on a hill and picture the troubled conferences which must have been held from time to time on lonely windswept heights to consider whether one stretch of road would link up with another out of sight – and with no binoculars or precision gauges to aid them. Occasionally they blundered. Those who have travelled north out of Yorkshire along the A.1., then called Dere Street, may have noticed a curious hiccough in the road just north of Scotch Corner. There two sections did not meet and a short stretch of road at an unexpected angle had to be built to link them. It was left to our own time to correct this 1,000-year-old blunder. A study of the Ordnance Survey's map of Roman Britain leaves one marvelling that mistakes of this kind were so few among the maze of roads they built during their stay in Britain.

It is an interesting exercise to follow a straight stretch of Roman road and to find the point at which a more recent diversion to meet a new need has pursued another course. Here and there in Yorkshire it is possible to trace the long-lost track through fields long used for cultivation. Often, of course, the straight line of the Roman road has provided modern planners with a direct course they have taken over, expanding it to cope with modern traffic. Even the early bridges across rivers have been utilized and enlarged on Roman foundations, as at Corbridge in Northumberland and probably at Doncaster.

As I have said, use rather than beauty has been the guiding rule of road builders from Roman times to our own, which is why our new 'walking ways' part company with the roads wherever possible. Although the Pennine Way and the new Cleveland Way pass through country which contains many minor Roman remains those early builders saw no necessity for a road there. Such tracks as remain, like the Neolithic ridgeway, may have been used by them as short cuts, but not for any delight in the countryside. And although the Romans had signal stations down the Yorkshire coast from Huntcliff to Filey they built no road to link them, and certainly none for the purpose of enjoying sea views. Now when we find a long-forgotten path over the fells, or a bridle path through the trees, or a deserted moorland lane which now serves no useful purpose, we can be thankful that we at least appreciate what seemed to be missing in those far-off days, a sense of scenic beauty.

The enjoyment of wild nature is a comparatively recent pleasure. Until the seventeenth century mountains and woods, waterfalls and other natural phenomena exercised no charm. Mountains were "horrid". Caves produced shudders. Torrents and lonely places were awesome. Then came a change. Poets and travellers became enthusiastic about our scenery. Where there once was fear they found romance, and the countryside instead of being sinister and dangerous was found to have beauty and delight. Now we seek out wild nature and are anxious because there may not be enough left to go round. Perhaps it was not coincidence that this new attitude appeared with the improvement of the roads and communications which ignored it. Wordsworth sang the natural beauty of Lakeland, and his sister Dorothy, in her diary, extolled the pleasures of her Yorkshire journeys at the very time Telford and Macadam and John Metcalf (Blind Jack of Knaresborough) were making it easier to move about our roads. Ruskin deplored the railways but drew attention to the architectural and other treasures of the county. Richard Jefferies wrote his essays on wild nature when railways were booming. So as the countryside became more accessible without danger and in increasing comfort, there grew up an appreciation of the wilderness and the lonely places at the time their wildness and loneliness were threatened. Even our modern road-builders, let it be said with gratitude, are doing something to break the monotony of the new motorways by landscaping and tree planting.

There is little doubt that the worst period for our roads was that following the Roman withdrawal when their network of highways was neglected, smaller ways overgrown and bridges allowed to decay. So far as is known no roads were built in Yorkshire for several centuries. It was all part of that desolation which settled upon this land when the Romans left Britain to itself and when their villas and farmsteads fell into increasing ruin and their military towns "became the haunt of wild fowl", as an old scribe put it. The successive waves of

Saxon and Scandinavian invaders were so busy pushing their way in and creating their settlements that they had probably little time and no inclination for road building. Where a Roman road remained usable they gave it the Anglo-Saxon name 'street', which still lingers in Yorkshire place-names.

Later, as these new communities became established and their need for contact with one another increased, what one might call the typical English lane grew up, finding the easiest way over streams, avoiding bogs and woods which have long ago vanished, circling this obstacle and that, to arrive at a hamlet or farmstead now lost without trace. I remember a few years ago taking part in a survey of existing footpaths round a Yorkshire village. There were dozens of them that led nowhere in particular and made the most extraordinary twists and turns in the process. Once they had been important and their convolutions had meaning to our 'rude forefathers'. This, rather than G. K. Chesterton's surmise that "the rolling English drunkard made the rolling English road", was probably the origin of many of those lanes and tracks which wander so illogically over our Yorkshire countryside. Long-distance travel on these tortuous ways must have been near impossible, even on horseback, and local contacts both difficult and dangerous. When one thinks of the remarkable feat of Saxon Harold who marched his army of some 3,000 men all the way from the south of England to Stamford Bridge on mere tracks to repel the invasion by Hardrada and Tosti and then had to march his army back again to battle with Norman William at Hastings, the question arises: may it not have been the ordeal of this double journey which led to their defeat and decided the whole pattern of the future England?

Although the Normans were great castle builders and had a strong sense of organisation and method – the compilation of the *Domesday Book* survey is evidence of this – they did not, apparently, attempt much road building. Their conception of the king's highway was limited to the right of passage for the king and his subjects over all the land. They were, however, concerned about bridges, and they began repairs and construction of many river crossings which have left us a legacy of medieval bridges. The church often had a hand in this. Archbishop Gray, of York, as early as 1228, offered indulgences to all who contributed to the building of a bridge over the Wharfe at Otley, the forerunner of the present bridge.

ON THE ROAD: *1, A turnpike road*
                           2, A sixteenth-century bridge at Barnard Castle

Stamford Bridge was a timber bridge in the time of Harold and remained so until the early eighteenth century, but the famous Ouse Bridge at York may have been stone from a very early time as it had to withstand constant heavy floods and indulgences were offered for its repair. The church also encouraged the building of chantry chapels on sound bridges, as can be seen at Wakefield and Rotherham.

The time of the first building of our bridges is usually lost beyond recall. The phrase so often to be met with in old documents is "there is and hath been time out of mynde a bridge". And that is as far back as one can go, although anyone who wanders far in our rural areas is likely to come across stone clapper bridges still in use which may go back to a still remoter past.

It was on such undrained tracks and lanes and over the few bridges that our traffic was slowly carried down the centuries. Along these ways went humans and their goods, cattle, sheep and great flocks of geese. The pace of the horse was the fastest known travel. And so the state of our roads apparently remained until early in the eighteenth century. Pack-horses carried such goods as could be split up into two-and-a-half hundredweight loads – and this included iron ore, wood for smelting, corn, coal, wool and woollen goods. The 'bell-horse' led the way to warn other travellers off the tracks or 'causeys'. The problem of foddering such processions of thirty or forty horses – or 'jaggers' as they were known, giving us many Jagger Lanes today – must have been stupendous, for frequent overnight stops would be necessary on long journeys where the daily limit could not have been more than twenty miles. The number of pack animals on our Pennine roads was very large, yet strangely there is little evidence of stabling or other accommodation to be found.

Yet a new era of faster travel was on its way. Private coaches appeared increasingly in the early eighteenth century, particularly in the vicinity of the towns and mainly for the use of the wealthier classes. Cumbrous waggons were built to carry coal and textiles and had to make their way on almost unusable roads. In 1740 a Bill was promoted, backed by manufacturers and merchants in Leeds, Wakefield, Halifax and Selby, to improve highways that were described as virtually impassable in the winter months. Stage waggons (like the covered waggons of 'Western' films) holding up to thirty people transported the less

VIEWPOINTS: *1, The tower of York Minster*

well-to-do. Mail coaches carried letters and sometimes passengers longer distances at faster speeds, hence the term 'post haste'. These were in time ousted by regular posting houses and time-tables, in turn giving us the familiar phrase 'slow coach' and, more unexpectedly, 'flying machines' for the fast coaches – an odd anticipation of the future. At Easingwold and Helmsley, as well as at York and elsewhere, can be seen examples of the old coaching clocks in inns that were once posting houses, and in the few Yorkshire newspapers of the time are lurid accounts of horses shying, of wheels coming adrift and of coaches being snowbound or overturning. Occasionally there were races between rival coaches. Two, 'The Pilot' and 'The Telegraph', left Leeds for Birmingham at six o'clock in the morning and raced all the way. On one occasion both coaches made the distance between Leeds and Wakefield in twenty-five minutes, frightening all the cattle along the route.

How perilous was such travel can be discovered in the diaries and letters of many travellers of the time. It was not easy even to get into or onto the coach. The wealthier passengers were crowded into a close box after climbing some portable steps, with little room and much close proximity (in which, as the historian Dr. Whitaker, remarked, helpless individuals were at the mercy of a drunken brute), with straw on the floor and little or no light. The cheaper sort travelled on the roof or even in a luggage basket behind; the first was cold and insecure, the second dangerous to limbs if not to life as the luggage bounced and tossed with the passengers. Springs were for long unknown on coaches either for the wealthy or for the fare-paying passenger, and as most roads were little better than farm tracks and often like ploughed fields one can understand Dr. Johnson's remark that "no wise man will go to live in the country unless he has something to do which can be better done in the country".

A certain Mr. Du Quesne, a social, kindly man, wrote to Parson Woodforde in the middle of the eighteenth century: "I steal a few minutes to aquaint you that, After numberless Disappointments, Difficulties, Dangers, Distresses and Vexations, I arrived here on Friday at 2 o'clock, with dislocated Joints, sore Bones, Bruises, and black and blue arms and sides, and concussions of the Brains from the most rough and disagreeably Hill Roads that ever were passed."

Inevitably this traffic brought a demand for better roads,

just as increasing motor traffic does today. Parishes or townships were then expected to look after their own roads, but not unnaturally felt it unjust that village purse and village labour should be called upon to provide facilities for travellers from outside their bounds. So the turnpike trust system was evolved, by which stretches of road were to be improved and re-surfaced and tolls based on the type of transport were to be collected at each end of the allotted stretch to pay for the work. We have to go back to the reign of Charles II for the beginning of turnpikes. A series of Acts of parliament empowered local magistrates at Quarter Sessions to levy tolls to maintain the highways. The results, as so often happens, fell far short of the intent. It was not until some forty years later that a system of private turnpike trusts was devised to raise capital for the repair and maintenance of stretches of road, the interest and capital repayment to be financed out of the tolls. A typical set of such tolls was as follows:

For every horse drawing any carriage	8d
For any horse drawing any waggon with wheel tyres more than six inches wide	4d
For every horse	2d
For empty carts	2d per horse
For every drove of oxen	8d
For every drove of calves	4d

In the making of such turnpikes that remarkable Yorkshireman, John Metcalf of Knaresborough on the Nidd, made his contribution. He was born in 1717 and lived to be 93, and from his sixth year he was totally blind as a result of smallpox. Yet he lived a more than normally full life. He could find his way about many miles of his own countryside before he was 10. He learned to swim, ride a horse, and play the violin, all to such good purpose that he rescued several folk from drowning in the Nidd, rode to hounds and earned his living by fiddling at Harrogate hotels. He boxed, wrestled, played bowls and travelled on horseback as far afield as Whitby, Newcastle and London. He started a carrier service between York and Knaresborough, fought on the Hanoverian side against the Jacobites, and when the war was over looked about – and the phrase can be used almost literally – for a job. It was propitiously at the time when there was strong agitation for better roads around his home town of Knaresborough. The occasion found the man. He tendered for the contract and, presumably because his many abilities impressed the authorities, received it. From that moment his real career began. Highway building at Knaresborough, Boroughbridge and Harrogate led to other contracts in Yorkshire, Lancashire, Cheshire, Staffordshire and Derbyshire. Most of the roads into Yorkshire bear evidence of his work, which included the bridging of rivers, the crossing of bogs and the building of embankments – all directed by a man who felt his way by a long staff, tested the soil and the stones by feel and made detailed plans that his own eyes could never see.

Much of the work of 'Blind Jack' came in the early days of turnpikes, when, as I have said, the local parishes bore the cost. It was not until a few years before his death and when in some parts of Yorkshire, including the Knaresborough and Harrogate area, there were angry outbursts against their cost and the restrictions on travel they appeared to involve, as well as opposition from farmers who felt their land was threatened, that the Turnpike Act became law permitting the formation of private trusts.

As an example of how this system worked we may look at the Keighley to Kendal highway, the history of which was pieced together by the late J. J. Brigg over forty years ago. On this highway, we are told, before the turnpike roads were made and when waggons came into use, about thirty packhorses arrived at Kendal from Settle every week. The existing road was described as being "from the narrowness thereof in many places and the nature of the soil very ruinous and in great decay and, not only impassable for wheel-carriages, but very dangerous for travellers". The Keighley-Kendal Turnpike Trust of forty "qualified gentlemen" was set up in 1753 and raised capital at $4\frac{1}{2}$ per cent interest, to be used on the remaking of the road and recouped out of the tolls. Contracts for this were given out, and for a time the scheme contributed greatly to the improvement of the old road and the creation in parts of a new one. Bad corners were cut out, steep gradients by-passed, and toll bars erected (a few of which still remain as private cottages along the road). But the increase of traffic did not always keep pace with the cost of maintaining the roads. Before long the Keighley-Kendal Trust had incurred a debt of over £30,000, a very considerable sum then. Besides, many travellers found the paying of consecutive tolls on a long road journey both costly and inconvenient and sought to by-pass the toll bars by taking to obscure lanes round them. Many toll bars

were resited to catch these evaders of payment. Things went
from bad to worse. There was difficulty with the bank, the rate
of interest on the capital was reduced, and the amount spent on
the road fell almost to nothing.

The final blow to this and other Turnpike Trusts came at the
very time when Macadam, Telford and others were bringing
new ideas to road-building and surfacing. This was the dawn of
the railway age. In its last years the Keighley-Kendal turnpike
road was, for a large part of its length, rivalled by the new
'little North Western' railway line from Skipton to Lancaster.
And this was typical of what was happening all over the
country. All the great build-up of road travel which had
emerged from the days of medieval neglect to a network of
highways, vastly improved minor roads, regular stage coach
services, and all the amenities of coaching inns with their
Dickensian company of jovial landlords, obsequious coachmen
and ostlers, pretty serving maids and mischievous stable boys,
vanished as the railway lines spread their tentacles. As
Macadam said (and Ruskin later echoed) "the calamity of the
railways has fallen upon us".

Some Travellers

Across these thresholds and along these roads came the early
travellers to Yorkshire. Many of them have set down their
discoveries in a strange world where speech, customs, food and
life itself was so greatly different from that of their home
towns. All these years later we can see our own land through
their eyes, share their experiences, attend as they open their
hearts on this or that issue, and picture our Yorkshire heritage
as it was growing and developing.

Not all these visitors are as helpful as we would wish. Many
of their diaries and journals resemble those we ourselves keep in
these hurried days – just a note of destinations, business, and
perhaps the weather. Others are compounded of trivialities,
amusing in themselves but telling us nothing of places or people
or events. But here and there comes in a traveller with the true
topographer's eye. He is not concerned with the loss of his wig
on the way, nor the discomforts of his lodgings, nor is he solely
an antiquarian probing the stones and vallums or the epitaphs
of the past. Instead he travels through a tract of country and
repopulates it. Like the time machine of Mr. Wells, he can take
you back down the centuries and depict the town, the village,

the countryside as he saw it. Out of the throng of visitors who jolted and trundled and bumped their way into the county we can best dip here and there into a few of their records and impressions.

One of the earliest travellers who entered through Bawtry and Doncaster, in a journey which took him on what would, even today, be an illuminating 'sampling itinerary – to Tadcaster, York, Thirsk, Northallerton, Richmond, and across country to Sedbergh and into Lakeland – was that curious character 'Drunken Barnaby'.

In his book *Travel in England,* published a quarter of a century ago, Thomas Burke calls him that "odd creation whose creator cannot certainly be named". There is little doubt, however, that this was the nom-de-plume of Richard Brathwaite, a gentleman of North Country stock, a high churchman and the author of nearly fifty books of which the only survivor is *Drunken Barnaby's Four Journeys to the North of England,* published in 1638. He was a Royalist who suffered fines for his loyalty during the Commonwealth, but this did not prevent him travelling widely in the twenty years from 1610 to 1630, during which time he made his four journeys and recorded them originally in Latin, later translated into doggerel verse in English. From whence he derived his *nom-de-plume* is something of a mystery, although there is an old ballad which contained the lines:

> Barnaby, Barnaby, thou'st been drinking
> I can tell by thy nose and thy eyes winking
> Whoop, Barnaby, take't for a warning
> The drunk overnight are dry the next morning.

Brathwaite was certainly a convivial traveller with a dislike of Puritans, not unexpected in one whose journal is outspoken and even lewd in parts. He has an eye for scenery, as at Keighley in the Aire valley

> Thence to Keighley, where are mountains,
> Steeply threatening, lively fountains,
> Rising hills, and barraine valleys.

He notes too, the foibles of local characters, particularly the clergy and the magistrates; observes minor industries (now often forgotten) like sausage-making at Redmire in Wensleydale, knitting at Aysgarth, and pin-making at Aberford.

He tells us at the outset that he went out to see

> Bridges, fountains, mountains, vallies,
> Huts, cells, hillocks, highways, shallows,
> Paths, towns, villages and trenches,
> Chaste, choice, chary, merry wenches

and this last line gives us a clue to one of his interests, amorous adventures, which he details in a style which shocked his contemporaries but which in these permissive days amuses rather than disturbs.

It is his third journey which holds the reader most closely because of his observations along the way. At Pontefract he noted the crops of liquorice which provided that town with an industry that has lasted to our own times;

> Thence to Pomfrait; as long since is,
> Fatall to our English Princes.
> For the choicest Licorice crowned
> And for sundry acts renowned;
> A louse in Pomfrait is not surer
> Than the Poor through sloth securer,

which we have today as a Yorkshire proverb, "Snug as a louse in Pomfrait".

Perhaps it was his entry into the county through Bawtry, where he may have heard the story of the saddler hanged for leaving his liquor, which stirred him to set down at York the still older story of the "piper who played after he had been hanged". In this case it was the 'executed' man who had the last laugh, for on being teased before the event that it would stop his playing for ever, the piper told his tormentors to wait and see:

> All which happen'd to our wonder,
> For the halter cut asunder,
> As one of all life deprived
> Being buried, he revived,
> And there lives, and plays his measure,
> Holding hanging but a pleasure.

Drunken Barnaby remains one of our most amusing visitors.

Daniel Defoe, as has already been noted, found his entry by Blackstone Edge a century later an ordeal, but that did not prevent him noting the character of the country. When he had descended from the heights he could write:

I must observe to you that after we passed the second hill and were come down into the valley again, and so still the nearer we came to Halifax, we found the houses thicker, and the villages greater in every bottom; and not only so but the sides of the hills, which were very steep every way were spread with houses. ... After we had mounted the third hill we found the country one continued village, though every way mountainous, hardly an house standing out of a speaking distance from another, and as the day cleared up we could see at every house a tenter, and on almost every tenter a piece of cloth, kersie or Shalloon, which are the three articles of this country's labour.

"Tenters" were, of course, the racks or fences on which the beaten or 'fulled' cloth was hung to dry after being scoured or dyed, and which has given us the phrase of being 'on tenter-hooks'.

The travels of Defoe make excellent reading, even though, as is widely held, he did not himself visit all the places he describes. Some of his material was secondhand. Some of it may have been fiction. Even the late G. D. H. Cole, who edited his travels, declared "Everyone knows him for, one of the world's greatest liars, with a peculiar art for making fictitious narrative sound like truth." Yet as a Yorkshire historian wrote to me some years ago, "He lied, but he lied very well," and even his masterly fictions provide for us a picture of the country in his time that is not completely remote from the truth.

Another traveller of a very different sort was the doughty John Wesley. In his years of journeying he must have been the most knowledgeable user of our English roads, for somewhere in his *Journal* he says that he had just covered some 2,400 miles on horseback in seven months, and his frequent achievement was sixty miles in a day on fearful roads, in all manner of weather and with no great thought for accommodation at the journey's end, for his immediate purpose was to preach the Gospel – which in itself frequently brought him rough treatment.

About 200 years ago the poet Thomas Gray, who wrote the famous "Elegy" and also an "Ode on the Death of a Favourite Cat", visited Gordale Scar in Malhamdale. This was long before hikers and holiday folk discovered it as a place for scrambling and picnicking and, incidentally, a dump for litter. He had been first to the Lake District and came by the northern threshold into Yorkshire. The poet arrived first at Ingleton, which he described as "a pretty village situated very high and yet in a valley at the foot of that great creature of God, Ingleborough". Here he dined at an alehouse with two local notables, "one of them 6 feet $\frac{1}{2}$ high, and the other as much in breadth". He apparently found the dales roads a little unnerving in his horse-drawn transport, as he records: "I went up the steepest hill I ever saw a road carried over in England, for it mounts in a straight line (without any other repose for the horses than by placing stones every now and then behind the wheels) for a full mile."

He stayed two nights at Settle at an inn "which pleased me much" and then went by chaise to Malham, "a village in the bosom of the mountains, seated in a wild and dreary valley". From there he had a guide to lead him to the horrors to come.

The first thing he noticed were goats on the edge of the great cliffs leading into the Scar: "One of them danced and scratched an ear with its hind foot in a place where I would not have stood stock-still for all beneath the moon." He was impressed by the great waterfall which gushes from a hole in the rock and by the stream that rattles like a torrent down the valley, as well as by the yew trees growing out of the rock face. What really stirred him, however, was something else: "It is that rock on the right, under which you stand to see the fall, that forms the principal horror of the place. From its very base it begins to slope forwards over you in one black and solid mass without any crevice in its surface and overshadows half the area below with its dreadful canopy."

Although he stood four yards from the cliff, to his alarm drops of water from the overhang above fell on his head. He gazed at "loose stones that hang in the air and threaten visibly some idle spectator with destruction". The impressionable poet was torn between admiration for the awesome spectacle and fears for his own safety. "I stayed there (not without shuddering) a quarter of an hour, and thought my trouble richly paid, for the impression will last for life."

One can imagine how thrilling a story he made of this on his return to his London haunts of civilisation in 1769, probably embroidered in the telling over a glass at an alehouse. What one cannot imagine are his comments could he but see the coach parties clambering over those rocks and round that waterfall today. And what would he have said of the modern potholer who revels among such "horrid" cliffs in total darkness hundreds of feet below ground? Although the poet was a worthy traveller he still found scenery horrific and wild nature a little disconcerting.

Following the poet came a musician. Twenty years after Gray's visit, Charles Dibdin, a composer and singer, made a

Musical Tour of England, performing in assembly rooms and halls, attracting the public by locally printed handbills, and offering popular ballads as his stock-in-trade:

> Sweet ditties would my Patty sing,
> Old Cherry chase, God Save the King,
> Fair Rosemy, and Sawny Scot
> Lillibularo, the Irish Trot,
> All these would sing my blue-eyed Patty.

Towns not the countryside obviously drew this traveller in search of an audience, and his comments markedly reflect the response he found.

Had Wakefield ever been praised so highly as it was by Dibdin when he visited it? "There is such a spritely cleanliness about it that the inhabitants seem as if they were born for the real purposes of life," he wrote. "The vicinity of Wakefield is filled with opulent and respectable inhabitants, all of whom inherit or have accumulated fortunes by trade. Their manners are simple and unaffected; their conversation is polished, and in their musical pursuits they go my way to work and praise everything that pleases them upon reflection."

At York, alas, he was swindled by an imposter, and he noted that that city had "many churches but little devotion; fine clothes and spare purses; a magnificent prison always full; and a Theatre Royal where they perform at a constant loss". At Northallerton he was unlucky with a damp bed, but Scarborough he praised as "one of the prettiest seaports I have ever seen". Which rather suggests that he found there good audiences for his performances.

A more famous traveller, who brought his wife with him, was that upright Cavalier and High Churchman, John Evelyn, who rode into the county on horseback in the mid-seventeenth century by way of Tickhill and Doncaster. "Tickel", as he called it, he mistakenly regarded as in Nottinghamshire, but he said the town and castle had "a very pleasant prospect". He was much impressed by Doncaster "where we lay this night, a large and faire Towne, famous for greate Wax-lights and good stockings. The next day we pass thro Pontfract, as the Castle (famous for many seiges both late and antient times, and the death of that unhappy King murder'd in it) was now demolishing by the Rebells; It stands on a mount, and makes a goodly shew at a distance."

Someone must have introduced him to an old Yorkshire

custom, supposed to bring good fortune, for they stopped on the road "to drink at a Christal Spring, which they call Robinhoods Well. Neere it is a Stone Chair and an Iron Ladle to drink out of Chained to the Seate." From there they travelled to Tadcaster and on to York, noting that the land round about "is goodly, fertile, well-watered and Wooded Country, abounding with Pasture and plenty of all provisions". After a day in York they set out for Beverley, where "a very old Woman shew'd us the Monuments, and being above 100 years of age, spake the language of Queen Marie's daies in whose time she was born". And so to Hull, where, as a Cavalier, he was critical of the "Hothams refusing enterance to his Majestie" – an act which touched off the Civil War. The two travellers left Yorkshire by crossing the Humber, "the weather was bad, but we cross'd it in a good barque over to Barton".

John Evelyn was an observer on the grand scale, and the edition of his diary published by the Oxford University Press runs to over 1,100 closely printed pages. We can only regret that his time in Yorkshire was so short. He had a close rival, however, in another indefatigable traveller, John Byng, better known as Lord Torrington, who spent a good deal of every year after leaving the army in 1780 wandering about the country and recorded his experiences in twenty-four journals. Like so many others he came on horseback up the Great North Road. He was probably the first of our notable travellers to carry a map, for, as he said, "none could inform you", and maps were then becoming available. He had a critical eye, and taste when it came to hospitality. His first stop was at Doncaster, where, unlike John Evelyn, he found the inn "nasty, insolent, and with city stabling", and as he disliked city life this was strong condemnation. At Pontefract he fared better with "a good stable, a good parlour, and an intelligent landlord". When he neared Ripon there were traffic problems not unknown today.

> Meeting many cows and calves driven along I dreaded a Fair at Ripon, and my fears were soon confirmed: for when I entered Ripon the market place was crowded by cattle and holiday folk. I got a good stable, and a good parlour, wherein I could see the tedious fun; after parading the Fair and staring at the booths, the misses, and the Scotch cattle, I sat down to a good dinner – trout and roast fowl.

One of the best meals of the journey was at the 'White Swan' at Middleham and it sounds appetising nearly 200 years later: boiled fowl, cold ham, Yorkshire pudding, gooseberry pie, roast loin of mutton and cheese cakes. He adds to the privacy of his diary a qualm about the price he will be charged. "A better dinner I never sat down to", he writes that evening, "but I fear that the charge will be heavy – 1s. 6d. at least."

Byng travelled through the Yorkshire Dales – after making a diversion to York which he did not greatly enjoy – and was fascinated by the natural beauty of the landscape – in which he proved himself a forerunner of later visitors to these parts. He was ecstatic about the country round Hackfall where the "romantic River Eure frames its broad and rapid course", adding that "nothing can be more grandly wild and pastoral than the unexpected view of this river". He also appears to have taken intelligent interest in monastic ruins. Of Easby Abbey in Swaledale he notes, "there cannot be a more complete, a more perfect ruin; about every part of it did I crawl and every part of it could I trace". He completed his tour and made his exit from Yorkshire by way of that road which runs through Gisburn into Lancashire.

So the long cavalcade of visitors came and went, jotting down their pictures and impressions of the North Country and allowing us to see through their eyes Yorkshire as they found it down the centuries. Of them all, I must admit, my favourite is that lively lady Celia Fiennes, with her shrewd mind and eager pen and immense vitality. Landscape and wild life, industry and trade, architecture and the arts, people and health all interested her, and she had a passion for "spaws" and taking the waters. Celia came of a notable Puritan family and had a link with Yorkshire in that she was the niece of Constance Fiennes, who had married Sir Francis Boynton, of Burton Agnes in the East Riding. She made her two journeys in Yorkshire in successive years, 1697 and 1698, and, unlike John Byng, she had no map and often found it "very difficult to find the wayes here".

She came on horseback. On her first journey she rode from London up the Great North Road, visiting Nottingham on the way and liking it so much that she used it as a standard of comparison for other towns. So she came to Doncaster and made her famous remark, "here Yorkshire begins, and here the Musick welcom'd us into Yorkshire", although what the music was she does not explain. She visited York, Harrogate, and Ripon, and then doubled back on her tracks to York again, and on to Hull, Burton Agnes and Scarborough, taking good roads and bad as they came and rarely complaining except to say that the road from Knaresborough to York "is the worst riding in Yorkshire". Whether she meant that as a pun on the three Ridings I am not sure, but it is in keeping with her character. On her second journey she crossed the northern doorstep to Richmond, then by Boroughbridge and Harrogate to Leeds, and south to Elland and out of the county over Blackstone Edge.

York was the first place to stir her comparison with Nottingham:

> It stands high but for one of the Metropolis and the See of the Archbishop it makes but a meane appearance, the streetes are narrow and not of any length, save one which you enter of from the bridge that is over the Ouse which looks like a fine river when full after much raine . . . the houses are very low and as indifferent as in any Country town, and the narrowness of the streetes makes it appear very mean. Nottingham is so farre before it for its size.

She enjoyed looking down from a tower of the Minster and at "a vast prospect of the Country at least 30 mile round". Inside the Minster "there is the greatest curiosity for Windows I ever saw they are so large and so lofty, those in the Quire at the end and on each side that is 3 storys high and painted very curious".

At Harrogate she notes the many different springs of water. One was "the sulpher or Stinking spaw, not improperly term'd for the smell being so very strong and offensive that I could not force my horse near the well". Naturally she took the waters and drank a quart each morning for two days. She believed they were beneficial "if you can hold your breath so as to drinke them down". From Harrogate she paid a visit to Copgrove where St. Mungo's Well offered another sort of "spaw" wherein she could bathe, and, although she disliked the "Papists fancyes of it" as a holy well, she dipped her head "quite over every tyme I went in and found it eased a great pain I used to have in my head". She arrived in Ripon on market day and noted that provisions were very plentiful and cheap and naturally compared them with London prices. "In the market was sold then 2 good shoulders of Veal, they were not very fatt nor so large as our meate in London but good meate, one for 5 pence the other for 6 pence." Crawfish were on sale at "2 pence a Dozen so we bought them". The inns did not impress her as they did John Byng for she declares they "are very dear to strangers that they can impose on".

After visiting Newby Hall, which she greatly admired and where she "dranke small beer four years old – not too stale", she continues her travels into the East riding, approving Beverley "which is a very fine town for its size, its prefferable to any town I saw but Nottingham", visiting Hull where she looked in at Trinity House, then a hospital for seamen's widows, and venturing on a trip on the Humber, and eventually rode on to Burton Agnes, the house of her kinsfolk, the Boyntons.

A sad mishap at Darlington preceded her second journey into Yorkshire, "I lost some of my night-clothes and little things in a bundle that the Guide I hired carry'd," but she enjoyed her ride through lanes and woods to Richmond, "though I must say it looks like a sad shatter'd town and fallen much to decay and like a disregarded place". Perhaps she had forgotten Nottingham by this time; certainly she no longer makes comparisons. Leeds she admired for its large clean streets and good houses all built of stone, some with gardens and steps and with walls round them. "This is esteemed the wealthyest town of its bigness in the Country, its manufacture is the woollen cloth, the Yorkshire cloth in which they are all employ'd and are esteemed very rich and very proud." She approves the local custom whereby when you bought your ale you were given a slice of hot or cold meat or else butter and cheese. This was apparently a market-day custom "at the sign of the Bush just by the bridge", and she regrets that she missed it. "Had I known this and the day which was their Market, I would have come then."

Strangely, she avoided Halifax because of its stony roads and because she had been told of its "Engine" for the summary execution of criminals. "I resolved not to go to that ragged town." So she came to Blackstone Edge, "noted all over England for a dismal high precipice and steep in the ascent and descent on either end", and on to Rochdale in Lancashire, where we leave this observant and talkative traveller who tells us so much about the county as it was some 200 years ago.

From Coaches to Trains

When Charles Dickens and his companion, Hablot K. Browne, came north in 1838 to gather material and local colour for *Nicholas Nickleby*, they travelled by coach from London to Grantham where they "found everything prepared for our reception". It must have been a chilly ride, for the month was January and the weather was bad, and even worse on the next stage, for on 1st February Dickens wrote to his wife: "Yesterday we were up again shortly after seven a.m., came on upon our journey by the Glasgow mail, which charged us the remarkably low sum of six pounds fare for two places inside.... As we came north the mire grew deeper. About eight o'clock snow began to fall heavily, and as we crossed the wild heathes here-about there was no vestige of a track."

Fortunately there was compensation in North Country hospitality when they arrived late at night at 'The George', a once famous coaching inn at Greta Bridge: "To our great joy we discovered a comfortable room, with drawn curtains and a most blazing fire.... In half an hour they gave us a smoking supper and a bottle of mulled port (in which we drank your health), and then we retired to a couple of capital bedrooms, in each of which there was a rousing fire halfway up the chimney."

Dickens must have worked assiduously in gathering his material and filling his notebooks, for two days later he is in Darlington, having travelled there by post-chaise, and has joined the Newcastle coach which travelled down the Great North Road to York, on its way to London. He remembered the pains and trials of coach travel all his life. Speaking many years later at a dinner of the Newspaper Press Fund he recalled his early reporting days:

> I have often transcribed for the printer from my shorthand notes important public speeches in which the strictest accuracy was required, and a mistake in which would have been to a young man severely compromising, writing on the palm of my hand, by the light of a dark lantern, in a post-chaise and four, galloping through a wild country, and through the dead of the night, at the then surprising rate of fifteen miles an hour.

Nine years after his Greta Bridge journey by coach he wrote a letter, still preserved in the railway archives at York, asking for the reservation of four first-class compartments on the London to Manchester train and saying that "a large party of gentlemen connected with literature and art propose going to Manchester on a public occasion by the ten o'clock train on Sunday morning next". In the years that were to follow he became an habitual train-traveller, visiting his friend Charles Smithson at Easthorpe Hall, near Malton, Lord Normanby at

Mulgrave Castle, near Whitby, and others, giving public readings of his books in almost every county, and on pilgrimages in search of backgrounds for his stories. Some of these railway journeys must have been as gruelling as his earlier coach travel. In Forster's *Life of Dickens* it is noted that

> at Harrogate he read twice in one day (a Saturday) and had to engage a special engine to take him back that night to York, which having reached at one o'clock in the morning, he had to leave, because of Sunday restrictions on travel, the same morning at half-past four, to enable him to fulfil a Monday's reading at Scarborough. Such fatigues became matters of course; but their effect, not noted at the time, was grave.

Perhaps it is a pity that Dickens, who lived through and experienced this remarkable travel revolution from road to rail, did not make it the theme of a major book, for its impact both socially and commercially was far-reaching. The distance between London and York was no longer a matter of days but of a few hours. In 1700 the journey from London to York took a week. The turnpikes reduced this to four days seventy years later, but even at the peak period of coaching the journey by the 'Rockingham' coach took twenty-three hours from the 'Saracen's Head' at Snow Hill to the 'Golden Lion' in Briggate, Leeds. The 'Union' coach took an hour longer. And when the two concerns amalgamated in 1840 they could not improve on this time. The number of passengers declined, and the service ceased entirely in 1844. The 'Lord Wellington' coach from Newcastle to London, which took thirty-one hours, had ceased three years before, and we are told that on its last journey "It drove into Darlington empty, into Northallerton empty, into Thirsk empty, and the proprietors saw the end had come."

What amazes us now is not the speed of the trains but the speed of the revolution. Within a few decades the railway network had become an accepted part of existence, with its own great companies, its own laws, its own uniforms and police system, its own inexorable time-tables, its vast terminal stations with waiting rooms, refreshment and luggage amenities, its marble halls for directors, its Pullman coaches and its apparent immutability. Ruskin and others might protest. A few wealthy men might struggle against the proximity of the new lines to their estates and when compelled to accept the inevitable, plant trees to shut out the offending sight, as many did in Yorkshire. But to all appearances the railways had come to stay, and in

those exciting years from midway last century to the beginning of this there was scarcely a moment when new lines were not being planned, built or extended somewhere in Yorkshire. In the western Dales, across the Plain of York, through the industrial region of the West Riding and along the coast tracks were laid, stations built, signal wires erected.

Yorkshire had railways of sorts in the form of tramways with cog-wheels at some of its collieries from the middle of the eighteenth century, but the first passenger railway was the Leeds to Selby line which opened in 1834 and made the journey twice a day. At first these pioneer lines were short lengths linking two or three towns, each maintained by its own company – not unlike the development of the Turnpike Trusts already referred to. Carriages were primitive, being little more than trucks, roofed for first class, open for the rest. When the gentry travelled they brought their private carriages and had them placed on open trucks. 'Booking' meant literally writing down the journey in a book whose counterfoil was the ticket. The brushing off of dust and cinders after a journey was a matter of course.

Enthusiasm for this new form of travel grew as the tracks lengthened. The 'railway mania' seized the North Country, as it did the rest of England, and there followed an orgy of buying and selling railway stock and shares the like of which had not been known since the days of the South Sea Bubble. Once again the occasion found the man in Yorkshire. There appeared on the scene George Hudson, a York linen draper, who was born in 1800 and was a respected tradesman in the city. Unlike John Metcalfe, he had no physical handicaps, but he suffered from an over-whelming ambition. A fortunate legacy when he was still a young man came at the time when he could foresee something of the possibilities of the new railways, and he was soon on the boards of the companies being formed in the north. Association with George Stephenson and others stimulated his dominant idea of making York a great railway centre, for which it was well situated. From an interest in the York and North Midland Railway, which linked the city with Normanton and the south, his empire spread, not without opposition from the rival empire of what became the Great Northern Railway. He linked York with Darlington and later with Scarborough, and by amalgamation and acquisition created the North-Eastern Railway Company.

FARMING WAYS: *1, Raking up in Teesdale*
2, In Wharfedale

So the era of the great railway companies came into being. Hudson himself came to grief, although honours poured in upon him. He became Lord Mayor of York, Member of Parliament for Sunderland, the owner of a great estate in the East Riding, and earned the title of the 'railway king'. There can be little hesitation in saying he 'earned' the title (although Carlyle called him a "big swollen gambler") for it was his foresight and ability which placed York and Yorkshire so firmly upon the railway map and stimulated much that was to follow. He over-reached himself by his ambition and died in 1871 in some disgrace, but he was no less a victim of the craze for railway speculation which overwhelmed so many of his fellow countrymen. His service to our railway system has received a final honour – oddly in this motor age – by the naming of the new northern headquarters of British Railway at York 'Hudson House'.

There can be no doubt of the far-reaching effect of this railway revolution which eliminated the stage coach as completely as that had eliminated the traveller by horse and by foot.

J. S. Fletcher, the Yorkshire historian, writing at the end of the First World War of the expansion in communication and transport over the previous 150 years, could say enthusiastically:

> By the development of road, of railway, of canal, of shipping, distance was lessened, far-off places were put in communication with each other, man's opportunity of going quickly from his own door to wherever it was necessary he should travel were extended, and the maker of goods, the grower of produce, found it possible to avail himself of his desired markets. It has meant more than is easily conceivable that a man can travel from Leeds to London within four hours, and that he can send his wares wherever he likes in quick time, and that merchandise can be brought to his workshop and factory from the very ends of the earth.

Inevitably there was opposition from those who mourned the passing of the coaching inns and who feared the ruin of the countryside, the noise and the smoke, and the increasing pace of life. There were objectors to branch lines in the Yorkshire Dales and in the moorland valleys. It was said that, although travel would be faster and more comfortable, the age-old pattern of rural life and husbandry would be shattered, the true foundations of life would be lost for ever. Looking back now in the midst of a new transport revolution we can see the matter in better perspective.

To the great cities and towns of Yorkshire, to the collieries and steel works, the mills and the factories, to the industrial areas generally, the coming of the railways brought a transformation greater than anything previously known. The railway revolution stimulated the industrial revolution. As a recent writer has put it, "In transport the revolution in scale went furthest of all . . . the real unit of production, of passenger – or ton – miles, increased from the two-man coach or waggon, to the fleet of boats, and finally, since the train could not operate as an independent unit, to the whole railway company, or even, after the rolling-stock clearing house system of 1844, the whole railway network."

Yet, although the revolution was far-reaching in the urban areas, the effect on our countryside was limited. When all the lines had been laid and the trains were running there were still vast stretches of Yorkshire almost as isolated as they had been in coaching days. The villages remained much as they were, untroubled by trains. The local carrier would go to the station for parcels, but would still deliver them by hand at cottage doors. Expresses rushed by on main lines to far destinations but did not greatly concern the farmer in his fields – except that he put his watch right by their regular appearance. The immemorial round of the seasons went on: ploughing and seed-time, lambing and harvest. Old customs continued without much change. An annual outing or even a trip to the seaside by train became a possibility, but it had not the attraction for the rural areas that it had for the towns. Conversely, trains brought more visitors into the country, but they did not stay long; they went back on the last train at night.

For both countryside and town something more radical and revolutionary was looming, and that was the internal combustion engine. We who are older can still, perhaps, recall the horse-drawn growler at the station, perhaps even a hansom-cab. We can recall cattle being driven to markets on foot along rural roads. We can remember when the chief traffic on our roads were the horses and cyclists, and when speeding on a bicycle was an offence against the law. We can remember when the blacksmith shoed horses and when youth hostels were reserved for walkers, or 'hikers'. We can remember these things if we are not distracted by the noise of cars and motor-lorries on the road outside our window or the sound of a jet-plane overhead, which are the signs of our new revolution.

Away on the moors of North Yorkshire set amid a sea of heather, purple in autumn, dark brown in winter, is the well-known Saltersgate Inn, whose story typifies the changing way of the world. Originally 'The Wagon and Horses', it was remote and deserted save for the little traffic on the ancient road between Whitby and Pickering. This was probably the 'gate' or road by which the monks of Whitby obtained their salt, then a scarce and heavily taxed commodity, and almost certainly there was a hostelry there from the earliest times when the salt would be carried on pack horses. Later it was a calling place for stage coaches, with a resident farrier in attendance. Nearby is Gallows Dike, which suggests a more sinister story. A couple of miles away an old track leads to Robin Hoods Bay on the coast, once called the Fish Road, along which the fishermen brought their catches. But almost certainly more than fish travelled that way. Brandy and gin brought in from the bay was smuggled along that road out of sight of the preventive men and doubtless exchanged for tax-free salt which the fishermen needed.

There followed long years of desolation when the railways drove the coaches off the road and the smugglers ceased to call. Grass grew again on many of these forgotten moorland highways and mine host languished. Now that same highway has become a busy motor road carrying traffic every day of the year and crowded with picnic parties during the summer months. And within sight are the great radomes of the radar early warning station as a symbol of the new age. Every farmer in the area has his car and his tractor and his mechanical baler and can visit the old inn for his drink in the evening.

In the East Riding recently I saw something I thought had gone for ever – a man ploughing with horses. It was a glimpse of an older Yorkshire when time went more slowly than today. There may still be many horse-drawn ploughs at work in the arable parts of Yorkshire, just as there are still places in the Dales where they use horses for haytime. But the motor-powered machine is winning. Almost in the next field to the horse-plough was a mechanically-propelled contraption which was picking up straw-bales and stacking them neatly, as if by hand, on to a wagon.

On my way home I looked in at a cottage where I was shown

an old photograph album in which was a faded picture of the whole family lending a hand in the harvest field. It was taken, I was told, a few years before the First World War. This family assault in the harvest field was a reminder that even in those far-off times when there was no shortage of labour on the land, the gathering-in of the crops, because of the vagaries of our climate, was a difficult and urgent undertaking that sometimes necessitated the mobilisation of all hands.

But the real interest of the photograph to me was the evidence that even the 'good old days' were not entirely good, or at any rate not particularly comfortable. All the pitchfork-carrying men (except for a couple of obviously truly rural farm hands) were wearing starched white collars of considerable height and presumably unyielding stiffness. The ladies were wearing voluminous frilly summer skirts, which must have been fearfully hot in the open fields, and loose floppy hats which appear to require ribbons to hold them in place. It must have been difficult raking up or doing anything except look sentimental in that garb.

Not only transport has been transformed by this new revolution; it is our whole way of life. The accepted things and habits of today are the oddities of tomorrow. I often wonder what our grandchildren will find the strangest bygone of our 'modern age'.

2

Down the Coast

Old Father Humber – Folk Talk – Spreading the News

When Operation Neptune was launched by the National Trust a few years ago to preserve the beauties and amenities of our coastline we woke up to the fact that we had some 2,000 miles of it to enjoy. Two thousand miles sounded ample until an ingenious statistician calculated that if all the nation's car owners wished to sit in their cars facing the sea only one in five would have a front view of virgin coast. If we all decided to claim our bit of beach at the same time it would amount to three or four inches each.

There have been occasions when I felt that Yorkshire's 5 million population had decided to try the experiment on its own 120 miles of coastline, strung with gay resorts as varied in colour and style as beads on a young girl's necklace. In the days when our seaside resorts were served by railways, and often had their special excursion platforms for high days and holidays, the seasonal rush to the nearest coast from the industrial areas was something to marvel at. But the motor cars which have brought about the decline of our railways have extended holiday-making to a wider area. Modern motorways, assisted by the ubiquitous motor coach, have tempted people further afield, so that today you will hear Yorkshire voices in Dunoon or Clovelly as certainly as you will hear Scottish or South Country voices in Whitby or Scarborough or Bridlington. The pull of the bird-haunted cliffs stretching all the way from near the mouth of the Tees to Flamborough head, and the temples of pleasure at their feet, still draw the family parties and the honeymoon couples, but nowadays not only from Yorkshire but from every part of Britain.

This is all part of that discovery of the seaside which began in Georgian times with the improvement of roads and coach travel at which we have already looked. Smollett writing *Humphrey Clinker* in 1770 took Mr. Mathew Bramble to Scarborough, where his servant Humphrey pulled him out of the water to save him from drowning. He also attended the subscription balls. Sheridans's *Trip to Scarborough,* produced at Drury Lane a few years later, took Lord Foppington to the same spa. Only the well-to-do could afford coach travel to the coast until the arrival of the railways. Then Victorian England saw the rise of the popular holiday which transformed our largely deserted coasts and gave us the family watering place, the promenades and the piers, the winkle stalls and the pierrots.

Unlike their Lancashire counterparts, Blackpool and Morecambe – which were insignificant coastal villages transformed by man's artifice at a comparatively late stage and in the briefest of time into gigantic pleasure centres – Yorkshire's coastal resorts emerged gradually and almost imperceptibly from being small but busy harbours as easier travel and the discovery of seawater as a way to health began to draw the wealthier type of visitor. Doctors recommended regular dips in the sea (with adequate precautions) as the summer antidote to winter wear and tear and for unwise excesses, as well as being an amusing change from drinking the waters at Harrogate or Bath. This called for reputable hotels and well-managed lodgings as well as the elegant amusements of inland resorts. So esplanades and pavilions and music rooms, at first Georgian and then Regency, appeared some little distance from the workaday harbours but along the same coastline. An esplanade offered scope for gentle exercise and a view of the sea. Hotels on the grand scale, and with grandiloquent names, offered food and comfort, music and company of the right sort, and a sense of aristocratic splendour. They can still be seen flaunting a nostalgic charm at all our larger resorts, and at some of the smaller ones too. They were followed in Victorian times by the lesser houses which grew up on the landward side of the resorts, offering more and cheaper accommodation "with delightful prospect", if not with sea view. They came with the bathing tents and the pleasure boats and the entertainments at the Spa.

For generations of Yorkshire folk a long line of coastal resorts has been a near approach to the kingdom of heaven on earth. Each has its distinctive character and its devotees. In the north, where the romantic river Esk joins the sea through the gap between the Abbey-topped east cliff and the built-up west cliff, Whitby has often an ethereal beauty. Its background of woods and moorland provides a natural foil to the miles of storm-battered scars and sands. Activity in the tiny harbour, where there is still a lively fishing industry and occasional foreign ships loading or unloading, makes an extra attraction for the family holiday party. Even when the railway connected it with the rest of Yorkshire it was never overcrowded (perhaps another resemblance to the desirable kingdom), and the long approach to it from any direction conferred a pleasant sense of remoteness.

Since the closure of one of the most picturesque lines in Britain – from Pickering through the deep valley of Newton-dale that was a legacy of the Ice Age – Whitby has become still more remote to the point of complete winter isolation. Perhaps this may help to maintain its marked individual character of seacoast charm and historic association, provided the recent 'development' of amusement arcades in place of the old fishermen's cottages and the erection of a tall T.V. mast on the skyline where once the abbey and the ancient St. Mary's Church were the only features are not the precursors of still more 'progress'. The abbey was founded in 657 on a site given by King Oswy of Northumbria, and will be for ever associated with the name of its famous Abbess Hilda, who was so saintly, legend tells, that she could transform snakes into stones. Its original name was Streoneshalh which, like Strensall, near York, meant 'Streon's nook of land', and it flourished until the Danes sacked it about 870. The abbey made a deep mark on our history as within its walls was held the synod in 664 which fixed the date of Easter.

By comparison with the stately beauty of the abbey, still evident in its present ruin, is the curious jumble of the nearby St. Mary's Church, with its high pews, many galleries and general air of hotch-potch which Mr. Gordon Home once said was like "a nightmare beehive", but which a more recent visitor, Mr. Nikolaus Pevsner, has described as being "hard to believe and impossible not to love". It has a remarkable three-decker pulpit, which, I take it, may have started at normal height but grew up to cope with the occupant's need to see his audience in the added galleries, and perhaps to keep an eye on what went on in the high box pews.

I have always observed a strong pride in Whitby's history among its inhabitants, perhaps because in the red-roofed older part of the town its past is the dominant feature even today. The market hall, the names of streets like Baxtergate and Flowergate, the relics of old whaling and shipbuilding days; all of these link the place with a vigorous and lively past which is not forgotten. In some of the old low-ceilinged timber-framed houses and shops you have to be careful indeed that you do not literally bump into history. There is still a spa on the West Cliff once famous for its mineral waters, which were so potent that they inspired one taker to verse: "Whitby, a poem; occasioned by Mr. Andrew Long's recovery from jaundice by drinking of Whitby Spaw Waters." On the opposite side of the Esk are remnants of the old boat yards where many a fine ship was built.

Whitby's hero is the explorer and navigator, Captain James Cook, who was born in 1728 at Marton, near Middlesbrough, but who served his apprenticeship to a Whitby shipowner and must have sailed often in and out of the harbour. A bronze statue of him which overlooks the harbour is, I am told, the only statue of this notable seaman in Britain although away on the Cleveland hills, overlooking the little village of Great Ayton, where he went to school, is a more formal monument known to all locals simply as 'Cooks'.

The chief literary association of the town is, of course, much older, in the person of Caedmon, whom some have called 'our first national poet' and of whom it is written "he did not learn the art of poetry from men but as the gift of God", both high claims that owe much to the Venerable Bede's story – which he had from hearsay. The story is, however, picturesque enough to be believed. Caedmon, according to Bede, was an elderly cowherd at the abbey and was ashamed that he could not sing like other men when the harp went round the hall in the traditional entertainment on winter evenings. When he went to bed one night troubled by his failure he dreamt that he heard a heavenly voice saying "Sing, Caedmon, sing." He answered that he had no song. "What shall I sing?" The reply came, "Sing to me the beginning of all things." And the words came as he dreamt. So when next the harp went round Caedmon sang his "Song of Creation", which impressed even the Abbess Hilda so that she encouraged him to compose many Scripture stories into Saxon verse. He died in 680, and a modern cross at the top of the famous 199 steps up the East Cliff com-memorates the 'Father of English Poetry'. It must be added that there is reason to believe that Caedmon was not a Yorkshireman but probably a Welshman, but he remains a part of Yorkshire's heritage. No one these days is likely to carry a copy of Caedmon to read on a visit to Whitby, and of course it must be remembered that Caedmon's verses, like most of the early poems, were passed down as the spoken word, only to be written on parchment much later by a monkish scribe.

Curiously, in modern times, most of the writing about Whitby is by women authors. Required reading now is more likely to be Mrs. Gaskell's novel of whaling days, *Sylvia's Lovers,* or the stories by the Whitby-born authoress Mary Linskill, *Between the Heather and the Northern Sea* and *The Haven Under the Hill,* or the many novels by Storm Jameson. A new author, again a woman, whose family has lived in the Whitby district since the sixteenth century, has produced in four volumes a lively fictionalised account of Whitby since the days of Captain Cook's first voyage, in which the life of the town and harbour, the fierceness of the wind on the moors, the peace of the Eskdale woods, the excitement of the building of the Pickering-Whitby railway line, and much else is portrayed with a loving regard for the town, its people, their superstitions and their traditional ways. Brenda English has created in these four books – *Into the North, The Gabriel Hounds, The Goodly Heritage,* and *The Proper Standard* – a complete library of Whitby life and lore.

In one of these she writes of that spectre which long struck terror into the hearts of those who lived on the wild moors of Cleveland. A Constable encounters a girl wandering near the old churchyard on the hill when a thunderstorm breaks over the sea and rolls inland, shaking the very cliff.

And then, behind it, dimly and from far away, came a faint cry, high-pitched and on the verge of hearing. Tense with a new fear, the Constable leaned forward, shading his eyes and searching the horizon beyond the sea. As he looked, a fitful gleam of light showed something moving from the north; something V-shaped.

"It's them! God save us, it's t'Gabriel Hounds! He seized Marie by the hand. 'Come, get thysen felted (hidden)".

The Gabriel Hounds, often referred to as Gabbleratchets, have haunted many generations of folk on the North Yorkshire moors. Their noisy passing overhead at night was held to presage death to the hearer or to one of his family. They have loomed as large in its folklore as they do in the night sky, and I can aver from personal experience that they can send an eerie shudder down the spine, even if one is aware that they are only a flight of wild geese. The churring of the night-jar, or fern-owl, can be equally disconcerting on a lonely moorland road, although when staying once at a little cottage on the Whitby-Guisbrough road I found their nightly performance a pleasant soporific when safely in bed.

Most of these ancient fears of apparitions and evil spirits have now gone from the moorland folk, although tales are still told of hobs and elves and witches who could turn themselves into hares if pursued. On the coast, however, superstitions still linger. I was told at Whitby only a year or so ago that some fishermen would not put out to sea on a Friday for fear of ill-luck, nor did they approve of onlookers counting boats as they sailed out between the piers. If fishing nets are stretched out to dry or fishing lines are being straightened a fisherman's wife will never step over them, but always lift them up and walk underneath. If her husband came into the house and saw a teacup inverted on the table he would regard it as an ill omen, and to see a pig while on the way to his boat would mean certain bad luck with his catch. Such beliefs were once universal all the way down the coast to Flamborough, which for long was an isolated and close community where almost every casual act could be construed as a good or bad omen. One strange custom there until recent times was the 'raising of the herrings'. When the men went to sea their womenfolk dressed themselves in men's clothes and danced or sang in the village street. This for some unknown reason ensured a good catch, but both herring fishing and 'herring raising' are no more. Whether in some way this custom had any link with the well-known Flamborough sword dance, in which the men danced while the women sang, I have never been able to discover.

Northwards from Whitby the cliffs continue beyond Boulby, and then the coastline declines to the sands of Saltburn and Redcar, popular resorts for Teeside workers. This top corner of Yorkshire once provided many fortunes from its soil, as old ironstone mines, jet workings and alum quarries bear witness. The scars remain if many of the fortunes have gone, as anyone will discover if they travel to Boulby Cliff (682 feet), the highest of all the precipices which guard the English coast. This old ransacking of the earth for its mineral treasure may prove only the introduction to a new chapter of development on a much more massive scale. There are plans to open up extensive potash mines around Boulby, where it is believed there is enough potash to meet all Britain's requirements and leave some over for export. The hinterland of this coast from Whitby northwards is now being jabbed by drills, like pins in a pin-cushion, in search of minerals, oil and gas, and when the land runs out the search is continued in the sea itself. The menace of all this to an area of great natural beauty – much of it is already included in the North York Moors National Park, although that seems to count for little against economic progress – can be seen in the far from beautiful chemical plants round the mouth of the Tees and the coal-blackened coast of Durham further north. The prospect is not inviting if, as may happen, the plant necessary to the new industry comes to the very threshold of Whitby itself.

Just as Whitby lost its railway link with Pickering with the closure of the line down Newtondale – a group of enthusiasts is at present struggling to acquire and re-open this as a private venture – so its rail connection with Scarborough went with the scrapping of the attractive coastal route through Robin Hoods Bay and Staintondale. In place of glimpses from the railway carriage of little fishing villages and sleepy stations with names that were synonymous with summer holidays the traveller now has a motor service across the moors, purple in summer and black velvet in winter, with a sight of the new age in the early warning station at Fylingdales, with its gigantic golf-ball-like equipment and miles of wire fencing. Scarborough meets you if not half-way then many miles from the resort itself with its outliers of holiday suburbia, houses, shops and bus routes, which is probably the proper way to be greeted by a once-romantic small watering-place now evolved into a sophisticated holiday centre.

This is not to deny its romance or its charm.

Scarborough is a very pretty Sea-port town built on the side of a high hill, the Church stands in the most eminent place above all the town and at least 20 steps you ascend up into the churchyard; the ruins of a large Castle remaines, the Walls in compass severall acreas of ground that feeds many beasts and milch cows, the hills on which the Castle stands is very steep and severall trenches over one another round the walls, all one side of the Castle stands out to the sea shore a good length, its open to the main ocean and to serve the harbour there is a mole or half moone, two, one within the other ... the sand is so smooth and firme that you may walke 5 or 6 mile on the sand round by the foote of the ridge of hills, which is the poynt by which all the Shipps pass that go to Newcastle, or that way.

So wrote Celia Fiennes after her visit in 1697. Take away the beasts and milch cows and replace them with houses and the picture remains true. Scarborough is still a fine town although the adjective 'pretty' has now been transformed into something more regal as befits the 'Queen of Watering Places'. The old town on the South Bay which the seventeenth-century traveller knew is now swallowed in new building, but the castle remains dominant and the harbour is still attractive. And there can be found some of those Georgian, Regency and Victorian edifices which, with all their frills, are as charming as some old maids. What has been added is another town on the North Bay – where Miss Fiennes, if she had peeped round the castle wall, would have seen nothing but fields and scrub land and probably more beasts and milch cows. Ever since her visit the place has been growing, and the end is not yet. From the time Harold Hardrada landed at Scarborough in 1055 and burned the original little town under the hill – founded by his predecessor, Thorgils Scarthi – by throwing down fire brands upon it, thus compelling the natives to rebuild their homes, I doubt if Scarborough changed greatly in the next 600 years. Certainly such old drawings and prints I have seen do not indicate many differences. The castle was built in the reign of King Stephen. The harbour was extended. The church was rebuilt after its destruction during the siege of the castle in 1645. But it remained in essence largely a fishing village.

The turning point was the discovery of the spa waters. It all started when Mistress Farrow, "a sensible intelligent lady" walked along the shore about 1620 and observed that some of the stones lying in the bed of a stream running from the cliff were stained an unusual colour. She tasted the water, decided that it had remedial qualities, and "it became the usual physic of the inhabitants". A discovery of this sort soon becomes talked about, particularly when Harrogate's medicinal waters were drawing visitors, and "Spaws" were becoming popular. So the fame of Scarborough water spread and "several persons of quality came from a great distance to drink it". Miss Fiennes noted that on the "sand by the Sea shore is the Spaw Well which people frequent . . . its something from an Iron or Steel minerall". A century later, when Thomas Hinderwell wrote his

History and Antiquities of Scarborough, there was a "Spaw Season", and it was offering the added attraction of sea-bathing from bathing chariots, "curious contrivances of houses on wheels for the better convenience of bathers".

A few miles from Scarborough beside the river Derwent and at the entrance to the lovely Forge Valley is something left from a still earlier time, the first of many pele towers we shall find in Yorkshire. Known as Ayton Castle, it was built when the danger of raids by the Scots was very real and when strong towers to serve both as dwelling houses and fortresses sprang up all over the north, south of the Border. Some had their entrance at first floor level, like a lighthouse or those round towers in Ireland, reached by a removable ladder, and with a walled enclosure for the protection of animals. Others, like Ayton, had a strong door at ground level with a narrow interior staircase having a sharp bend in it suitable for easy defence. The first floor provided the living quarters with sleeping quarters on the floor above.

In more peaceful years many of these towers had a more comfortable mansion added to them and became 'stately homes', but their defensive origins are easily recognisable. If this part of Yorkshire seems far removed from the Border it must be remembered that the invaders came deep into Yorkshire, ravaging and burning as they went. Scarborough itself was almost destroyed, apart from the castle, and a body of Scots under Robert Bruce travelled as far south as Beverley. Pele towers incorporated into larger houses or still standing as ruins, often utilised by farmers as store places, can be discovered across the country as far as Morecambe Bay.

Although many who motor down the Forge Valley will give only a passing glance to the shattered walls of Ayton Castle, its acquisition by Scarborough Corporation has at least helped to preserve what remains and has enabled indefatigable local archaeologists to make many finds of pottery, glass and metal, and even an ancient dovecote with "a layer of guano 12 inches thick still with the active smell of the poultry-house".

South of Scarborough one meets two disturbing factors in our coastline: the first is a recent development, the second centuries old. We come to the first of these at Filey, which remained in the 'select' stage of resort growth much later than its neighbours. To its ornate hotels came wealthy visitors with their families and 'nannies'. Because of its seclusion and pleasant sands, it was always regarded as 'an ideal holiday place for the children'. It still retained enough of the old fishing days to be attractive. It had pleasant walks to the long rocky promontory called the Brigg. So it remained up to the First World War, and partly so to the second. Then came that widespread change of taste in living, in which the bungalow was preferred to the house, the caravan to the boarding house, and the mass pleasures of the holiday camp to the family holiday. And all of these new preferences struck this part of the Yorkshire coast hard. On the outskirts of Filey is a gigantic holiday camp. In many of the little bays between there and Hornsea are clusters of bungalows. And towns, if not cities, of caravans, have appeared in every permitted place – and there are many of them. Whether or not we approve of this desire to 'get away from it all', usually in company with others of like mind, it must be said that the Victorians, with all their ornate building and pseudo-splendour, did not disfigure our coast. They had regard to the pleasantries of living and a sense of dignity which today we have lost. We have replaced this so often with a disfiguring rash of building and general spoilation.

This rash has spread southwards along the coast, surrounding the historic town of Bridlington, with its charming priory and busy harbour now lost in the garish trappings of a modern holiday resort. You have to search diligently for any trace of the old amid the bingo halls and the dance palaces of today. You have to wander into the old town a mile inland to find the graceful priory, still so beautiful in itself that one wanders how magnificent the far more extensive monastic buildings must have been before Henry VIII's commissioners had them demolished. If you travel a few miles out of the town to Sewerby you will find a substantial mansion and gardens converted by Bridlington Corporation into a delightful pleasure place complete with civilised amenities.

You have not to go far along the road to be aware of the bungaloid epidemic, the caravan sites and the modern ways of holiday-making. My own memory of Bridlington is one of boyhood, when the few terraces of stone-built houses which flanked the town marked the end of habitation. The rest was sand, miles and miles of it, with the great cliffs of Flamborough Head on one side and a vast sweep of unmarred coastline on the other as far as the eye could see. At the harbour side you moved in a world of fish, which you would taste fresh from the sea later in the day. Stolid, leather-faced fishermen handled the baskets and boxes and occasionally threw out strange large-eyed sea monsters for which they had their own names. The only concession to the holiday maker was a pleasure steamer and rowing boats for hire. That, now, seems worlds away.

The other development, which was happening then although I was not aware of it, is that Yorkshire is steadily losing some of its broad acres along this part of the coast below Flamborough. It is a process which has continued for many centuries at varying speeds. Some years ago a number of datum posts were driven into the low cliff edge from which measurements could be taken. Five years later several of the posts had disappeared altogether. Erosion by the sea had taken bites of anything up to sixty feet as far south as Withernsea. To walk along the beach here is a geology lesson, for these falls of boulder clay expose layers of Yorkshire coast that were laid down in early periods of time. To attempt to live near the edge of the cliffs, as is done by the owners of weekend chalets and bungalows at Skipsea and elsewhere, requires a high degree of brinkmanship. Your garden or your front door may disappear overnight, and you may follow unless you have emergency plans.

Complete towns with lovely names like Auburn, Hartburn and Owlthorne – spoken of in old records as "places of fair fame" – now lie beneath the waves, and an old man I met on this coast not long ago pointed seawards to where a farmhouse stood in his youth. That same night I slept in a bed at Hornsea which shuddered noticeably when waves struck the sea wall several hundred yards away. I wondered how long it would be before someone pointed out to another inquirer where this house had stood before the sea claimed it. It is all part of that geological tilting process which experts tell us is continuing to lift the west side of England and lower the east, so that while Harlech Castle in Wales has an old water-gate now far above sea level, villages in Yorkshire are gradually slipping into the sea.

Of half-a-dozen piers which once graced this long coastline only one, at Saltburn, remains. Storm damage and havoc created by ships swept out of control have brought about their end. Great gales frequently wash away shore installations in winter where in summer the holiday crowds bask in sunshine. It is always a surprise to find the southern extremity of this coast, that long pebbly bank which runs down to become Spurn

LINKS WITH THE PAST: *1, The Caedmon memorial at Whitby*
2, Captain Cook's memorial at Whitby

Head, still intact after centuries of battering. Yet it remains with its lighthouse and bird sanctuary to guard the entrance to Yorkshire's ancient river, the Humber.

Old Father Humber

On a day of scurrying clouds and frequent squalls I stood on the Corporation Pier at Hull – a place of glass and fancy ironwork which might well be mistaken for a bandstand or an unusual conservatory – and watched the pilots going off to boats moving in the River Humber. A fierce wind shook the framework of the glasshouse and sharp outbursts of rain swept across the wood-boarded floor so that I was driven to shelter in an alcove where an old greybeard has already ensconced himself. Silently we both watched through the rain-mist the procession of great ships, listened to their sirens, and smiled at the antics of the pilot boats as they tossed and bounced on the churned-up water and weaved about the larger vessels like sheepdogs rounding up a flock in a country lane. Then the old chap in the alcove, who had never spoken a word, though he nodded silently when I joined him, turned up his coat collar and began to move off.

"I tell you, mister," he said vehemently, "there's no greater river in Britain than Old Father Humber and his family, and that's a fact."

And with that he was gone.

As I contemplated this great river highway I realised the strength of his claim. A glance at the map of Yorkshire will show how the Humber gathers its waters from almost every corner of this infinitely varied county. They come from high limestone fells and heather-clad moors, from dark industrial valleys and from broad rivers in the plains flowing beneath ancient castles and through historic cities. Swale, Ure, Ouse, Nidd and Wharfe, Aire, Calder, Don, Hull, Rye and Derwent – what a lovely assembly of family names. And these are not all. Look at a larger map, and there you will discover that Humber has other and distant branches of the family gathering up the waters of Lincolnshire, Derbyshire, Nottingham, Stafford, Leicester and Warwick. That downward tilt of the land from west to east, the erosion of softer rocks, the capture of lesser streams by greater, the effect of glacial ice barriers, all of this brought the waters to the flat lands of the Humber estuary and so to the sea.

ON THE COAST: *1, Fisherfolk at Filey*
                       2, Scraping whalebones at Hull

I marvelled that day, not for the first time, at the greatness of this vast river system which has shaped so much of our Yorkshire story. At many places along the lonely coastline, which at Spurn Point, as we have seen, juts out to guard the meeting place of the Humber and the North Sea, you can lose count of time, not just of minutes but of centuries. There is little to tell you whether you are in the first century or the twentieth. A Hull trawler puts out for the Iceland fishing grounds and disappears from view, as fishing boats have gone out far back in time. A cargo boat or a tramp steamer passes along the horizon and is gone – only the smoke instead of sails dates it. Then there is nothing but the restless sea and the white birds over the waves. At any moment, it would seem, a long high-prowed ship like that discovered at Gokstad in Norway, propelled by narrow-bladed oars with a single red and white striped sail to aid steering, might come into sight with its complement of fair-haired Vikings armed with battle axes and swords such as have been found as far away as Orkney, Dublin and York. For just so did they come 1,000 and more years ago, these sea-rovers who knew every 'vik' or inlet of the sea not only in their own land but down the coasts of Scotland and southwards to the Humber. They were one of many waves of those who down the years descended upon this desolate shore to raid, pillage and destroy this land, but who stayed to call it home, just as centuries later exiled English kings came with their followers to regain their thrones.

Into this great estuary of the Humber came the earliest invaders. First, the Saxons and Angles, who for long had harried the eastern coast, some as tip-and-run raiders, some as settlers in small bands along the coast, others spreading inland as family groups. They explored the Humber and its tributaries, forming more settlements and giving them names based on individual persons or families with a termination indicating possession – like Brantingham, Wintringham and Hovingham – as we might say 'Brown's farm'. Occasionally they took an existing Celtic name and added their termination to it. By these names one can trace their footsteps. They progressed steadily along the Dales rivers and into the Plain of York, probably conflicting greatly with the few natives already there, and dropping new names or adding to old ones as they went. Later waves of Anglian people went further into the valleys, enclosing open land, clearing spaces in the forests and building settlements. By looking for the three significant words they applied to these holdings their movements can be traced over a wide area of Yorkshire. The three key words are 'ton', a family farm on open land enclosed by a fence or hedge; 'ley', a clearing in woodland; and 'ham', a farmstead. By noting the incidence of these words on a map it is possible today to discover what was then forest but now is open land, what areas they cleared with much labour, and which areas they found easiest to cultivate and on which to establish their farms. An illuminating example is the row of 'tons' in the place-names running along the north side of the Vale of Pickering, which rather suggests that their early founders had a keen eye for a south-facing slope for their agriculture. They knew which was the sunny side.

From the ninth century onwards successive invasions by Danes and Norsemen continued the story, bringing 'thorps' and 'bys' into the place-name picture: so we have Danish names like Scosthrop, Fridaythorpe, Kirkby (which marks a Christian Church influence); and the Norse 'erg', as in Sedbergh, or its variation 'burgh', as in 'Skarthi's burgh', now Scarborough. Modern visitors to Norway are familiar with the *saetrs*, the mountain summer pastures where sheep are run and hay is grown. Their conterpart can be found in the little villages of Wensleydale already mentioned, for as we have seen Norsemen came into the North over the Pennines as well as into the Humber. Although there are still older Celtic and Roman names to be traced in towns and villages on the map, and although the Normans in their turn brought French names to the Yorkshire scene, Anglo-Saxon and Scandinavian names predominate, certainly in the rural areas.

We have already seen how the sea's erosion of the coast from Flamborough to Spurn Point has eaten into the land, and this applied to the Humber itself. In more senses than one it could not have been easy for these invading settlers from across the sea to establish a foothold in these lands, for a score of places along the riverside were literally washed from under their feet. Old records carry the names of villages no longer existing—Pensthorpe, Sunthorpe, Frismarsh and Withfleet are some of the places of which there is no trace today, as well as the historic Ravenser, which remained long enough to be represented in Parliament and to be the landing place of exiled kings. Those who know their Shakespeare will find it referred to under the name of Ravenspurg:

> The banished Bolingbroke repeals himself
> And with up-lifted arms is safe arrived
> At Ravenspurg.

Only a cross once erected in the place to mark the landing-place of Henry IV and now moved to nearby Hedon remains as evidence.

Such knowledge as we have of the burning of monasteries, the desecration of relics, and the terror they brought, suggests that each of these invasions from across the sea must have seemed a catastrophe at the time to those already settled in the land. King Alfred is on record as saying of them that they were as bad as a cattle plague, which in a land dependent on cattle must have been a grim verdict. The original Celts resented the coming of the Saxons and Angles, although being few in number they probably did not come greatly into contact with the invaders. Within two centuries the Anglian folk developed their own culture, and life went on reasonably smoothly. The Venerable Bede, writing then, said, "Our times are so calm and peaceful that many of us, high and low, have given up the use of arms and prefer the tonsure and monastic vows. . . . What will be the end of this, the age to come will see." He spoke too soon, for little more than a century later the pagan Danes arrived, ravaged the east of Yorkshire, captured York and set up their own kingdom with that city as its capital. Archbishop Wulf fled from their attack and found safety at Addingham, in the Wharfe valley, which as its name implies was an Anglian farmstead untouched by the Danish invasion – as were many of the remoter Dales settlements.

Even while the invasions from across the North Sea were in progress, the restless Norsemen had raided the Scottish islands and explored the western coast as far as northern Ireland, where Olaf the White set up a Norse kingdom in Dublin in 852. From there it was an easy venture across the Irish Sea to the Isle of Man and to the coasts of Lancashire and Cumberland, from which they penetrated not only the Lake District but the Pennines and Yorkshire as far east as York, from where they set up their own establishment. Thus, linking up with invasions from the east, a Norse kingdom based oddly on Dublin and York replaced the Danish rule. An uneasy kingdom it must have been, for it had eighteen different kings in less than a century, but it gave us much of the pattern of future development in the shire.

How much contact these invaders, who became settlers, kept with their homelands is uncertain. The Ouse and the Humber were probably used by ships linking them with Denmark and Norway, though the same rivers seem to have cut them off from their kinsmen to the south in Lincolnshire. Scarborough, Whitby and the Tyne appear to have been used as ports by the Viking kings in York. Doubtless the Norse liking for rougher mountainous country inclined them to prefer the north, leaving the marshy lands at the foot of the Wolds to the Danes.

You may often be told that Yorkshire folk do not take easily to strangers – or "off-cummed uns" as they are called – or you may hear that a newcomer to any place must be "summered and wintered and summered again" before he is part of the community. Indeed, it was said of me when I moved from one part of the county to another. Yet it is curious how easily new people, new ideas and new cultures are assimilated into our life. I suspect it largely derives from this long story of successive waves of incomers which set the pattern of northern character and created a people able to exercise an infinite patience.

The pagan Danes were absorbed by the Angles and accepted their Christian ways; they intermarried and adopted many of each others characteristics. After the initial onslaught by the Vikings, the Norsemen found themselves part of a new community and settled in it. Some who came through Ireland had even been Christianised by the Celts they conquered. This process was curiously aided by differences in their ways of farming settlement. By nature, as I have remarked, the Norsemen preferred the higher lands and steep valleys in the fells; the Angles and Danes had found their place in the lowland plains and broader river valleys. They could live without too much interference. Here and there conflict continued, and a recent writer has suggested that the custom of 'first-footing' still observed in Yorkshire on New Year's Eve by which a dark man must be first across the threshold to bring good luck derives from the Celt's repugnance to the blond Angle or Saxon. The same writer notes that on parts of the East coast "it is thought desirable that the first foot should be fair, which may originate in Angle prejudice against his swarthy predecessor".

That may be so, but it is possible to travel from east to west across the country and find adjacent villages, one with an Anglian origin, another with a Danish termination to its name and, not far away a Norse 'saeter', suggesting that each community, while having its home territory, lived in due time with a good sense of neighbourliness. Where there are groups of similar names they probably originated in the first settlements of the incomers. There is a story in almost every one of these place-names and a dialect link with the earlier peoples. For example, we have many Grizedales, a link with the Norse pig-keepers, who kept their 'griss' in the dales. Skipton and Shipley and many similar names are derived from the Saxon 'sceap'. A common Dales name for a stream is the beck, which is still used in Norway.

A North Riding farmer once complained to me that one of his men was "as idle as a stee", which is a stile across a path. 'Keslop' which is a Dales term for the rennet used in cheese-making is from the Anglo-Saxon 'ceselib'. Trollers Gill, a spectacular ravine in Wharfedale, may link us with the Scandinavian 'trolls'. The grafting of the new upon the old, with here and there a lingering trace of an ancient legend or a strange superstition, enshrines much of the folk-lore of York-shire.

And not only place names and folk life, but folk speech, too. The Rev. M. C. F. Morris, who gave a lifetime to the study of the Yorkshire dialect, declared: "the home of our folk-talk lies on the other side of the North Sea. It is to the land of the Norseman that we must look for nearly all the component elements of our dialect ... speaking roughly I should say that at least three-fourths of our Yorkshire words may be traced either directly or indirectly to Scandinavian origin".

Folk Talk

When a number of Barnsley youngsters were recently brought in to play as schoolboy extras in a sound film to be shown in this country and in America their speech bewildered the film men. Not only did they pursue the familiar elision of all schoolboys whereby "put them in here" becomes "pur-remineer" or "astagorratanner" means "have you got six-pence", but they dropped naturally into the dialect so that "gerrit in t'goil 'oil" had to be translated as "get the ball into goal". Not only American audiences, who believe all Englishmen speak either 'upper-class' English or pseudo-Cockney, but even our own South Country viewers would have been mystified. So the film had to be given a new sound track for 'foreign' audiences. The original unadulterated track was kept for showing in Yorkshire.

Dialect is dying here, as elsewhere under the standardising influence of radio and television and through the greater mobility of people, but enough remains of the old words and forms of expression to puzzle the stranger. These remnants are like the artefacts dug out of archaeological sites, they are the surviving elements of the unwritten speech handed down from our early invaders through long generations. They can still puzzle the experts, and fragments are being lost all the time. It is nearly a century since J. Orchard Halliwell FRS. compiled a *Dictionary of Archaic and Provincial Words* going back to the fourteenth century and collected from all parts of the country. My copy is in two volumes totalling nearly 1,000 pages of small print. In the hundred years since this appeared it is probable that enough words have fallen out of our dialect speech to fill another two volumes. It is comforting that the technical developments which are banishing our dialects are being enlisted to preserve what is left. In the 1920s gramophone recordings were made of samples of Yorkshire dialect speech to illustrate the variations between one district and another. These have now been improved upon by tape recordings. The Yorkshire Dialect Society, founded in 1897, has been steadily putting into print old dialect writings and encouraging new writers to keep the tongue alive. The English department of the university at Leeds has devoted long and careful study to its linguistic roots while a Folklife department is at work on its social aspects.

If you travel across the county from, say, Holderness in the East Riding, through Cleveland in the North Riding, and arrive in Leeds in the West Riding you will have passed through some two dozen recognised dialect areas, where words, pronunciation, and forms of expression vary, and, with luck, you may have heard some samples of the speech. If in the Whitby area you hear that someone has been "up since cock-leet to get t'weshin done" it means only that someone rose early for wash-day. In the West Riding you may hear a downtrodden husband declare, "Aw've bin raddlin' t'carpets for t'wife ivvery wick end", which indicates he is "stalled" (tired) of beating carpets with a stick every weekend. In

Holderness they have a rounder speech than in the West, as in this from a local dialect poet:

> Whin I gor hoired et Beacon Farm a
> year last Martinmas,
> I fund we'd gor a vory bonny soort
> o'kitchen lass.
> And so I tell'd her plooin' made me
> hungry – that was why
> I awlus was a leatle sthrong on
> pudden and on pie.

These variations tend to be lost as they all have a common origin. The late A. Stanley Umpleby, who was an authority on the Cleveland dialect and wrote much in that form, many years ago sent me a note on how these variations overlap.

Cleveland dialect [he wrote] is spoken over a rather wider area than Cleveland proper. With minor variations it is spoken throughout the Plain of York and the country east thereof. Actually there is remarkably little difference between it and the East Riding. East Riding folk largely drop the article 'the' whereas, of course, we abbreviate it to 't'. (In Lancashire this becomes 'th'.) Actually, each is a relic of the old Northumbrian language and a word like 'croon', for instance, is common to Holderness and to the others. 'Croose' (elated) is found in the East Riding and in Cleveland and in both Burns and Allan Ramsey, and there are dozens of similar examples. The Scots are, I find, very surprised at these things, but the early Scottish poets, Dunbar, Barbour and many another wrote, as they said in Englysse and not in Scots at all.

Umpleby's reference to the Northumbrian language takes us back to the days when speech was developing from a purely tribal thing into some sort of uniformity. There grew up three main dialects, northern, midland and southern, and our northern or Northumbrian speech included the Lowland Scots as well as Yorkshire, as Umpleby points out. 'Moose' for mouse, 'ken' for know, for example are common to both, and when the Yorkshire poetess, Dorothy Una Ratcliffe, called one of her collections of verse *From All the Airts*, she was using the word for wind direction known all along the Border. I have seen it suggested that had it not been for Alfred the Great what we might call 'broad Yorkshire' could have become standard English, for in the days of the great kingdom of Northumbria it was the important dialect. When Alfred came to the throne the centre of affairs moved south, and southern dialect became the accepted speech until after the Conquest. Norman influence moved the style of tongue north again as far as the Midlands at a time when Anglo-Saxon, French and the Latin of the wandering friars was being fused into one English tongue, which was the language of Chaucer.

It is of interest that Professor Adam Sedgwick, the notable geologist and antiquarian, once compiled a list of Chaucer's words still used in the remote Dentdale in his own and his father's time, including the familiar dales word 'shepen' (shippon).

The purist (and the Rev. Morris was one) maintains that only the speech of the North and East Ridings can be regarded as true 'Yorkshire dialect' as the industrialisation of the West Riding down the centuries, beginning with the rise of the woollen industry (which brought workers from the Midlands and elsewhere) and the mining industry (which brought labour from Wales and Scotland) and continuing importations from many other parts of the country, have 'polluted' the local speech. Only in the predominantly agricultural north and east is the original speech retained in any purity.

When it was decided to make the gramophone recordings already referred to, one of the test pieces selected as allowing the necessary variations in the sounds of vowels and consonants in different parts of Yorkshire was the old story of "The Moose and the Cat":

> Theer wur once a Moose, tha knaws, 'at 'appened ti fall intiv a cask o' aale, tha knaws. A Cat 'at wur on t'look out for its dinner cooms oop an' sees t'lahtle beeast swimmin' in t' tub.
>
> "Sitha, Missis Cat," says Moose. "If tha'll get me oot o' this tha can a'e ma. Droonin's sich a wat death – an' ah caant abide t'smell o' beer."
>
> So t' Cat she lets doon her taail, tha knaws, an' t' Moose climbs oop. T' minnit she's oot she runs tiv her 'oil an' sits theer a-winkin her whiskers an' nibbling her naails.
>
> "Fair dues! Fair dues!" cries t' Cat. "Tha sed ah might a'e tha!"
>
> "Aw," says t' Moose. "Aw," she says. "Missis Cat," she says. "Fooaks 'll say owt when they're i' liquor!"

And here is a story still told in Swaledale which illustrates the strangeness of the traditional tongue. A man from the dale had been taken by a friend to Leeds for the first time, and he was fascinated by the big department stores. After he had walked round for some time an assistant asked if there was anything he required.

"Nay, Ah doant rightly know," said the Swaledale man," 'ev ye owt terrible good, like?"

The assistant explained impressively that there were few things they did not sell.

"Way, noo", said the dalesman. "Tha can get me a stee for t'beaux an' a pair o' kreels."

It took some time and much explanation to discover that what was wanted was a ladder for the loft and a pair of devices of tough cord network on a frame of hazel branches for carrying hay.

I remember once attending a school speech day in Craven at which children from local villages and farms read, recited and spoke in excellent standard English. Afterwards I congratulated one boy on his good speaking. "Aye," he said, "it sounded allreet didn't it? But Ah allus speak proper Yorkshire when Ah get home." I suspect that the old dialect is used more widely by the menfolk than by women, perhaps, because it is more expressive. We are so accustomed in these days to sleek, smooth speech, that the gritty pointed speech of the moors and dales is the more effective when we hear it. The influence of radio and television is spreading, although whether the speech it often substitutes is more desirable is a matter of opinion.

Away from the towns, where there is a variety of local lingo and intonation so that it is quite possible to tell from overheard conversations whether you are in Hull, Leeds or Bradford, dialect has its special characteristics varying – probably according to some far-off predominance of invasion and settlements – from one area to another, so that not only pronunciation but words used for the same object differ. These have been recorded, studied, chartered and analysed in great detail by the University of Leeds and the results published in scholarly volumes. It is still possible for the ordinary wayfarer to note these lingering dialect expressions in our villages, as I did by chance one snowy morning recently when I heard this remark:

"By gow. Yon colly looks fair moithered. Ah reckon it don't like this sluthery weather".

I had called on a retired Dales roadman in North Craven, who, before he took on the job of maintaining the tidiness of many miles of highways and byways, used to drive a trap regularly from the village inn to the station two miles away meeting every train – over twenty a day where there are less than half-a-dozen now – and regale his passengers with stories and reminiscences. He looked down his garden path where sleety snow bore only my footprints to his door. The trees dripped, the sky was grey, and a blackbird with its tail outspread scratched vigorously in the frozen grass to find food.

It was not a collie dog my roadman referred to, as I first thought, but the blackbird. He was using the old dialect name which one rarely hears in these parts now. Around York and in the East Riding it is more often called "an uzzel", which is a pronunciation of 'ouzle', and in the West is generally "a blackie". When he said it looked "moithered" he was using the word in the sense of 'bewildered'. You will hear dalefolk remarking after some upset, "Ah'm that moithered Ah don't fairly know which road to turn." "Sluthery", of course, means 'soft' or 'sticky'. There are many "sluthery roads" after snowfalls in the Dales.

Many once pungent expressions like "yonderly" for absent-minded, and "threeapin" for contradicting, are now almost lost, and will probably disappear for ever when the older generation goes. "Minnin-on" was an expression once widely used in the sense of 'a reminder'. An old daleswoman used to tell me her husband "never needed minnin-on" when opening time came round. Curiously, the same phrase was often used for a morning snack or 'elevenses'. I presume the snack was a reminder of a bigger meal to follow.

"Dowly" is another wonderful word meaning despondent or low-spirited. A Dales doctor told me he had an elderly woman patient who became very depressed and unhappy. So he urged her to go out more often and mix with people in the nearby market town. She returned some time later and said she was no better. "Ah took thi advice, doctor," she said. "Ah've been out to three funerals in a fortneet and Ah'm just as dowly as ever Ah was."

"Thrang" for busy, "muckment" for trash and "slape" for slippery are words now seldom heard.

With them have gone some of those fine similies which were once so characteristic of Yorkshire folk – in the towns as well as in the rural areas. They summed up so much in so few words. We still talk of being "as fit as a fiddle" and "as clean as a whistle" but who remembers "to spin like a scopperil" (a top), "as straight as a yard of pump water", or to describe a girl who is "as fat as a butcher's dog", yet was "as nimble as a cat on a backstun" – a reminder of the days when oatcakes were baked on a backstone. I once complained to a farmer that it was a long road to his farm, "Aye", he said, brightly, "if it had been any shorter it wouldn't have reached." And a little later his wife remarked of a function she had attended: "Ah were that excited Ah felt in a hurry all over."

Yet occasionally even rural Yorkshire finds it difficult to keep up with the changing world. In a farm kitchen recently a woman busy ironing remarked in a worried voice, "These new-fangled irons fair puzzle me. You see, electric irons get hotter all t'time, while t'owd flat irons allus got colder. Ah'm fair gorstumbalised." At least, that's how she pronounced it.

As I have said, radio and television are ironing out differences of speech and giving us a uniform tongue, a process assisted by greater human mobility particularly in rural areas. Where a century ago a moorland family might see no one outside their own local community for months together, all speaking the same dialect that was almost a foreign language to the "off-cummed un", now every adult member of that family has some form of transport from a bicycle to a car, and over the remotest farm you will see a television aerial. The process had begun nearly a century ago when Joseph Wright, the remarkable millboy who became a philologist of international repute, began to collect specimens of local speech for his monumental *English Dialect Dictionary*. Groups of local enthusiasts assisted in the gathering, even then no easy task. Out of this grew the Yorkshire Dialect Society, formed in 1897, with the Marquess of Ripon as its first president. By the collection of glossaries of old trade terms varying from those of the Sheffield cutlers to the fisherfolk of the coast, and from the lead-mining industry to the farms, by recording the speech of surviving dialect speakers, and by the publication of poems, plays and stories in the vernacular, something is being saved of the harvest that was planted by those who sailed into the Humber long ago.

I doubt if any enthusiastic Yorkshireman would today envisage a return of the old vocabulary, although he sings "On Ilkla' Moor Ba Tat" on festive occasions and talks of a "reet good do" afterwards. But dialect is part of the county's heritage and tradition which links us with our forebears, their ways of life and their lore more intimately even than the stones and the artefacts which are so abundant in the county.

Local dialect poets, in whom the county has abounded since the seventeenth century, have done much to keep the old speech alive. I can remember when no entertainment was complete without a dialect reading or recitation. Old favourites were welcomed to regular repetition, even though the audience knew them off by heart. New pieces were given a critical hearing by knowledgeable listeners. Lamp or candle-lit readings round firesides pleased those whose daily speech was the dialect they heard read, and the finer points of humour, even though known by heart, were as much appreciated as the wise-cracks of a television comedian. The material came from the low-priced 'almanacks' and 'annuals' filled with stories, jests, poems, riddles which were published regularly throughout the county. Their contributors included many whose names became household words – Thomas Blackah, John Hartley, Samuel Laycock, Ammon Wrigley and John Castillo, to mention only a few. Some of their work was gathered up into slim bound volumes still treasured in rural homes and commanding a high price when occasionally they come on to the market. An anthology of this material was published by the Yorkshire Dialect Society a few years ago under the title of *White Rose Garland*. In it the editors point out that much of its subject matter "was an indictment of the ills and miseries that followed in the wake of expanding trade and a machinery-dominated economy", as well as that which came from a joy in the countryside beyond the industrial areas, where the birds, the flowers and the wind on the heath provided an antidote. And, of course, humour was always there, both in the poetry and in the tales that were told round the fireside and in the market place.

A strong sense of humour has always been marked in Yorkshire folk in all three Ridings. It can be seen in the story of "the Moose and the Cat", already quoted, and in a hundred similar traditional stories, like that of the farmer who advertised for a smart lad. A confident youth made his appearance.

"Ye're wantin' a smart lad, aren't yer? Well I'm 'im. Ah can dew ommust owt ther' is ta dew on a farm – milk, plew, sow, sarve t'hens and t'pigs – there's nowt yo'll hev 'ere at Ah couldn't manage."

"Tha duzzent hawf fancy thisen, anyway," said the farmer. "Can ta wheel a barra load o' sunshine?"

"Aye, easy enuff," said the lad, "if tha'll fill it."

It is evident in the "speyks" or sayings which are common currency in the towns and the countryside. To describe a wealthy man what is more apt than to say "He's that well-off, he's bow-legged wi' brass," or of a man who tries to keep up appearances on very little, "Ah reckon he nobbut has a spare suit except when he's i' bed."

It is probably this sense of humour, which fortunately can laugh at itself, that has fostered the delight in the daftness of Yorkshire folk, in which the normal ways of the world are ignored and folly becomes wisdom. Some legend of daftness would appear to be associated with almost every town and village in Yorkshire, though some places have achieved a reputation for being dafter than others. Austwick, a rural village in the West Riding, perhaps has a stronger claim to leadership than most. Its natives are known as Austwick 'carls', probably a corruption of churls, but later synonymous with queerness of behaviour, although the reason for this is no longer apparent as Austwick folk are as sane as other Yorkshire dales-folk. Some of their more memorable feats are immortalised in a rhyme which runs:

> Austwick carls
> Whittle to t'tree
> Bull o'er gate and
> Pig through t'stee.

The explanation is that many years ago Austwick was so poor a village that all the residents shared one butcher's knife, the whittle. This was hung in a tree in the centre of the village green, and when anyone wanted it and the knife had not been replaced he would shout, "Whittle to t'tree," meaning "Bring our whittle to the tree." This whittle also figures in another incident, for on one occasion the men of Austwick were working on the nearby Swarth Moor, with their only knife, gathering bracken for bedding. When they knocked off for a rest they had no place to put the knife, for Swarth Moor boasted no tree. After some discussion they stuck the knife into the ground, but to remember where it was they marked the place as being where a cloud shadow covered the spot. They were surprised later to have difficulty in finding the knife, the sky having cleared in the meantime.

In the matter of the bull and the gate there are two stories. The first relates that a local farmer discovered one morning that a young bull in one of his fields had caught its head in the gate and was bellowing with annoyance. Faced with this dilemma the farmer, deciding something should be done about the matter and not being able to push the bull's head back through the gate, cut off the animals' head to make the task easier. Legend has it that he was surprised when the beast died. But another and more likely story is that an Austwick farmer, wishing to get a bull out of a field, procured the assistance of several of his neighbours to help lift the bull over the gate. After trying in vain for some hours they decided to send to the village for more assistance, and when the farmer opened the gate to leave the field to gather his friends the bull followed, which, to the amazement of the Austwick people, solved the problem. Similarly when it was necessary to get a pig through a 'stee' or stile, and the pig proved larger than the gap the pig's owner broke down the hedge to make a way large enough. The same man of Austwick had to take a wheelbarrow to a neighbouring village and to save a hundred yards or so of travelling by the ordinary road he went through the fields and had to lift the barrow over eleven stiles.

Austwick is still known locally as 'Cuckoo town', from the story of Austwick villagers who tried to capture a cuckoo by building a wall round the tree in which it roosted – a weakness which was shared by a number of other villages in the south of England, and seems to have first appeared in print in a sixteenth century book entitled *Merrie Tales of the Mad Men of Gotham* – a village near Nottingham which still has its Cuckoo Hill.

Although Austwick outdistances all other competitors, there is no lack of runners-up for the daftness stakes. Cowling, in Airedale, can provide an example. There, after some years of controversy, it was decided that the church should be moved two or three yards to one side to overcome a tendency it had to slide. A team of well-made lads went to do the job and, having placed their coats on the grass, they walked round to the other side of the church and "got agate thrustin' ". Unfortunately, while they were busy pushing someone stole their coats. But they were unaware of this. When they had "pushed thersens to a standstill" they walked round to see what progress they were making. The blacksmith, their leader, looking in vain for their garments, wiped his brow and said: "Nay, what the dickens, chaps? We've shoved t'church on top o'our cooits. Come on, lets heave it back!" At the other side of Yorkshire the people of Whitby once showed they had an ability for daftness which ranks them high in the claim to fame. The mouth of the River Esk, upon which Whitby stands, has for long years had to be dredged free from the sand which threatened to silt up the harbour. Some years ago the old dredger began to show signs of wear and a new dredger was ordered. It was decided that the dredger should be given an official welcome and a brass band was engaged to play it in with appropriate ceremony. Unfortunately, the band made a sad mistake. Instead of going down to the pier head to await the arrival of the dredger by sea it marched off to the railway station and there stood patiently expecting the dredger to be disembarked on the platform.

Town bands seem ever prone to make mistakes in Yorkshire. It is recorded, I believe, of Brighouse, in the West Riding, that on one occasion its very famous band played at the Crystal Palace and won a trophy. Returning overnight to its home town the men of Brighouse decided that their fellow townsmen should not be left ignorant of the band's achievement and agreed to play "See the Conquering Hero Comes" as they marched in the early morning from the station to the centre of the town. But, in order not to waken the inhabitants while so doing, they also decided to remove their boots and march in their stockinged feet. The little mining village of Kippax has a reputation for doing peculiar things in a peculiar way. Not only is it reputed of them that they put up wire netting to keep the fog out, but also as the place "where they put the pig on the wall to see the band go past". What band it was or why the pig should be interested I have no means of knowing. But it is the sort of thing which they would be likely to do in a village where, it is said, at least one miner used to go to work with holes bored in the soles of his clogs so that the water could run out!

In the East Riding they frequently have snowstorms which isolate the Wolds villages for weeks at a time. Indeed, snow is their principal enemy. And the snowplough is their principal means of fighting it. Not very long ago one East Riding village decided that a horse-drawn snowplough was out of date in these progressive times. Instead they tried the experiment of sending out the snowplough hitched to the back of a steam roller. Not only was the job done in half the time but the roller made a nice smooth track on which the plough could slide so that it need not be forced through the snow at all. Another village had the brilliant idea of bringing out the tar boiler after a snowstorm, boiling the snow and pouring it down a drain. It was a farmer in the same part of Yorkshire who is reputed to have bent the barrels of his gun so that he could shoot marauding wood

FROM EARLY DAYS: *1, Sheep in the Three Peaks country*

                                   2, Appletrewick, so named in the Domesday Book

pigeons and sparrows round the corners of stacks in his stackyard. Legend adds that he bent them too far and shot himself in the seat!

It is not only the little villages of Yorkshire which have their peculiarities, however. There is a legend, which seems to have some foundation in fact, of a worthy alderman of a city council in the West Riding suggesting, when the subject of buying a gondola for the local park lake was under discussion, that they should buy two and let them breed. Of a city not far away there was a similar discussion on certain civic property, and one worthy councillor suggested that a verandah would be a useful addition. "What's the use of getting one of them?" asked the chairman. "There's nobody can play it if we do."

I have a suspicion that much of this lore of native daftness was perpetrated, or perhaps even invented, in times when the telling of tales, like the reading of dialect poems, was a source of local entertainment, just as the ballad singers and minstrels and jesters of an earlier age went the round of the great halls and castles. It was also a way of proclaiming the superiority of one community over another, as in the multitude of local rhymes still remembered in many parts of the county. For example, it was said that:

> Folk who live on the Plain of York
> Use a scythe for a knife
> And a rake for a fork.

Two villages on the Plain were held up to ridicule in a verse which said:

> Well and Snape
> Wheer they grin and gawp
> And bray hard water soft
> Wi' a clooase prop.

Carefulness with money was derided – or was it envied? – at Great Ayton, near Middlesborough, where it was said "Yattoners wade over t'beck to save their brigg," and of three other villages it was declared:

> If you wish to find a fool
> And do it without mistake,
> Take the first you meet in Stillington,
> In Easingwold or Crayke.

This heritage of nonsense is a rich store in Yorkshire, and it may have been one of the 'daft ones' of the county who figured in a famous tailpiece by Bewick when he portrayed a man

COUNTRY CHURCH: *The village church of Thornton-in-Craven*

sawing a bough from a tree while sitting on the wrong end of the bough. Fame comes to men and places in strange ways and for strange reasons and perhaps one kind of distinction is as good as another, but I doubt if any other county can claim so many communities whose reputation is proudly founded on daftness.

Spreading the News

In these days of 'instant news' it is difficult to imagine a time when men had nothing to communicate, even in dialect. Primitive peoples living unto themselves in tiny isolated communities had no need for wider communication than a call or a shout could provide. Such news as there was would not extend beyond tribal bounds. Whether it was conflict with other tribes, or barter and exchange between them, which expanded their world we have no means of discovering, but there must at some time have arisen the need to know of the affairs of others and hence to communicate. It must have taken a long time for the news of the first Roman landing in Britain to spread far beyond the beach-head. Probably tribes living in Yorkshire knew nothing of it until the Roman troops themselves appeared a century or so later, even though by that time the Brigantes had an organised way of life with a king or queen and a system of currency, and some contact with other tribes. It was left to the invaders to provide the first network of communications.

Successive Roman invasions were accompanied by the creation of forts and military centres linked by foot and chariot communications on the roads they built. York, for example, was the headquarters of the Ninth Legion and from this base a wide area of the north was controlled, so that a great deal of the road traffic must have consisted of messengers. The development of lead mining and other industries under Roman control presupposes a regular system of information, probably of visual signals.

When after three centuries of Roman occupation Saxon pirates began raiding the east coast of England the necessity for improved communications must have become pressingly obvious, and one can imagine many worried conferences at the headquarters of the official who was given the title of Count of the Saxon Shore and the task of coping with the new menace from across the sea. The outcome was a series of signal stations along the Yorkshire coast from the Tees to Filey and probably farther south linked in the north with York and Malton, where there was a big fort and camp, and with the Roman fleet on the Humber which could be called upon to repel the invaders.

These signal stations, or their remains, can be seen today at Huntcliff, Goldsborough, Peak (near Ravenscar), Scarborough and Filey. Not too far away are the Cawthorn Camps, near Pickering, which provided a sort of base for the area, all of which have been excavated and mapped. There is evidence of violent struggles against the raiders at some of these signal stations. At the bottom of a well inside the Huntcliff station were found the bones of the defenders, including women and children, and the remains of wearing apparel. Some of the stations must have had an unpleasant time.

The method of signalling used in these towers has been much debated, but it seems to be generally agreed that some sort of pole or mast bearing a semaphore was erected on each, so that in effect a continuous visual link was established, possibly with a fire signal at night. This would apply not only to the coastal stations but to cross-country links with York, Catterick, Brough and other forts, so that the countryside must have been sprinkled with these tower signals not unlike the radar masts and booster-stations of our own time. Thus does history repeat itself.

It is not improbable that this visual method of passing on news was one of the legacies the Romans left us, for the beacon fire has a long history which leaves little gap between the exodus of the Romans and the early use by their Scandinavian successors of fire signals. There is an Old English word 'beacen', a sign (from which we derive 'beckon'), and the Norse 'breck', a raise or hill, which may confirm early acquaintance with the method. Certainly the Scots used beacons as a warning of the approach of the English when the Border was a 'debatable land', and had a code by which the significance of the fires should be understood. Lord Coke is on record as saying that "the erection of beacons, light-houses, and sea marks, is a branch of the Royal Perogative; the first whereof was anciently used to alarm the country in case of the approach of an enemy, and all of them are signally useful in guiding and preserving vessels at sea by night as well as by day".

Prominent hill-tops are today often designated Beacon Hill, particularly in coastal regions, and although a study of place-names does not reveal many of them recorded before the sixteenth century, there is no doubt that along the south coast a beacon system operated very early against French raids. Early beacons were, doubtless, fires of locally handy and hastily gathered materials, but were later carefully planned. We have it stated, "Before the reign of Edward III the beacons were but stacks of wood set upon high places, which were fired when the coming of enemies was descried; but in his reign pitchboxes, as now they be, were, instead of these stacks, set up; and this properly is a beacon."

Beacons came into their own in Yorkshire in 1588, the year of the Spanish Armada. Long before then England had expected an assault on her territory by the Spanish fleet. As G. M. Trevelyan points out, "In the twenty years before the coming of the Armada, ocean sailing and the tactics of the broadside has been perfected by English seamen." One of the preparations on land had been the perfecting of "an early warning system" of beacons around the coast and inland to muster troops and defences. Macaulay's famous poem relates the picturesque result:

> For swift to east and swift to west the ghastly war-flame spread,
> High on St. Michael's Mount it shone: it shone on Beachy Head.
> Far on the deep the Spaniard saw, along each southern shore,
> Cape beyond cape, in endless range, those twinkling points of fire.

and so it continued:

> Till Skiddaw saw the fire that burned on Gaunt's embattled pile.
> And the red glare on Skiddaw roused the burghers of Carlisle.

Along the Yorkshire coast there was a chain of beacons, so linked that each gave the signal for the lighting of others. For example:

Hernewell, 2 beacons, is seated upon a hill half a mile from the sea, and they give light to Easington two beacons and Danby beacon.

Easington, 2 Beacons, is seated upon a hill called Racliffe, and they give light to Brotton beacon and Danby beacon.

Danby, is seated upon a hill about four miles from the sea. It giveth light throughout all Danby forest, Westerdale, Glaisdale and Egton lordship, and can give no further light southwards for hills and dales.

It was ordered that the beacons should be watched diligently by wise and discreet men living close by, so that there should be every day two persons and every night three persons in attendance. On the appearance of ships of doubtful purpose, after consultation among the wise and discreet men, one beacon only should be fired. If a great number of ships appeared with intent to invade, two beacons had to be fired, which was a warning to keepers of inland beacons to fire one of theirs and "that every man in charge put himself in armoure and be redy". In an extreme emergency three beacons were fired – where there were three together – and this was the signal for the general lighting of beacons everywhere and the hastening of men "with all speed to the place or shore from whence the fyrst lighte was given". Such a muster of men in the East Riding brought together an infantry force of 1,600, which included calivermen, pikemen, hillmen and bowmen.

Not many of the beacons remain intact with their fire-baskets and receptacles for holding tar barrels, although most of their sites are known. I have a vague memory of one standing in the Whitby area when I was too young to know much of its purpose, and I have assisted in heaving material for a giant bonfire on to the top of Ingleborough, which once had its own beacon linking the Yorkshire chain with Lancashire. But this was to celebrate a coronation rather than to communicate bad news.

Although far from the coastal region, the West Riding had many beacon hills. Nowadays young people climb Beamsley Beacon in Wharfedale to see the sun dance, which it reputedly does on Easter Day. But there was a time in the mid-seventeenth century, when a Dutch invasion was feared, when beacons were prepared on Beamsley, on Buckden Pike, on Ingleborough and many other hills, though it does not appear that they blazed into the night sky even when the Dutch ships appeared in the Thames. Instructions had been issued by the authorities that there must be sufficient fuel to keep them blazing for twelve hours.

It was about this time that York Minster was utilised as a beacon site. An old account of the Minster, published in 1740, says that "In the year 1666, by Order of the Duke of Buckingham, a Turret of Wood was erected, covered with lead and glazed, on the top of the steeple (on the central tower). This was to put lights into upon occasion, to serve as a Beacon to alarm the country, in case the Hollanders or French, with both which Powers we were then at war, should attempt to land on our Coasts." There is no evidence that it was ever lit.

We are accustomed to the daily round of 'alarums and

excursions' to which the press, radio and televsion treat us. When these were fewer I presume it was natural they should be taken more seriously. So in the days when Napoleon was Europe's menace the volunteers who had been recruited in the Yorkshire dales drank their evening ale with one eye on the nearest beacon. There the lonely watchman sat beside his heap of fuel. Perhaps his sense of responsibility enlarged his fears that 'Boney' was on his way, for one night when the custodian of Penhill Beacon in Wensleydale saw a far-off glare in the direction of Roseberry Topping in Cleveland, he kindled his fire and piled on the fuel. Throughout the dale men bade their families farewell, grabbed their weapons, and set off to repel the invader. They reached Thirsk before they discovered the Roseberry 'beacon' was no more than a barn fire. However they were publicly thanked for their alertness, and Napoleon himself was doubtless duly impressed.

Certainly after Napoleon's time the beacons were no longer kept refurbished. They vanished from use and often from memory, save as place-names. Other ways of spreading good and bad tidings came into being.

There seems to be no record of when the first printed matter reached Yorkshire. Ballads handed down from generation to generation recounted old gallantries and events. The monks penned their manuscripts in our abbeys and had their libraries of such writings. Caxton produced abroad, before he brought his press to England, the first printed book in our language – oddly *The Game and Playe of Chess* – between the years 1474 and 1475, but because of the rigid censorship of a kind not unknown in our modern world, the output of printed matter even of new-sheets must have been extremely limited. There was another difficulty, too, which arose out of the mixture of tongues spoken by those invaders from overseas whose descendants populated this land.

It is difficult for us to realise today that Caxton had no English language in which to print his books. So many peoples from so many lands had given us so many forms of speech and so many dialects that a farmer or even a clerkly man in our north-country would have had difficulty in making himself understood beyond his own small territory. As we have seen there was not just one Yorkshire dialect but many, widely spoken in limited regions until quite recent times. Caxton faced this problem and commented that the language had changed even in his own lifetime "and that comyn englysshe that is spoken in one shyre varyeth from another". As an example he related how a merchant from a ship held up in the Thames had landed in Kent to seek supplies of food, and particularly he asked for eggs. "And the good wyfe answerede that she coude speke no frenshe." Not until someone told her he wanted "eyren" did she understand his needs. "Lo," asked Caxton plaintively, "what sholde a man in thyse dayes now wryte, 'egges' or 'eyren'?" As the merchant's name was "Sheffelde" I have sometimes wondered if it was a Yorkshireman who set Caxton the task of deciding what was good English speech.

Such other news as reached the north came by occasional travellers and the few mails carried by postboys on horseback. As their speed, allowing for stoppages, averaged only three or four miles an hour such tidings as they brought were belated and often meaningless on arrival. It was not until "one of the greatest reforms ever made in the post Office" – as a contemporary described the carriage of mails by coach – came about in 1784 that general news began to reach Yorkshire within a reasonable space after its occurrence. Newsletters written in London and sent out in manuscript form to subscribers in Yorkshire was the accepted way of spreading the news. Such letters would be circulated among those neighbours who could read or would be read to those who could not until the paper was tattered and the writing illegible. Politics, foreign intelligence, some sport and news of the growing printed literature provided the contents of these journals. They were written and copied by hand by a considerable number of journalists and scribes scratching furiously with quill pens in dark rooms and cellars, for the work was not greatly remunerative. There were few coffee houses in Yorkshire at that time except in the larger towns, but where they existed the contents of the newsletters were read and argued over. The fact that a newsletter was subscribed for by the establishment was an added attraction to customers.

Printed newspapers appeared early in the eighteenth century. *The Leeds Mercury* came into being in 1718 and *The Leeds Intelligencer* in 1754, to be renamed *The Yorkshire Post* 112 years later. In other provincial towns there were papers bearing titles like *Courant, Journal,* and in Northern Ireland *The Belfast News-Letter,* all indicative of their origin as hand-written sheets. Heavy "taxes on knowledge" (by the Act of 1712 this was 1d on a full sheet and $\frac{1}{2}$d on a half sheet) as well as duties on the paper and on advertisements limited their scope and growth. Not until, the end of both licensing and censorship in the reign of William IV was there real freedom of publication for the dissemination of news. Speed in its transmission grew with the improvement of roads and mail services, it leaped forward with railway transport, and became almost instantaneous with the coming of the electric telegraph and later technical development. What might be called the 'unearthly' aspect of all this is found in the fact that news was once collected by balloon and is now disseminated by satellite through radio and television.

3

Stone upon Stone

Building The Churches – The Way of the Monks – York Minster

Not the least of the pleasures of travelling in Yorkshire is the variety of domestic building to be encountered in a day's journey. Eastwards from the grey stone villages and low solid farmhouses of the Dales country, with their barns and laithes solitary on the fellsides amid a maze of limestone walls, to the coloured brick and pantile-roofed houses of the Plain of York with here and there a thatch still remaining, and on to the great farmsteads of the East Riding, the pattern is continually changing. Similarly the traveller from the north to south will mark the transformation from the gay white-washed farm buildings of Teesside to the ancient and sombre cottages of the weavers on the Yorkshire-Lancashire border. Yet it is no less possible to discover a striking similarity of design in many regions dictated by the availability of stone or wood or brick, or reflecting local differences between industries, such as textiles, or mining or fishing, as well as the personal taste of the landowner or builder.

To interpret this variety we must recall a little history. We take some pride in the fact that we are an Anglo-Saxon people and that the England of today springs from the tradition they began after the Romans had departed. Our landscape began to take shape and our village emerge when Anglo-Saxon settlers erected their first groups of primitive homesteads surrounded by open fields cultivated in strips on ground they had cleared from the scrub. They were agriculturists by nature and not only tilled the ground but fed their livestock, particularly swine, on the beech mast and acorns and the young shoots of the forest, and kept bees for mead-making. They encouraged their sons to found new homesteads and bring more land under cultivation. Many such early villages can be traced in their original patterns in the western Dales, and the evidence of their strip cultivation is still visible on the low fell sides. Our landscape then must have resembled aerial photographs of primitive lands with dense forests, and here and there cultivated clearings and hutments.

In time the settlers found the inclination and the means for other things than cultivating crops and rearing cattle. In Yorkshire churches today Saxon work can be found, usually in the tower, indicating a place of worship that was venerable before the Normans set foot in England and reflecting the influence of Christianity on people who previously had worshipped a varied assortment of gods and goddesses. By the time of the Conquest there were well-established townships, named as they appear in *Domesday Book*, with a pattern of agriculture, worship, local government, and justice.

There was, too, a literature fostered by the early Saxon monasteries in the north. This suffered so severely, however, when the Danes raided these parts and burned the monasteries and their books that King Alfred despairingly declared: "So clean was learning gone out of the land that very few this side of the Humber could understand the meaning of their own Latin Service books, or translate aught out of Latin into English."

As we look upon the Saxon crosses which still remain and gaze at the fragments of Saxon epics like *Beowulf* which have come down to us after this destruction we can only guess at a way of life in which, while the peasants worked in the fields, the monks could write and illuminate their sacred books, write poetry and carve in stone and metal. Although we know the place of their settlements and their townships we can only presume that these early invaders used their skill as shipwrights in the construction of their crude homes, and occasionally some acquired skill in stonework, such as can be seen at Ledsham, in the West Riding, and at Hovingham, in the North Riding, where they erected their sacred places.

Little actual Anglo-Saxon building survives however, as, until much later, village housing was probably no more than dwellings of wood, wattle-and-daub or unshaped stones, with a turf or ling roof. Folk moots and the dispensation of justice were conducted for the most part in the open air for lack of adequate premises. Even the places of worship were still in many places built of local timber. When Coifi, the high priest of the old heathen faith, decided to turn Christian he rode to the temple of Goodmanham, near Market Weighton in the East Riding, threw his staff into the wooden building and urged his onlookers to burn it down. And when Edwin the King later followed suit and asked to be baptised the ceremony took place in a wooden church hastily erected in York which became the first York Minster.

Not until the coming of the 'cruck' building – which for the first time made the Englishman's home something more than a place of shelter from the elements – are we provided with evidence of how early villagers lived. Two bent trees, or a single tree trunk divided down the middle, were set up on end and joined at the top and middle to make a wooden *A*. Another pair was set a little distance away, and the two joined by timbers. Here was the framework of a building which could then be filled in with the usual wattle-and-daub, wood or stones, and roofed with turf or ling or straw thatch according to the locality. It was at last capacious enough to serve both as a dwelling place for the family and accommodation for the stock. Something similar I have seen in the wilder parts of Connemara in Ireland. Indeed over there, as I discovered from many who were born and brought up in such houses, there is great reluctance to move out of them into modern cottages provided by the authorities, "Sure, we were much warmer in the old ones," I was told.

From these cruck houses, which seem to have appeared widely in Yorkshire, the stone cottages and farms of today have evolved. Examples of the original structures have been saved and re-erected in several North Country folk museums, notably at Hutton-le-Hole, to which a still surviving structure at Danby on the North Yorkshire moors was transported recently piece by piece and re-erected, with its salt-box and witch post (to ensure good fortune) and thatched roof.

As the original cruck houses proved inadequate to the growing households additional bays were added, known today as 'outshuts', revealing their Norse origin – 'shot' or 'skot' meaning a part shut off from the rest. So emerged the long house, which has lasted to our own time, with the 'house-place' at one end with square window spaces and the shippon or byre for cattle (on a lower level to carry off the manure) at the other, this having only narrow slits for illumination and ventilation. Examples of these can be seen in Wharfedale and Airedale and elsewhere in the Dales. Thatch, which was a commoner form of roofing in the 'straw country' than in the pasture lands, can still be seen in the North Riding villages in the Harome, Pockley and Farndale areas, although it is fast disappearing. Of some forty occupied thatched houses remaining in the county, I believe over thirty are in the North Riding. Thatch has been displaced by pantiles, common away from the Pennine area, which were introduced early in the eighteenth century.

So the landscape developed as new invasions from Denmark and Norway in the ninth century and later increased the population. Division of Yorkshire into Ridings (or 'thirdings') probably came about at this time with a sub-division into 'wapentakes', administrative districts whose freemen met at regular intervals. I can very well remember seeing the remains of the ancient 'shire oak', where the Skyrack Wapentake was believed to have held its meetings 1,000 years ago, still standing, though long dead, by the roadside on the outskirts of Leeds. A plaque now marks the site, and is a reminder that observed custom rather than written law was the basis of Saxon life. It is tempting to picture the sort of nation which might have evolved had this way of life continued unbroken.

Nine hundred years after the Norman Conquest it is difficult for us to imagine the impact on that old way of life of a completely new culture. Previous invasions of this land had come from Germanic and Scandinavian peoples with something of a common outlook not too remote from our own. The Normans, although historically descended from earlier Norsemen, brought a legalistic Latin attitude of mind which they imposed upon the existing pattern. Not until Chaucer's day some three centuries later does England reassert herself, in G. M. Trevelyan's words, "as a distinct nation, no longer a mere oversea extension of Franco-Latin Europe".

More than one historian has called the Norman Conquest "a disaster for the North", and so it must have seemed to those then living in this part of the country. Faced by continuing rebellions three years after his defeat of Harold at Hastings, Norman William was as ruthless as some of the armies we have known in our own time. He came north through Lincolnshire, found the Humber held against him by Danes, so turned west, crossed the river Aire near Pontefract and advanced on York, which had been deserted by its inhabitants, He then swept north to Durham destroying every town and village on the way, creating a terrible devastation in which "the bodies of the dead were left to rot as none were left to bury them". Wild beasts roamed where farms and homesteads had been. The 'Harrying of the North' achieved its purpose of safeguarding his rule against any further rebellion. To consolidate his power William not only built castles himself, as at York, but bestowed territory widely distributed throughout the country upon his supporters, who themselves built castles to safeguard their rights. *Domesday Book* records that the county was held by nearly thirty "tenants-in-chief". Count Alan the Red's castle at Richmond, although greatly shattered, still stands high over the river Swale. You can see the ruins of the castle Ilbert de Lacy built at Tateshale (now Pontefract). Roger de Busli, who was given land in south Yorkshire and Nottinghamshire had the castle at Tickhill, which we have noted on one of our ways in. There were other castles, to a total of a dozen or more, scattered about the county from Scarborough to Conisbrough, and they must have inspired awe in the minds of those who lived about them. Certainly they were the outward signs of a new era.

The Norman castle was basically a stone tower or keep erected on a mound, built first by masons brought from France – some of whose distinctive work can be seen at Richmond – and then by men trained under them. Later the same skilled masons turned their hands to building the large number of Norman churches. It seems likely that the skills in wood inherited by generations of Anglo-Saxon settlers in its turn produced the carpenters. Out of this came the technique of building in stone and timber that provided improved domestic building and from which evolved in due time the great halls and stately mansions which today we pay our pence to visit.

With the coming of the Normans some of the original settled communities and their freemen lost their rights of pasture. No longer did the land belong to those who cultivated it, but instead it became a possession of the king, as a royal forest (not necessarily wooded) with severe forest laws to protect the king's rights, or was bestowed upon his followers whose vassals could be called upon for military service. What land was not thus allocated was 'let' to the original occupiers on conditions of homage and service. There is little evidence that this feudal system did much immediately to improve the living conditions of those who remained on the land, save that some would live in the newly-built castles as servitors or that an enlightened baron might provide somewhat better housing for both his vassals and his animals where both were equally valuable. On the other hand many of the primitive hovels were destroyed to make room for the new castles.

You can literally hear an echo from the old forest days at Bainbridge in Wensleydale, when every night from September to Shrove Tuesday, a horn is sounded to guide belated travellers, as in the time of the Forest Laws when roads and tracks were few.

Away from the devastated lands there would probably be little immediate change in the daily life of the people as a result of the Conquest. In the Dales much land was granted by William to his followers, but it was unlikely the owner was ever seen, unless he came hunting. A steward or bailiff would manage the estate, and probably sub-let it to the original occupant, exacting rent or services more strictly than the old pre-Conquest landowners had done. Personal names, now familiar in the Dale country, like Neville, Romille, Percy, Tison (presumably now spelt Tyson and someone who had lands at Malton as well as Grassington) first make their appearance as landowners.

After the castles and churches came the monasteries. Religious houses spread rapidly through the land in Norman times, at first simple in style and probably of wood, but soon of stone. The original Fountains Abbey was almost certainly largely built of timber from the adjacent woods; a few years after its first establishment it was almost completely burnt down and had to be rebuilt in stone.

As the countryside became more prosperous stone domestic buildings increasingly replaced those of timber, often on the site of the old cruck building. So as the Rev. William Harrison, wrote later in Elizabethan days: "Every man turned builder, pulled downe the old house and set up a new after his owne devise." The transformation was helped by the decline in the amount of work for builders and masons which followed the Dissolution of the Monasteries in 1539. Dated stones over the doorways of many farms and houses indicate how many were built in the sixteenth and seventeenth century, and these door-heads are often lavishly embellished with carving. No longer was building confined to a single storey, but by carrying up the walls still higher rooms could be added. Personal taste or local conditions influenced building styles. For example, in the Pennine area a problem which was not felt in the wooded country to the east was the shortage of long timbers. Hence stone is often used where elsewhere wood was utilised – a window seat in a Ryedale farm house is of wood, in Wharfedale of stone. Already the stone manor house or hall had appeared in increasing numbers as the house of the lord of the manor, who held the land for the king and was the equivalent of the modern landowner.

Castles originally established by the Conqueror were, as we have seen, at first little more than a 'motte and bailey' structure, then they grew into more permanent fortified structures as the Norman extended their grip. From the thirteenth century onwards even the barons who dwelt in them began to hanker after homes progressively more comfortable than cold and draughty castles. The needs of defence gave way to a demand for space and light. After all, wars might come and go, struggles between kings and barons might bring violence and bloodshed, but other things went on as well. Law, trade, literature, education and sport developed more and more under the inspiration of those who lived in halls and manor houses as the influence of the monasteries declined. So the castle lost its military character as alterations made it a more liveable place. In some, drastic conversions were made to the structure. To others domestic wings were added. Elsewhere new halls were built. These new buildings were at first just timber halls in which the family and retainers met and ate, with a subsidiary room for the master and his lady at one end and a kitchen and buttery at the other. This was the basic pattern for many centuries, even in stone. It survived into the days of pele towers, when homes along the Borders and deep into Yorkshire had to be protected against Scots raiders – the lowest floor of the tower was a defendable store place, with the hall above, and on a third floor, where it existed, the master's sleeping quarters.

It is worth while when looking at an historic house or even a farmhouse in Yorkshire to discover whether or not it has somewhere in its structure the remains of one of these pele towers, sometimes standing intact but often incorporated into a larger building. Nappa Hall in Wensleydale provides one example in which the tower has become a fortified manor house. Gilling Castle, Mortham Tower and Crayke Castle are others. Their derivation from the earlier Norman 'keep' is clear. Later events made Yorkshire a cockpit of baronial and political struggles and left most of our castles in ruins, but some great houses remained.

Unfortunately one of the best examples of a fortified manor house, Markenfield Hall, near Ripon, is rarely open to public view as it is now a farmhouse and has been for many centuries. Built very early in the fourteenth century it has a great hall, with a solar, with a kitchen below and vaulted stone cellars, and in a wing is the chapel and other rooms. Between the wings is a turret containing the stone stairs which led to the living rooms above. There is a gatehouse and moat, once spanned by a drawbridge. From this hall went one of those who fought at Flodden. As an old poem puts it:

> Next went Sir Ninian Markenfield
> In armour coat of cunning worke.

Many such halls were thus developed as time went on by the addition of other rooms: a chapel, sleeping rooms for servants, a minstrel's gallery, a bower for the ladies, the introduction of panelling and tapestries. Froissart, the Frenchman who travelled in this country in the fourteenth century and probably visited Yorkshire, speaks of our manor houses as being notably rich in tapestries.

As trade and industry thrived and the market towns grew in importance, wealth increased and the standard of building rose. The end of the monasteries, which had released a great deal of skilled labour, also added considerably to private wealth. The vast monastic estates were valued and sold, often at low prices, to merchants and titled families, who used them as sites for their residentces, built by the 'free' masons often out of the old stone of the monasteries. Other buildings were let to tenants on the new estates. The wealthier gentry added parks and gardens to their new mansions, and these developed into what we now call 'stately homes' – a far cry from the mud hovel and the 'cruck' house, or even of the first 'hall'. Yorkshire has an abundance of such great houses, most of them now open to public view.

Much of our Yorkshire domestic building is a legacy of Tudor times, when enthusiasm for the improvement of their houses spread among prosperous landowners and the new class of capitalist clothiers in the north. It was then that brick

BUILDING STYLES: 1, *Pebble-faced cottages*
2, *Stone-built houses*

became popular and began to replace stone in areas where supplies were available. It appeared late in the North Riding, but was widely used in the East. Indeed, there are houses in the East Riding where stone was used but made to look as much like brick as possible, being cut small and the joints emphasised. When the old great halls were rebuilt with new floors to cut off the upper part and so provide bedrooms, chimney stacks had to be installed to carry away the smoke which previously had been partly caught by a canopy over the great fireplace, or allowed to drift round the room. The traditional 'hall' gradually disappeared leaving us only the shrunken relic which appears in house agents' advertisements today: "Lounge, dining room and hall". Upper rooms called, too, for better staircases than the old stone spiral steps. When glass became available the old shutters over the windows were replaced.

Such houses were not always lived up to by their owners. In *Humphrey Clinker* Smollett describes one which

> though large, is neither elegant nor comfortable. It looks like a great inn, crowded with travellers who dine at the landlord's ordinary, where there is a great profusion of victuals and drink; but mine host seems to be misplaced, and I would rather dine on filberts with a hermit, than feed on venison with a hog. . . . I think I can dine better, and for less expense, at the Star and Garter, in Pall-Mall, than at our cousin's castle in Yorkshire.

One of the most charming examples of Tudor halls on an elaborate scale is at Burton Agnes in the East Riding, built at the turn of the sixteenth century at the end of the reign of Queen Elizabeth. This, of course, had far outgrown the primitive hall as we have seen it. Its form is that of a broad recessed front, between projecting wings with graceful bow windows, rising four storeys above the ground. A long gallery, which became popular in the larger Tudor houses, stretched the full width of the building with fine Venetian windows at each end. The whole building, with rosy brick walls and stone mullioned windows rises out of a beautiful formal garden of lawns and topiary. Close by, as if for comparison with the new, is the old hall, with a still older undercroft dating back to Norman times.

One can conjure up a pleasant picture of a wealthy Tudor merchant and his lady planning the rebuilding of an old hall, or even the building of a new, adding this or that amenity, devising a bow window here or some ornamental stonework there, deciding upon a new and impressive front door, and

BUILDING STYLES: *3, Brick-built weavers' cottages*

then, as the final touch, having their joint initials and the date carved over the entrance. Their descendants may not have been so pleased a century or so later when the fine glass windows which had been installed to bring more light into the new hall became liable for the Window Tax on all windows over six. This imposition, which lasted from 1697 to 1851, accounted for many of those bricked-up windows still to be seen.

The town craftsmen lived in well-built houses, the fore-runners of our present-day terrace houses, standing in reasonably orderly rows and lanes rather than jumbled together in haphazard fashion. Shops with open fronts, over which lived the merchant and his family and with accommodation for apprentices, lined the streets, which were, unhappily, usually filthy with garbage and with open gutters for sewage. It was as urbanisation became suburbanisation that we moved into our modern world.

Our towns grew out of the need for markets and shops and brought a larger community sense. Each building in the medieval townscape was erected to suit the individual owner and this gave it a lively variety lacking in our modern 'shopping precincts'. They did not always line up with the next building, and they overhung the street for the very practical reason that the weight of the outer wall balanced the weight of the people and goods inside. Yet as can be seen in York's famous Shambles, where the top storey on each side is within hand-shaking distance of its opposite number, there is a harmony in the variety. A street of such premises conveys a sense of living together, strengthened by the tendency to concentrate particular trades in particular areas. Progress was slower in the rural areas, but stone farmhouses and workers' cottages began to appear, largely of the same pattern as the old, but of cut and well-shaped stone where the local material permitted, as in the industrial area south of the Aire, or of rougher finish in the limestone Dales. Usually the chimneys were built on the roof-ridge, but a feature of Dales houses still to be seen are the stepped-up chimneys at the ends of the houses, rising like giant stairs to the gable end.

We have a picture of a well-built house of this kind in Emily Bronte's description of the exposed house on the moors which she calls 'Wuthering Heights', of which she says "the architect had foresight to build it strong: the narrow windows are deeply set in the walls, and the corners defended with large jutting

stones". She discovers the date-stone over the door – "1500".
Then she takes us inside:

> One step brought us into the family sitting-room, without any intro-
> ductory lobby or passage: they call it here 'the house' pre-eminently. It
> includes kitchen and parlour generally, but I believe at Wuthering
> Heights the kitchen is forced to retreat altogether into another
> quarter; at least I distinguish a clutter of tongues and a clatter of
> culinary utensils deep within. . . . The floor was of smooth white stone;
> the chairs high-backed primitive structures, painted green: one or two
> heavy black ones lurking in the shade. . . . The apartment and
> furniture would have been nothing extraordinary as belonging to a
> homely northern farmer, with a stubborn countenance, and stalwart
> limbs set out to advantage in knee-breeches and gaiters. Such an
> individual, seated in his armchair, his mug of ale frothing on the round
> table before him, is to be seen in any circuit of five or six miles among
> those hills, if you go at the right time after dinner.

Typical houses of this kind are a familiar part of the
landscape today in this part of Yorkshire.

Other distinctive styles can be seen in the textile area around
Halifax, where three or six-light heavily mullioned windows
with heavy dripstone above, built in the dark stone of the area
and with elaborate doorways, are common. By way of contrast
are the severe uncompromising houses of the Swaledale lead-
miners, almost undistinguishable from the grey-black fells
about them, while there is a romantic air in the colourful
village houses in Ryedale and the Vale of Pickering.

Among the most attractive rural houses I know is a row of
Tudor-style cottages with small mullioned windows, each with
a fine dripstone above, in the little village of Kettlewell in
Wharfedale. Although they were probably built much later
they indicate how the Tudor mode of building lingered on in
the north. An odd feature of these cottages, incidentally, is a
row of pigeon holes under the eaves. There are many similar
cottages in the same village built at any time between the
seventeenth and nineteenth centuries, which, because they are
built of local material, harmonise with their surroundings.

One feature of the spate of stone building in the sixteenth
and seventeenth centuries which rarely fails to intrigue the
visitor is the liking for carved lintels and door-heads so
noticeable in the Dale country. The sternest and most utilitarian village houses are frequently adorned with designs of
infinite variety, sometimes symmetrical, sometimes not. The
Craven area is particularly rich in these patterns. May they not

be an expression of one aspect of our Yorkshire character which might otherwise be unsuspected?

From many sources one can build up a picture of those who lived in the homes of our forefathers. Old inventories tell us of their furniture – large oak tables, stools and settles, a meal chest and wood and pewter tableware. Cooking was done over an open fire in the great hall until kitchens were added. The yeoman had his round of seasonal work in the fields, with visits to the weekly market and the annual fairs. 'Badgers', or travelling pedlars, bought and sold small quantities of commodities. As is common today, the countryman's wife played a large part in the economy of the home or farm. Butter and cheese-making, labouring on the land, the raising of medicinal herbs when there were few if any doctors to call upon – all of these had to be fitted into a round of child-bearing, household chores and the preparing of winter stores when salted food provided the only meat. I remember seeing somewhere an epitaph to a yeoman's wife:

> From my sad cradle to my sable chest,
> Poor pilgrim, I did find few months of rest.

In the larger houses and castles life was probably a good deal easier because of the abundance of serfs and menials. The man of the house could hunt, course, fish, attend to his lands and meet his fellow gentry in style, while his wife – who was often married when in her early teens – would train not only her own children but young girls sent from the yeomen and labourers' cottages for domestic service, and often keep an eye on the workers on the farmlands about the house. And to judge from many of the effigies and memorials in Yorkshire churches, she managed to find time to adorn herself in fine clothes, being the eternal woman.

Building the Churches

A glance at the map of Yorkshire will show how many villages bear the prefix 'Kirk'. I have counted nearly 150 in the West Riding alone. The North Riding contributes several dozen more, the East Riding slightly fewer. And then there are the place-names beginning with 'Church', like Churchtown and Church Fenton. Religion has always been deep-rooted in the shire and it has bestowed its music on the map.

Many of our churches are surprisingly old in time. We are

told that Christianity was introduced into these parts at the end of the sixth century, and there are venerable buildings where you will be proudly shown a bit of Saxon wall, or a tower, or, as at Ripon, a crypt beneath the cathedral dating back to 670 – or, most impressive of all, the remains of a Saxon monastery in the secluded village of Lastingham in the North Riding. Still more surprising, the ruthless and often barbaric Anglo-Saxon invaders, who made little or no use of the Roman roads and villas they found here and who avoided the deserted Roman settlements for fear of evil spirits, left in the North Country a remarkable number of most beautifully sculptured crosses – to which I have already referred – in an area from Bewcastle on the Roman Wall and Ruthwell in Dumfries to Ilkley and Dewsbury in Yorkshire. R. G. Collingwood, writing fifty years ago, recorded over a hundred such carved stones in this county alone. There once may well have been more examples of Anglo-Saxon piety, but when Norman William ravaged the North Country and left it "all waste" many architectural and other treasures must have vanished, as most of the pre-Conquest churches in the north were of timber, as we have already noted.

The oldest complete church in Yorkshire is probably St. Gregory's Minster at Kirkdale between Helmsley and Kirkby Moorside, which has a Saxon sundial still in its original position over the south door bearing the inscription (translated):

> Orm Gamal's son bought St. Gregory's
> Minster when it was all broken down
> and fallen and he let it be made
> anew from the ground to Christ and
> St. Gregory, in Edward's days, the King,
> and in Tosti's days, the Earl
> This is day's Sun marker at every tide
> And Hawarth me wrought and Brand priests.

This suggests that much of the present building, erected shortly before the Norman Conquest, was rebuilt from a still earlier church and may have been part of a monastery centuries older than the abbeys of Rievaulx and Fountains. I know of no other place in Yorkshire where the centuries slip away and you can yet be so aware of the long slow rhythm of time.

Not far from Kirkdale, at Lastingham, already mentioned, is the crypt of an unfinished monastery built to hold the remains of St. Cedd, who died in A.D. 664 and who had been trained at Lindisfarne, thus linking us with the earliest days of Christianity in Yorkshire. There are also Saxon remains at York, Hovingham, Stonegrave, Skipwith, Leathley and elsewhere scattered over the three Ridings. At Appleton-le-Street, a village so named because of its position on the Roman road from Aldbrough to Malton, is a church which has grown with the times. It began with a Saxon tower with bell-openings; added another storey to its tower a century later with a higher set of bell-openings and made a new doorway; added a north aisle in the thirteenth century and still later added a south aisle. Yet from outside it appears an uninspired austere building.

It was probably a desire to replace the churches lost in the devastation of the Conquest, as well as Norman piety, which began the spate of building that has left us a wealth of Norman churches. Well over 8,000, more than half the parochial churches of England, were built wholly or in part between then and the close of the Middle Ages, and the most a visitor can do is select those distinguished for their special features. Most of them were built on a simple rectangular plan of tower, nave and chancel, often without an aisle, and can frequently be found in this form in the East Riding, on the Cleveland moors and in the forest and vale country round Pickering, as well as in the West Riding.

Adel, near Leeds, has an aisleless church which more than makes up for its deficiency by its magnificent Norman doorway, bearing the original bronze ring which has on it a monster's head swallowing a man. Beautiful doorways, indeed, come in an embarrassing number in every part of Yorkshire and invite special study. In a tiny church at Scawton, near Helmsley, founded by monks from Byland in 1146, is a Saxon-style chancel arch but erected in Norman times, and this, too, is representative of a feature worth discovering in a dozen or more places in the country. The emergence of successive styles from the round-arched, rather ponderous beginnings to the pointed arch and increasing beauty of Early English work and its flowering into the perfection of the Decorated period is something for which we have to thank the Norman craftsmen and master masons and those to whom they passed on their craft. From each Riding it is possible to pick, almost at random, examples of the skilled work of early and late periods by such craftsmen. Brandsby, on the York to

Helmsley road in the North Riding has an English Renaissance church with a cupola and supporting columns that might well have followed an Italian model. Rotherham, in the West Riding, has a Perpendicular parish church that is one of the most outstanding in Yorkshire, although few travel to Rotherham especially to see it. Not far away is the equally delightful chapel on the bridge built in the fifteenth century. The East Riding is rich in them. Hull and Beverley alone can offer enough of architectural admiration to satisfy any traveller. Yet Howden church provides beauty in a variety of styles of different dates – a wonderful fourteenth century west front, fine and lofty nave arcades of the Decorated period, a noble Perpendicular tower. This bell-tower was reputed to have been made of great size so that it might be a refuge for the local people in the event of the river flooding over the lowlying land.

The 'king' of Holderness is the local name for the cathedral-like church at Hedon, now dominating a peaceful little village but once the pride of the 'fair haven' which had a greater importance than Hull. It has a great tower that is a landmark in a flat country. Not far away is Patrington, whose church is the 'queen' of the same area. There is a true distinction between them, for while Hedon is majestic, Patrington is both graceful and beautiful with one of the finest tall spires in the land. Its builder was Robert de Patrington, and it was the beauty of this church which probably brought him the appointment of master-mason of York Minster in the fourteenth century. Curiously, he was succeeded in this office by Hugh de Hedon, who, it is believed, was the builder of the church at Hedon. If so, good work in each case brought its just reward.

One of the most remarkable women of her age was Lady Margaret Hoby who was the Lady of the Manor of Hackness, in the valley of the Derwent not far from Scarborough. She kept what is believed to be the earliest extant diary ever to be written by an Englishwoman. It dates from 1599 to 1605 and is now in the British Museum. She died in 1633. Her monument, carved by Chantry, the Sheffield sculptor, can be seen in the beautiful church at Hackness, where you can find evidence of Saxon work and succeeding styles up to the Perpendicular east window. There is also an altar cross of oak from a chapel built by Lady Margaret's husband, who rejoiced in the name of Sir Thomas Posthumous Hoby.

Another church built on a Saxon site is that at Pickering,

whose tall spire is a landmark. It is a beautiful building reached by a flight of steps from the busy market-place, but its most notable feature are the colourful wall-paintings which probably date from the fifteenth century. They depict Bible stories and legendary scenes with a religious motive; St. George slaying the dragon, St. Christopher carrying the infant Christ across a stream, Herods Feast, the Seven Acts of Mercy, and many lurid representations of the demons in hell. These were pictorial versions, for worshippers who were illiterate, of the sermons preached from the pulpit. Like the lively carvings at Beverley and elsewhere they must have beguiled many congregations whose minds wandered from the spoken word. Because the Parliamentary troops would have found them too gaudy for Puritan times they were whitewashed over, and for centuries remained hidden. Not until the middle of the last century were they rediscovered – and Puritanism struck again. They were re-whitewashed and so remained for nearly another thirty years, when at last they were cleaned of their many coverings and restored to the vivid colours of the original artists. They occupy all the walls of the north and south naves above the arcades.

At the other side of the county in remote Langstrothdale is one of the two Yorkshire churches in which the rood-loft survives. This is at Hubberholme, which has been in turn an Anglo-Norse burial place, the site of a forest chapel, and is now a parish church. It stands so close to the river Wharfe that on occasions flood waters have lapped the pews, yet it has been a place of worship since long before our abbeys were built. The other rood-loft is at Flamborough on the East coast. It was here that the great rood or crucifix stood in full view of the congregation and was the boundary between the secular nave and the sacred chancel.

In all this centuries-long development it can scarcely be said that there is a typical Yorkshire parish church, for, as we have seen, the county offers an impressive variety with an immense contrast between one extreme and the other. Within a few miles you can discover a simple solid Norman church like Adel, on the outskirts of Leeds, while in the centre of the same city is the ornate Gothic seventeenth century church of St. John. Over a wider range is the austere stumpy village church at Grinton in remote Swaledale and the cathedral-like Decorated church at Patrington by the Humber. There are low-roofed stone-slated churches not far from those with high-pitched tiled roofs; square-ended Saxon buildings and others built to Romanesque plans; churches (mainly in hill country) with squat towers and those (in flat lands) with soaring spires – a difference once explained to me as obvious – that a spire would be dwarfed by the high fells but was a directional landmark in the lowlands.

Apart, however, from its long history of changing styles, a traditional Yorkshire imprint is not easy to trace for another reason. When building in stone replaced the old timber castles the few skilled craftsmen who came over with the Conqueror were probably adequate to oversee and train labour for the purpose. But it was not long before the first abbeys began to take shape, founded by the religious orders from France. Again these were at first mere wooden structures, but their translation into stone could not be long delayed. Conisbrough and Tickhill in the south-west corner were probably the earliest stone castles in Yorkshire, and the Benedictine monasteries at York and Selby the first considerable religious buildings. With the coming of the Cistercians Rievaulx and Fountains Abbeys were founded, followed by Sawley and Kirkstall. Such a spate of stone buildings of considerable size called for more and more skilled workmen.

The masons and builders travelled from place to place as teams of individual craftsmen of many skills – quarrymen, rough masons, stone carvers, labourers, tilers, woodmen and carpenters. They were under the control of a master mason, who made the working drawings and who maintained a lodge or headquarters while the work was in progress. It was only possible to work for part of the year and by November work stopped for the winter.

One can but marvel at the work of these unknown men who laboured so well that for centuries to come people will look upon their handiwork with a pleasure they are unlikely to derive from much of the building of our own time. They grappled with problems of material and of its transport by horse-drawn or ox-drawn vehicles. They had few mechanical aids, and their tools would be primitive in our eyes. Their pace, of necessity, would be slow, so that people must for long periods have worshipped in an unfinished church. Yet they were proud of their work and signed it with their mason's marks, still to be seen in churches and monastic buildings, before they moved on to a new site and new problems. They left their characteristic imprint, too, in the detailed mouldings and touches of humour which always repay a second look in any old church.

This sense of humour is particularly noticeable, probably more in the greater churches and cathedrals than in village churches, in the miserere carvings in the stalls. The word comes from the Penitential fifty-first Psalm, which begins "Miserere mei, Domine." Hinge up an ancient seat and beneath it you may find a carving, perhaps a caricature of the carver's workmate or an animal dancing or, more frequently, a pig playing the pipes. You can see both of these at Beverley and at Ripon. Some of these carvings seem incongruous in a sacred building – humans riding on animals, a woman thrashing a man, the Devil carrying off a woman – but they probably all had meanings and fables behind them the implications of which we have lost. At least we can be grateful that our forebears had an eye and a hand for humour.

Such similarity as can be found in early styles of early church building was probably due to this nomadic method of work. Later, when craft guilds were established in parts of the county with rules and regulations of workmanship, some purely local styles often dictated by local materials evolved and can be traced in different regions. Many of the bridges erected in these centuries were also the work of masons not engaged in religious or military building, and they, too, have a regional pattern.

One example of a vernacular style in church building can be found in the Craven area of the West Riding, where it is often difficult to distinguish at first sight one church from another. They are long low buildings, generally having a squat tower and square windows. Another group of Norman churches of distinctive character can be found around Driffield in the East Riding and further south a galaxy of large beautiful churches with fine masoncraft built out of the great agricultural wealth of Holderness. Other similarities can be found in each of the Ridings by a sharp-eyed observer, particularly when the churches were built before improved transport made long hauls of building material from outside the region possible.

Pride, genius and craftsmanship all went into the building of our parish churches. Doubtless a desire to build bigger and better than their neighbours was the stimulus behind some of the more ornate and expensive churches, as it was in the building of great windows and high towers. Local wealth had much to do with this, as in Holderness, and as can be seen by the large number of original Norman churches where funds were not available for their alteration. The story is still told of two adjacent villages where the tower of one church exceeded the other by a mere foot or two. It is said that the good folk of the lesser turned out by night to manure their tower to make it grow bigger.

Incidentally, what is often claimed as Yorkshire's smallest church, at Upleatham near Saltburn, is really only the remains of a large church which once held several hundred worshippers. The smallest complete Yorkshire church is probably that at Speeton, in the East Riding. The parish church at Hull is often claimed to be the largest in England, though I do not know if the claim has ever been substantiated. It is certainly impressive in its dignity today, although it has had a troubled history of desecration and neglect. There was a spell, during the Commonwealth, when it was shared by two rival sects, one worshipping in the choir and the other in the nave.

With the Dissolution of the Monasteries between 1535 and 1540 there was a slowing down in church building, as there had been earlier in castle building, largely because of lost impetus from monastic sources and also because the Church itself was under a cloud. So from that time the emphasis moved, as we have seen, to secular work in which the great halls and smaller manor houses as well as small domestic properties came into being. So many churches were built in those busy preceding centuries, however, that it has been estimated that there was one church for every 500 inhabitants at the close of the Middle Ages. Little wonder a marked lull in such building followed and lasted, indeed, until after the Napoleonic Wars, when a new building fervour grew up and gave us a multitude of town churches all built after 1800.

Just as much of the old stone from the discarded monasteries was used in the building of new houses, so some of the monastic church furniture found its way into nearby churches. In St. Mary's Church in Richmond are carved screens and stalls from the nearby Easby Abbey, including a grotesque piping pig which may have been a caricature of some forgotten flute-playing monk. At Aysgarth in Wensleydale is an oak rood-loft and reading desk from Jervaulx Abbey. Other relics from Easby can be seen in the nearby Wensley Church. Something like a 'disposal sale' of the stricken abbeys must have brought many clerical buyers in search of bargains.

One effect of the Reformation which is often forgotten was that the church ceased to be the pivot of community life in the old sense. Down the centuries the church had been a social centre as well as a place of worship. The chancel was the sacred area and belonged to the priest. The nave was the meeting place of the people, who could use it for weekend recreation as well as for Sunday services. There is evidence of such communal use in the frequency with which an inn is to be found not far from the church gate. Where no inn was available there was often a house where the wardens sold 'church ales' for refreshment between services and communal occasions. At Hubberholme in Wharfedale the inn was owned by the church. At Linton lower down the same dale is a group of houses known as Church Yett, which served the same purpose. These 'church ales' were an accepted source of revenue to meet the churchwardens expenses. When the monks were no longer there to look after the wandering poor the task fell usually upon the churchwardens, until, at the end of the sixteenth century, the Poor Laws created special overseers of the poor to work with the wardens.

The parish bounds were perambulated by the wardens each year to ensure their maintenance long before the days of maps. Most parishes had their 'poor pasture', which did not indicate a doubtful quality in the soil but which was let each year to the highest bidder for the benefit of the poor of the parish. I once attended one of these annual lettings at Hubberholme. The ceremony was held in the inn after a service at the church and was attended by most of the local farmers, who were held to constitute a 'House of Commons'. The 'Lords' sat apart in the inn parlour. This House comprised the Vicar and his two wardens. As bids were made in the Commons they were transmitted to the Lords, and eventually one was accepted by them when it reached the desired figure.

The churchwardens, too, had to maintain the church fabric and the bells, pay the dog-rapper to whip dogs out of the church, and keep a 'pinder', who gathered up stray animals in his pound and kept them there until they had been announced in church as 'estrays' and bought back out of the pound. They were sometimes responsible for the village cross and had to make provision for bastards, either by discovering the father and making him pay or passing the cost on to relatives of the child. All in all, the churchwardens' lot was that of considerable responsibility, if not a happy one.

One old custom in Yorkshire churches was the carrying of garlands before the coffin of an unmarried girl. An old ballad tells us that

> A garland fresh and fair
> Of lilies there was made,
> In sign of her virginitie
> And on her coffin laid.

The garlands were afterwards hung in the parish church. I have seen them in the church at Alne, and I believe at one time they hung in a number of churches on the Yorkshire coast.

If 'church ales' have disappeared so has the older custom of painting clock faces in blue and gold, and with less reason. Not many North Country churches observe this tradition today, although I have noticed that the Bronte church at Haworth has not forgotten it. The reason for this use of colour goes back, I am told, to the reign of Henry VIII, when an edict went forth that church clocks were to be painted "blew and the signs upon them gilte". These were the colours used in the making of vestments for Aaron and his sons, according to the Book of Exodus. Down the years they must have added a pleasant touch of colour to the greys and browns (and nowadays, black) of our parish churches. The floors of churches were, of course, strawed over, which is the origin of the ancient rush-bearing ceremonies still observed in the north.

The Way of the Monks

In a world which can transmit words and pictures through the air from a studio in London or elsewhere to a lonely farmhouse on the Yorkshire wolds the discovery not long ago of some beautifully coloured tiles on the floor of the twelfth-century Rievaulx Abbey in a hidden valley under the Hambleton Hills may seem an event of minor importance. Yet it is probable that the monks who first trod those newly laid tiles, an innovation brought over from Normandy, were no less stirred by them than we were by the first coloured television pictures. They induced that sense of wonder which comes with all new ideas. And as we walk over them today we can, in the right mood, share that same wonder some 800 years later.

To move among the ruins, now fortunately considerably restored and preserved after years of neglect, of abbeys like

Fountains, Rievaulx, Jervaulx, Bolton, Roche and Kirkstall, is to catch a glimpse of another age. Yet it will remain only a glimpse without an imagination which can picture something of the ritual of the daily round, the teeming activities – religious, industrial and social – closely regulated by bell and service, and the hopes, fears, sorrows and rejoicings of those who lived within their walls. We have to try to construe the language of the stony remains which are left to us, aided by such writings of the time as remain.

We must first rid ourselves of the notion that our old abbeys were planned as artistic showpieces in idyllic settings by men whose aim was sanctity in the midst of beauty. Almost always the site of their sanctuary was in remote unwanted land, "uninhabited for all the centuries back, thick-set with thorns, lying between the slopes of mountains and among rocks jutting out on both sides", as ran an early description of the banks of the Skell, where the monks of Fountains settled. Or as William of Newburgh wrote of the site of Rievaulx, "a place of horror and vast loneliness". Tracks had to be made, swamps drained, woods cleared, timber cut and stone quarried as the pioneer monks carved out of the wild a place for their community.

Life in the monasteries was compounded of many devotions, much manual labour and little sleep, conducted strictly according to the Rule of their order. One can still picture the monks descending the night stairs from the dorters, or dormitories, for the midnight service, gathering in the chapter house in order of seniority round the abbot for praise or reproof, eating in the refectory where "no noise is to be made; if there are nuts, they are not to be cracked with the teeth but privately opened with a knife", or warming themselves in winter in the calefactory where the rare comfort was not to lead them into "scurrilities or idle words and those exciting laughter". There were few gaps in a round which began at midnight with the night office and ended after vespers and supper with early bed in order to be ready for the next midnight service.

In between there were the canonical services of matins, lauds, prime, terce, sext, none, and compline, as well as High Mass and chapter meetings. Special duties fell to the sacrist (vestments and plate), the precentor (services and singing), the cellarer (whose life was not a merry one of cakes and ale but included the physical well being of the inmates), the almoner (doles for the needy callers), the kitchener and the infirmarer and many minor officials.

The monks themselves not only worked inside the monastery. They had to supervise the work of others. One thing is not easy to picture in these days of deserted ruins, and that is the monasteries' importance as employers of labour. In the fields, barns, stables, mills and workshops so many lay workers were employed that they outnumbered the monks. Their lands spread over many thousands of acres, increased by gifts to the monasteries by wealthy benefactors, until it was said that the monastic lands totalled one-fifteenth of all England. At Rievaulx in the time of Abbot Alred there were some 140 monks and not less than 500 lay brothers, so that, as a contemporary account has it, "the church swarmed with them, like a hive with bees".

The monasteries dominated not only religious activity but agriculture, crafts, industry, education and most early forms of social service. Their power, like that of the barons, lasted for many centuries. To a simple people, whose largest building hitherto had been a village church or here and there a castle, this new emanation in their land must have been not merely awesome but bewildering. To the most unlikely and, to a farming community, the most worthless land, came groups of monks bearing deeds of gift from a wealthy baron anxious to ensure the safety of his soul or to make a thank-offering for good fortune, or merely to find a remote refuge. In a short-time buildings, first of wood and then of stones, arose on land cleared of scrub and trees. Bells would toll, services would be held, labouring men would find jobs, travelling men and clerics would visit the place, and gradually a great stone church would arise built by masons and craftsmen from afar. Older folk would doubtless shake their heads, as they do over developments today. New generations would take it for granted. But it all made an indelible mark on the face of the land.

Each order of newcomers had its own characteristics. The Cistercians were well represented with abbeys at Rievaulx and the nearby Byland, at Fountains near Ripon, at Kirkstall in the Aire valley, at Roche at the southern entrance to Yorkshire, and at Meaux near Beverley (although there are only scanty remains here). They believed in austere living and hard work, and were responsible for extensive sheep farming and wool production. Among the tasks of the Cellarer at Fountains was the storage of vast quantities of wool in the cellarium which remains almost unchanged beneath the abbey today. The Benedictines were scholars and teachers and had abbeys at Whitby and at Lastingham (from which they later moved to St. Mary's, York, and from which a group broke away to found Fountains under the Cistercian Rule). Only one abbey remains of the Cluniac order, which had much greater ritual than the rest. This is at Monk Bretton near Barnsley. Augustinian Canons founded Bolton Priory and Bridlington Priory, as well as a priory at Guisborough and one in the Derwent valley at Kirkham, of all of which some remains can be seen. At Newburgh, near Coxwold, and at Nostell, near Wakefield, there were priories but these have now been incorporated into houses.

One of the saddest orders to modern eyes was the Carthusian, whose Priory or charterhouse at Mount Grace still stands in remarkable completeness off the road between Thirsk and Stokesley. Here the heavily cowled monks lived in absolute seclusion, less like a community of monks than a collection of hermits. Each monk had his own cell; so built that even his scanty food was delivered to him by an unseen lay brother. Behind the cell was a garden in which he could work. His devotions were performed alone save for a single church service. This order was a return to the earliest form of Christian solitary, and an air of sanctity grew up around it so that even after the Dissolution it was a place of pilgrimage for many of the old faith.

Each of these monastic houses has its stories and legends, sometimes still kept alive by ceremonies as at Ripon, where, each August, 'Saint Wilfrid' rides a white horse at the head of a procession through the streets as a reminder of the safe return of the original saint from the Holy Land. In the Saxon crypt of the abbey is a narrow niche through which a woman can pass to prove her purity. At Beverley there is the shrine of St. John, whose sacred banner brought victory to the forces of King Athelstan and King Edward I in their battles. The banner no longer exists, but you will be shown the bracket on which it rested. At Fountains you will be told of a company of monks who seceded from St. Mary's Abbey at York, in revolt from its laxity, and who after much wandering settled under a giant tree beside the River Skell, where later the abbey rose. Indeed, you may even be shown the tree under which it all began.

RELIGIOUS HOUSES: *1, Fountains Abbey*

Wordsworth wove several poems around legends he heard on his visits to Bolton Abbey. At Selby they recall the legend that it was a vision of Saint Germanus which decided the site and the building. And at Newburgh Priory it is said that Oliver Cromwell's bones are hidden in the building.

Jervaulx Abbey was originally founded by Cistercians in 1156, not on its present site but at Fors, in upper Wensleydale. It throws light on the character of the early dales folk that they resented this intrusion by foreign monks. Several times they attacked and destroyed the original buildings. It was not until one of the Earls of Richmond, hunting in the nearby woods, sought rest and food at the primitive abbey buildings and was told of the persistent hostility of the local folk that a solution was found. Whether or not the meal and comfort provided for him was unusually good, legend does not disclose. Apparently he was in beatific mood, for he offered the monks a new site several miles away, and here the present abbey was erected. Perhaps after all there was something good about the food, for one of the remarkable features about the new abbey was the enormous fireplaces in the kitchen, where many joints could be roasted on spits one above the other.

Both Kirkham and Rievaulx owe their existence to that outstanding lord of Helmsley, Walter l'Espec, who built the first in memory of a son who fell from his horse at the place where the Augustinian abbey was built, and who later founded Rievaulx, the first Cistercian abbey in the North, as a place to which he himself could retreat. Byland was first built on a site in Ryedale, but the bells disturbed the monks of Rievaulx not far away. "At every hour of the day and night the one convent could hear the bells of the other, and this was unseemly and could by no means be endured." So the monks moved to a new site; the original one being known today as 'Old Byland'. The second site soon proved no more acceptable, so they moved again, to the place where the ruins can still be seen. Even then trouble was not over, for some 200 years later the abbey was attacked and pillaged by the Scots.

Well over 200 sites of abbeys and monastic institutions, founded by the four main religious orders as well as communities of nuns, canons and priests and the houses of Knights Templars, have been discovered in Yorkshire. Mr. Kenneth Wilson, who has listed these, notes that the earliest monasteries in England were Celtic foundations which later came into

RELIGIOUS HOUSES: *2, The Cistercian abbey of Rievaulx*

3, Mount Grace Priory

conflict with the Roman church introduced into Britain by the Benedictine missionary, St. Augustine, in A.D. 597. The differences continued until the Synod of Whitby in A.D. 664 and from that time the Roman church prevailed.

As well as monastic houses, bishoprics and minsters and churches were created, but the major part of religious teaching was for long carried out by itinerant priests who erected wooden crosses at their preaching places, later to be replaced by the stone crosses which still exist. It is not easy in these days to picture these travelling friars, who depended upon charity for their keep, wandering the countryside, preaching from their crosses and providing for many people their only live contact with organised religion. As G. M. Trevelyan points out, "teaching and preaching often amounted to very little in an English village so far as the resident priest was concerned, though Mass was regularly performed". This deficiency was to a large extent supplied by the preaching friar on his regular beat, who could hear confession and give absolution. Many 'Friar' place names spread over the county provide evidence of their widespread travels. Near Doncaster, for example, there is Friars Close, named from the White Friars, and a Grey Friars Road, from a group who had a friary at a bridge nearby. Black Friars had a house on the Yorkshire-Lancashire border near Saddleworth, where there is a Friar Mere. Near Pickering in the North Riding there is a Friars Ditch, and both York and Beverley have streets named after them. Whitefriars is today a busy road in Hull.

The tracks, probably following prehistoric ways, used by these travelling friars as well as by the monks on monastic business, can be traced in many parts of Yorkshire. Often they have become modern tarred roads, but there are still green ways over the moors little changed from what they were when monks or lay brethren drove sheep along them to winter pastures or to the monastic granges. 'Monks trod' is a footpath name still linking us with five centuries ago. Abbotside in Wensleydale marks an old possession of Jervaulx Abbey, and it was from the milk of ewes fed on these pastures that the first Wensleydale cheese was made. Many a rambler has crossed Fountains Fell wondering at the name, but not linking it with the abbey many miles away whose sheep were pastured there. On the old road near the abbot's lodging at Bolton the ghost of a monk is still to be seen, according to local belief.

Many thousands of holiday makers visit Bolton 'Abbey' in the valley of the Wharfe each summer. In the hey-day of railways, waggonettes and carriages would line up alongside the station a mile or so away to convey parties of visitors to the ruins, and competition was keen almost to the point of violence among the waiting drivers. It is still a popular centre for coach and car parties, offering picnic spots by the river, an exciting crossing by stepping stones, walks through the woods, and always the attractive ruins as a background for family photographs. Few of the visitors leave without remarking on the beauty of the scene, and on the good choice of the monks who built there.

In this instance their comments are probably correct, despite my earlier remark about the savage beginnings of our monasteries. This corner of the Wharfe must always have been a beautiful place, and the beauty of the original buildings in newly-wrought creamy stones as compared with the rather sombre browns and drab greys of the present weathered ruins must have been overwhelming. Again, this was not the original site. Land at Embsay, some miles away, was given to the Augustinian Canons by Cecily de Romille of Skipton Castle (of the family of one of the Conqueror's followers), in 1120 and a start was made on buildings there. Some thirty years later they decided to move to new land, provided by the same family, at Bolton, and building went on intermittently for the next four centuries, providing almost permanent work for masons, carpenters and others in the district. Incidentally, the word abbey is a misnomer, although now universally used, for it was as an Augustinian Priory that it was built, ruled not by an abbot but a prior.

One important difference was that the Augustinian Canons were priests and much more free than monks of other orders to go outside the conventual buildings, to take services at churches in the district, and even to travel to towns and markets for the buying of food and wine and trading in wool. Further, a great many estates in the Wharfedale area were bought by or given to the priory and were managed from granges, so that unlike many other monastic areas there must have been a considerable coming and going of monks among the villages.

I have already referred to the extensive sheep-rearing pursued by the monks of Fountains. At one time they had many thousands of sheep on the moors of Fountains Fell, Malham and Littondale. Coverham Abbey also had pastures rights in Littondale, as did Sawley Abbey. Bolton soon established its own flocks, both for wool and for ewes milk, and considerable sums of money were involved in sales and purchases. Inevitably there were were conflicts over grazing rights between one monastic house and another, and between the granges and flockmasters of one abbey and another, sometimes ending in blows. On one occasion, at least the monks of Fountains were fined by a commission of abbots for damaging a mill at Litton belonging to another abbey. A minor trouble was that milkmaids who attended the ewes were often a temptation to the lay brothers, and one monastery recommended that only old or ugly women should be employed for the purpose.

It was in the nature of things, no doubt, that as the monasteries grew in size they also became wealthy. They were among the best organised institutions in the country. They were the recipients of gifts in land and money from the benevolent as well as those who regarded a gift to the church as an insurance policy for the hereafter. Their properties rose in value with the increasing wealth of the nation. And all this brought a laxity and widespread indulgence which would not go unobserved in the outside world. The Prior of Bolton rode forth in state with a retinue and the entry in the Prior's House Book recording 2,000 gallons of wine purchased in one year could scarcely have been a secret and must have caused much headshaking. The quality of charity which stirred the first monks of Fountains to give away their only food to a beggar had fallen to a low pitch when the accounts of Sawley Abbey showed only a few shillings spent on benefactions to the poor in one year. The reformation had wider causes, but it would appear that there was a canker at the heart.

How the Dissolution of the Monasteries affected Bolton Priory might be taken as typical in general of all our Yorkshire monastic estates. It is not true, save in a few instances, that the buildings and estates were scrapped, the prior or abbot killed and the monks ejected to become beggars, while all their wealth was confiscated. Actually Bolton Priory was badly in debt at the Dissolution, largely because it had been living and trading beyond its means. Like many others it had pledged several years' wool crop ahead against loans. Discipline was no longer observed as we saw it in its early days at Rievaulx and elsewhere. Luxurious living was not unknown. And in some cases abbots, having a shrewd idea of impending trouble, had sold, or given away, some of the outlying estates as a 'hedge' against possible personal needs later. When the Dissolution came the Prior of Bolton and his officers and monks were given gratuities and pensions. The property was valued and either sold or leased – in the case of Bolton to the Earl of Cumberland – the bells were sold to neighbouring churches, and the nave of the Priory church, being regularly used by the local inhabitants, was preserved as the parish church when the rest was pulled down. It is still in use as a church today. Tenants of priory lands were for the most part left undisturbed.

Similar treatment was bestowed upon the small Benedictine nunnery at Marrick priory, in Swaledale. At the Dissolution there was a prioress and sixteen nuns in residence and all received life pensions. The will of one of these nuns, who lived in retirement for nearly twenty years, is quoted by Speight in his *Romantic Richmondshire,* and from its contents one suspects that some at least of the priory's furnishings must have found its way into her home. In this case the priory estate was given to "one of the king's council-men in the north".

The reduction of the monasteries took many years to complete, and their fabrics were used over a long period as a quarry for other building. Much beauty was thus destroyed which would have given delight today. Yet, although it marked the end of an age, the Dissolution also symbolised the beginning of a new one. Not only the stones were used to new purposes, but the new ideas which brought about the end of monastic establishments accelerated a social change in the countryside. From this time dates the age of expansion. In place of the old abbeys there were new and stately homes. Semi-feudal monastic estates were developed by progressive farmers. Trade found new outlets. Poets, playwrights and philosophers moved into a new world, not truly without some loss but also with great gain.

In one sphere, however, the immediate loss was heavy. Before there were schools of medicine in our universities the religious houses were the custodians of such medical knowledge as had survived from the earlier days of ancient learning. We are told that in the ruins of Pompeii were found delicate surgical instruments which indicated a high standard of skill and knowledge, but their use and purpose had long been forgotten. A long process of crude experiments, much superstition and human folly, and an incredible amount of suffering, had to be endured to re-create a new surgical and medical science. Saint Benedict declared that "before all things and above all things, special care must be taken of the sick, so that they be served in very deed, as Christ himself, for He saith 'I was sick and ye visited Me' ".

So in general the infirmarer ranked high in monastic establishments, not only for his work among sick inmates but in a wider sphere as one carrying on a tradition of good treatment and who worked with the almoner in the dispensation of medical charity. Apart altogether from the community life at abbeys like Rievaulx and Bolton, their crafts and industrial activities from wool to mining, from agriculture to milling, must have brought in a stream of major and minor casualties for treatment.

When leprosy spread to this country with the returning Crusaders it was the monks who staffed the lazer-houses and insisted on the strict cleanliness and hygiene which eventually stamped it out. The place-name Spital usually marks the existence of a hospital, as at Spital Bridge near Whitby (where I once discovered a 'Hospital Farm'), and various Spital Moors, Spital Houses and Spital Gap. Naturally, invoking the aid of saints ranked high in monastic treatment and the saying of masses were recognised medical treatment, along with fasting and the use of 'worts' or plants.

Such treatment must often have been extremely primitive, sometimes unspeakably so. Blood-letting was a universal cure-all, performed either with the lancet or with the aid of leeches. In some monasteries it was the custom for monks to attend every quarter for blood-letting, which was regarded as a not unpleasant relaxation of the daily round. This was not long confined to monasteries. It was practised in moorland farms as well as by wealthy townsmen who paid 'chirugeons' highly to bleed them and to give them and their families 'vomits'. I believe that George IV was bled before his coronation to fit him for the ceremony.

It is a legacy of this religious background to medicine which is largely responsible for naming our hospitals after the saints – St. Thomas, St. Bartholomew and Bethlehem – a pleasant custom which we are discarding in the days of regional boards and less significant names.

York Minster

"Most remarkable and worthy seeing is St. Peters Cathedral, which alone of all the greate Churches in England, had best been presev'd from the furie of the sacrilegious. . . . It is a most intire, magnificent piece of Gothic Architecture: The Skreene before the Quire is of stone, carv'd with flowers, running work and statues of the old Kings." Thus John Evelyn, describing in his diary a visit to York Minster in August 1654.

How many times has one walked out of the bustle of York with its ancient narrow streets, its thronged pavements and bicycled roads, its antique shops and modern restaurants, and its strident and anachronistic supermarkets, into the cool hushed darkness of the Minster, to become conscious of its "intire magnificence", of vast, lofty space, of tracery-topped columns, like a still forest of stone, of soft gentle colour as light filters through the glorious stained glass, and perhaps of the deep reverberation of the great organ and the voices of choirboys at Evensong. Past, present and future seem at such moments to be merged into one unity: a sense of timelessness in which the services and the ritual are as natural as the seasons, and as eternal.

Yet it is time which has ravaged the Minster itself. Each passing century has taken unrevealed toll of the structure. Immense weight has shifted its hidden foundations, unnoticed cracks have appeared in its massive columns, joints have slipped out of alignment. The whole great edifice has been on the move until its very existence is now threatened. Although, like the Forth Bridge, it has always had its devoted army of men busy on perpetual maintenance, it has reached a stage where only a major operation can save its life. The whole structure has been surveyed and measured using modern techniques undreamed of by its builders, revealing the fearful extent of the danger to the building. Delicate 'tell-tales' reveal the movement of the structure. Long plumb-lines hanging from far up in the roof betray how greatly out of the vertical the building has slipped. Borings into the pillars reveal the depth of the cracks in the stonework. And regular checks by technical assistants mark its continuing movement. Like a human being facing drastic surgery, it appears to the onlooker that only a miracle can save the life of the patient.

The critical examination of the whole structure began in 1965, when Bernard Feilden was appointed Surveyor of the

Fabric, and the study took two years. Deep into the foundations men probed. High on to the roof and great towers they climbed, measuring and sounding, noting changes in parts of the building where previous inspections had been almost impossible. Devices hitherto unknown were used to estimate the extent of the movement in the Minster. Ancient records were searched for evidence of its building and structural changes, and they showed that historical time lies literally at the root of the Minster's troubles.

On this site originally was a Roman building – a temple or a military establishment. It may even have been a religious site earlier. Then came the first Christian church erected in the time when Paulinus was Archbishop. Edwin was king and had overthrown the king of Wessex, so becoming ruler of Northumbria with his throne at York. He had taken a vow to adopt the Christian faith and, after his victory and return to York, his wife and Paulinus persuaded him to make an open declaration about his change of faith at a ceremony at which he would receive the official letters from the Pope confirming the establishment of the church.

Then came a hitch, for when a day was appointed for the ceremony at York at which the King would make his declaration it was found there was no old temple or sacred building large enough for the occasion. To quote an old chronicler: "A little Oratory of Wood was therefore thrown up in the very Place where the great Church now stands, and dedicated to St. Peter; in which on Easter Day, being April 12, 627, One hundred and eight Years after the Coming of the Saxons into Britain, the King and his two Sons, Osfrid and Edford, whom he had by a former Wife, with many more of the Nobility, were solemnly baptized." Soon afterwards a stone building was erected round the oratory, which itself was based on the older Roman remains. This was the first of many such structures which succeeded each other after fires, neglect, great storms and the coming and going of armed men had destroyed existing fabrics.

It was on top of all these foundations, partly of timber, partly of Roman stone, that the first Norman church was built. This endured until the thirteenth century, when the building of the present Minster began – again on the old foundations. In the 250 years from 1220 to 1472 the builders of this Minster, often several generations of one family, added stone to stone, creating the transepts and the bell tower, the nave and chapter houses, the great central tower and the two towers 200 feet high over the magnificent west front. Inside, other craftsmen down the centuries erected the stained glass, carved the choir screens, built libraries and hung the great bells. Yet deep below ground the very foundations were unstable.

There was a sense of dismay in the county when its peril became known, and the late Lord Scarborough, the Minster's High Steward, sent out an appeal for £2 million to save it. Suddenly it appeared surprising that so vast a structure had remained intact so long on such fragile surroundings. It was discovered that some of the great piers were resting on a base of ancient logs. The water table – which lies beneath all our buildings – had varied in level down the centuries alternately wetting and drying the structure below ground. Some of the stained glass windows had bowed out by several feet. The towers themselves were endangered.

Now the surgeons have carried out their drastic operation. The foundations have been excavated and replaced deep below ground by men in safety helmets. Stone and metal and concrete have been forced into the footings, some of the stone used in the reconstruction coming from the ancient quarry at Sherburn-in-Elmet which supplied the original material for the Minister. The pillars have been strengthened and much of the roof replaced. After long months when the sounds of digging and welding and the roar of dumper trucks down the aisles was the only music echoing through the lofty building, the surgical treatment has ended and the ancient Minister has been given a new lease of life. Peace and serenity have returned and with them the steady pilgrimage of visitors from all parts of the world. This lovely jewel in Yorkshire's heritage gleams again.

4

Moors and Dales

Markets and Fairs – Music Makers – Digging Up the Past

Far far off us, in the western sky, we saw shapes of Castles, Ruins among groves, a great spreading wood, rocks and single trees, a minster with its tower unusually distinct, minarets in another quarter, and a round Grecian Temple also; the colours of the sky of a bright grey, and the forms of a sober grey, with a dome. As we descended the hill there was no distinct view, but of a great space; only near us we saw the wild and (as the people say) bottomless Tarn in the hollow at the side of the hill.

Dorothy Wordsworth wrote this in her journal in October 1802, describing the return homeward from the wedding of her brother William to Mary Hutchinson at Brompton, near Scarborough. She had not attended the ceremony and had thrown herself on her bed until it was all over. The event had taken place at eight o'clock in the morning, and after breakfast William and his wife and Dorothy set out by road for Grasmere. They paused for two hours at Kirkby Moorside while the horses fed, passing the time by reading the gravestones. "There was one to the memory of five children, who had all died within five years," noted Dorothy. Cheerful reading for a young bride!

The vantage point at which they stopped for the view is known to every traveller who makes this journey across Yorkshire today, although the modern motorist is often more concerned with the 1 in 4 hill of Sutton Bank than with the scenery. There are few finer prospects in a county which can offer a multitude of viewpoints. At the foot of the Hambleton Hills which mark the division of the moorland country of the north-east from the dale country of the west, is the broad flat strip of the Plain of York before the fells rise in the far distance. The minster Dorothy Wordsworth saw may have been York. The "bottomless Tarn" was the little lake of Gormire beside

Sutton Bank. Behind them a few miles away was Helmsley, where they had spent the night and visited the ruins of Rievaulx Abbey – "Dear Mary had never seen a ruined Abbey before except Whitby." Hence their late arrival at the viewpoint. When they descended the hill and arrived at Thirsk, on the plain, a light they thought at first was the moon proved to be a bonfire in the market place to celebrate the thirty-eighth birthday of a local worthy who had fathered an heir to the estate.

Because the inn was full they had to move on to Leeming Lane, on the Great North Road, where they arrived in the dark at eleven o'clock and, not surprisingly, "were not very well treated". They had travelled almost from the Yorkshire coast, along the Vale of Pickering which marks the southern foot of the Cleveland hills, and so to the sharp edge of Sutton Bank. Next morning they were off again across the plain to Middleham and its castle at the edge of the dale country. Here they entered Wensleydale about which Dorothy became lyrical. "The vale looked most beautiful each way. To the left the bright silver stream inlaid the flat and very green meadows, winding like a serpent. To the right we did not see it so far, it was lost among trees and little hills." They had a good view of Bolton Castle for they had to spend some time imprisoned in their post-chaise while the driver went for another horse. Typically, they compared their lot with that of Mary Queen of Scots, who had been imprisoned in the castle, and William wrote a sonnet about it: "Hard was thy durance, Queen! compared with ours."

On through Hawes, Garsdale, Sedbergh and Kendal they travelled, looking at Aysgarth Falls, having "a Bason of milk at a publick house", popping into churches, eventually arriving home at Grasmere at six o'clock in the evening of the third day after leaving Brompton. It was a journey of well over one hundred miles as the crow flies, and much more as the post-chaise meanders, over rough stony roads, and must have been a severe undertaking even in days when families like the Wordsworths thought little of walking from Grasmere to Ambleside to collect letters or up the long road to Keswick to take tea with Coleridge.

This way across the middle of Yorkshire remains almost unchanged in essentials nearly 200 years later. It is untouched by industry and for the most part traverses an unspoiled landscape. Contrary to the accepted view of Yorkshire, you will scarcely see a factory chimney, never a pit head, and no conurbation larger than a country market town. Age-old villages cling to hillsides or their cottages line a by-road or huddle round a village green with a chuckling stream not far away. Such changes as have come since the Wordsworths travelled this way are minor ones. On market days cars and buses bring in buyers and sellers to the little towns where once they came by cart or wagonette or, earlier, on horseback. Holidays stimulate a surge of motor traffic, but this for the most part prefers the main roads to the wandering but deserted byways. More noticeable perhaps is the new noise overhead, for war days left on the plains a legacy of aerodromes where training flights are still carried on, though you are likely to see rather than hear gliders swooping over their club's head-quarters along that very edge from which the travellers gazed.

In a physical sense this broad Plain of York separates two halves of Yorkshire; the millstone grit and the mountain limestone of the Pennine heights and the dales which run from them, and the North Yorkshire moors of Jurassic limestone, which rise to the 'cliff-lands' called Cleveland. The glacier-carved plain between, known in parts as the Vale of Ouse, the Plain of York, the Vale of Mowbray and Tees Vale, is of magnesian limestone with soft red marls and sandstones and is more richly cultivated and wooded. It divides the country from north to south. Through it runs the Great North Road, avoiding the hills on either side.

These two halves of Yorkshire present their contrasts. All the way from the coast on the north-eastern side heather covers the moorlands, in the winter dark and brown, almost black, for mile after bounding mile. As the high land of Cleveland descends from its heathery escarpments to the Vale of Pickering the rolling moors are cut into deep wooded valleys, still unspoiled. From the east in order are Newtondale, Rosedale, Farndale, then a gap to Riccaldale, Ryedale and Bilsdale. Along the top runs the Esk valley eastwards to the sea at Whitby, the rest run south. Each of these dales has its special appeal. Daffodils grow in Farndale and Riccaldale, filling the valleys in spring with a golden carpet. Newtondale once had its own picturesque railway line linking Whitby with the rest of Yorkshire, now alas no more. Rosedale, down which runs the river Seven (for the dales are not, as in the western lands, called after their rivers), once had an abbey for nuns, but its stones must now be sought in the houses and farms in the valley. It, too, had one of the oldest ironworks in the country. There were mines here in the thirteenth century, and forges for the working of the metal. It has just lost its last relic, the 'Chimney', a landmark for many miles around with, beneath it, grass grown mounds where I have gathered specimens of slag discarded I know not how long ago. The rest of the valley is a beautiful green hollow.

In Ryedale is Helmsley with its castle, built by Robert de Roos, Lord of Helmsley, at the end of the twelfth century, and thereafter passing through many historic hands. It was besieged and taken by the Parliamentary army in 1644, when Sir Thomas Fairfax held it for the King for three months before surrender. One interesting feature is the very marked change of colour in the stonework where the walls were raised still higher to keep out the marauding Scots.

In one of the many Scots raids on Ryedale inhabitants of the villages round Pickering banded together, not to oppose the raiders but to buy them off. They had to promise to pay the sum of 300 marks, then a very considerable sum, and provide hostages to ensure payment. Alas, once the Scots had departed the locals were not anxious to pay up, and it is recorded that the hostages languished many years in the hands of the Scots and then were not heard of again.

One of the castle's notable owners, though not a very desirable one, was George Villiers, the second Duke of Buckingham, who was described as "one of the wildest rake-hells in English history". After many matrimonial adventures he fell into disgrace, drowned his sorrow in heavy drinking, and retired to his Yorkshire home at Helmsley Castle. Here hunting provided his relaxation, and led to his death. While out riding his horse dropped dead beneath him, a sinister omen for a superstitious horseman. He waited by the roadside and caught a chill which affected his ravaged body so swiftly that he could not reach his castle at Helmsley. He was taken to the house of one of his tenants at Kirkby Moorside and there died, not perhaps as the poet Pope so grimly described:

> In the worst inn's worst room, with mat half-hung,
> The floor of plaster and the walls of dung.
> On once a flock-bed, but repaired with straw,
> With tape-tied curtains, never meant to draw.

The house was never an inn and indeed can still be seen, now greatly altered, in the market place. Yet it was a miserable end that should please the moralists, of a lord "more famous for his vices than his misfortunes after having been possessed of about £50,000 a year".

A brief entry in the parish register records the death thus:

1687 – April 17th, George Vilaus, lord dooke of bookingham,

which gives a clue to local pronunciation at that time. A legend is still told of a ghostly duke who still rides in pursuit of a ghostly fox over the moors between Helmsley and Kirkby Moorside. Fox hunting has continued in this region ever since, for the mixture of moorland and farmland, wooded valleys and hillside copses makes it good fox country.

This thinly peopled land was a populated area long before the tread of Roman troops was heard along the Great North Road which borders it on the west, or over the Roman road on Wheeldale Moor near Levisham. Barrows and burial howes are marked thickly on the map of the high moors. There are earthworks, megaliths, cairns and remains enough to keep an archaeologist happy for life. Indeed it did just that for the late Dr. Frank Elgee and his wife, who devoted all their days, and many nights too, to exploring this vast area and hunting up evidence of prehistory back to the Old Stone Age. Still earlier remains show that this and other parts of Yorkshire had an animal population before the ice Age shaped much of its present landscape.

Perhaps it is something of the spirit of these ancient peoples on these remote moors which kept alive until almost our own times a belief in ghosts and witches and boggarts as well as the flying barguest I have earlier referred to. These animistic pagan beliefs were deep-rooted in these parts. You can still find witch posts in the area, usually made of mountain ash and marked with a X, placed between the door and the chimney to prevent the witch going through the house, which she must do to bewitch it. It was a common custom when churning to throw a pinch of salt over the head into the fire to keep evil spirits away. When you passed the home of a reputed witch you kept your thumb in the palm of your right hand to keep off evil spells. And if a witch appeared in the form of a hare, a common disguise, you shot it with a silver bullet made out of a melted-down coin.

Even in summer daylight these moorlands can be lonely places, and on winter nights when easterly gales blow over them and whine through the heather or batter at the red-tiled stone cottages a host of wild stories and legends spring into life. Here and there among the heather are ancient stone crosses and still more ancient and queerly shaped natural rocks which bear names like the Badger Stone, Bridestones, the Old Wife's Neck, as well as many standing stones from the Bronze Age. They had a symbolism at which we can only guess today. An old legend links two notable features on the moors above Pickering. One is Blakey Topping, a cone-shaped hill – for the hills are called 'toppings' in these parts as they are called 'knotts' in the west of the county. The other is a basin-shaped hollow called the Hole of Horcum.

The story, told by Frank Elgee, is that a local witch had sold her soul to the Devil on the usual terms, but when he claimed it she refused to give it up and flew over the moors with the Devil in hot pursuit. As he could not overtake her he grabbed a handful of earth and threw it at her. He missed his aim and she escaped, the hole of Horcum remaining to prove where he tore up the earth and Blakey Topping to show where it fell to the ground. Curiously, a track which still leads from the hole to a Bronze Age settlement on the way to the topping is known as the Old Wife's Way. Which suggests that many of the Old Wife stones may be linked with witchcraft.

No evidence of extensive witch-hunting as happened on the Lancashire moors round Pendle and elsewhere has come down to us in this region. Here witches were accepted as a part of life only to be avoided when they were likely to interfere in one's personal affairs.

There is still a touch of the old superstition remaining in the rather dismal "Lyke Wake Dirge", sung by those who each year complete the forty-mile Lyke Wake Walk across these North Yorkshire moors from west to east, for the Dirge is one of the oldest dialect funeral chants marking the flight of the dead person's soul over Whinny Moor. Another, longer, walk has been recently established under the name of the Cleveland Way, which begins at Helmsley and sweeps in a great curve along old tracks and drove roads across the Cleveland hills to the coast at Saltburn and continues down the coastline to Filey. It is a continuous footpath nearly one hundred miles long.

Witches are being ousted nowadays by trees, for, although

there is still plenty of wild moorland remaining, the men and machines of the Forestry Commission each year turn over more uncultivated land, drain it and plant it and create vast new forests where any witch would be lost, unable to see the witch wood for the trees. For lesser mortals the Commission has organised well-marked forest trails open to the public. These trails run for many miles in the area between Thornton-le-Dale and Scarborough through woods clothing what were once heather-covered moors and now forgotten valleys. Tens of thousands of acres are already dense woodland, with here and there a farm clearing still remaining. More acres have been planted and maintained by private landowners. So that this has now become what one visitor described as the "Black Forest of Yorkshire".

To ancient man the central plain between the moors and the dales must have been far more of a barrier than it is today. Low-lying and swampy for the most part, with the ancient forest of Galtres filling much of the vale between York and Northallerton, and with no well-marked forest trails to help him, the most intrepid of our forefathers must have dreaded crossing from one side to the other. He must have feared the deep forest and found it difficult to negotiate the bogs and marshes. Only near York was there a glacial ridge which became a well-worn way and probably accounted for the site of that city itself. Now it has so many crossings that the Great North Road, which runs north and south through the plain, is provided with underpasses and overpasses to keep its traffic flowing while the cross traffic goes through.

Towns and villages in this strip of Yorkshire, broad at its southern end, narrowing near Northallerton, and then broadening out again towards Teesdale, have a richness and security which comes from a fertile land. They have had their troubled moments of history, the traffic of armies to the wars, the return of broken and disillusioned forces, political and personal strife. But their prosperity has continued. It has a mature rhythm which comes from ordered labour in a land of plenty. Yet place names like Sutton-on-the-Forest, Barton le Willows and Ainderby Mires (which was once Ainderby-in-the-Mires) indicate its earlier woods and swamps. Leland speaks of this country as "shaded in some places with trees, in other some a wet flat, full of moist and moorish quagmires".

Sydney Smith was the witty rector of Foston and built

RELIGIOUS HOUSES: *4, The Augustinian priory at Bolton*

himself a house at Thornton-le-Clay (which speaks for itself)
nearby. He it was who, when preaching a charity sermon,
declared that Englishmen were distinguished for generosity and
the love of their species. Alack, the collection which followed
was not up to expectation, so he added a rider that he should
have said they were distinguished not so much for love of their
species as of their *specie*. And when a local squire, after a
fruitless argument with the rector, declared "If I had a son who
was an idiot, I'd make him a parson." Smith replied, "But I see
that your father was of a different opinion." He must have
been a big pulpit draw.

Easingwold, now a quiet market town, was once the busy centre
where the Swainmote Courts were held. This was a court of
verderers of the Forest of Galtres which tried poachers and
regulated the affairs of the forest. The town continued to be
important until the end of the coaching era, and at one of the inns
you will be shown the vast stabling which was needed to cater for
the traffic then. When the railways came Easingwold tried to
maintain its place by founding its own private railway company,
but although it carried local traffic, it could not compete with the
main lines. Now even the main road by-passes the town and only
its old-world houses and doorways recall the busy days.

Until recently, Thirsk, which is at a meeting place of main
roads, had its modern nightmare of traffic—literally as well as
metaphorically. Its large cobbled market square was so full of
vehicles all day long that parking was almost impossible for the
visitor. By night, too, the same square became an overnight
parking ground for lorries and giant road vehicles of all kinds,
coming in, moving off, and 'revving up' at all hours. Now a new
by-pass and out-of-town parking space enables you to see Thirsk
as a delightful town, with old coaching inns, a weekly street
market, and a pleasant little stream, the Cod Beck.

The square itself is of a pattern common in towns here-
abouts, and indeed of market towns all over Yorkshire. It is
broad and roomy, but with bottle-neck approaches which
enabled it to be easily guarded when looting Scots came down
from the north to steal cattle, goods or womenfolk. You will see
the same pattern at Easingwold, at Bedale, and at Northallerton in the Vale of Mowbray to the north. We shall meet it
again at Leyburn in the Dales. It is less noticeable in the
eastern side of Yorkshire we have just left.

The Plain of York merges into the Vale of Mowbray without

RELIGIOUS HOUSES: *5, An interior view of York Minster*

notice, and I have failed to discover anyone who knows the dividing line or even whether one exists. Its physical features are the same; all part of that rich flat area between the hills. Perhaps the northern half has less historic territory but many villages, old halls and houses in this region are worth a visit, having so much of our heritage to reveal. Catterick, for example, dates back to the Roman fortress of Cateractonium, it is still a great military camp, and it has one of the county's many racecourses. Cowton Castle, often ignored, dates back to the Conyers family in the days of Henry VI. Hornby Castle was built for the St. Quintins in the fourteenth century. The whole area was once in the powerful barony of Mowbray.

Today its chief town is Northallerton, the capital of the North Riding and as such the administrative centre for schools, libraries, drainage and other services, including a prison. At times I feel that all this modern machinery of local government operating from the County Hall and many other buildings fits oddly into a town with a notable history of kings and queens and armies and raiding Scots. Then I give myself a nudge as I realise that this and all the vast wartime flying activity that was centered in this region – when men from many lands flew their sorties and returned, or did not return, to their home bases on these flat lands – will appear in the history books of the future and will no doubt make a stirring chapter for readers in what we hope will be a very different world.

On a windy Saturday early in 1965 the Pennine Way was formally opened at a gathering near Malham Tarn, at the head of Airedale, and 250 miles of footpath linked Edale in Derby-shire with Kirk Yetholm over the Scottish border. For the first time it became legally possible to walk almost the full length of the backbone of Britain and to realise what a nobbly spine we possess. The Pennines, running up to 3,000 feet, are truly the bare bones of geography, hard and uncompromising. There are far fewer trees here than on the eastern moors. By comparison, these Pennine moorlands are as bare as a shorn sheep. Even the valley pastures appear unfleshed of fertility, netted over with stone walls, and the fells above them places of great loneliness. You have to be made of stern stuff to tackle those 250 miles – at least at one venture.

The Pennine Way enters Yorkshire from the south near that Roman road over Blackstone Edge we have already noted as one way into the county. It crosses the white limestone country

of Craven to Malham and Ribblesdale, just missing Wharfedale, and then crosses Wensleydale and Swaledale, past the
cloud-touching Tan Hill into Teesdale, where at High Force it
leaves the county at its most northerly extremity.

Although it passes through historic and indeed prehistoric
areas, the Way reveals the landscape as a physical thing which
has shaped the life of men, from the mixture of peoples which
have chosen their territory in it, to the forms of its agriculture,
the nature of its buildings, and the layout of its villages and
towns.

There is a consistent pattern to the villages of the western
dales, quaint by comparison with those of the plain and the
moors. For the most part they grew up in the valleys on level
well-drained gravelly ridges, out of reach of the river in the
valley in flood time, but usually protected by a belt of woodland
above. Between the woodland and the limestone scars of the
dale side was sheltered land for their stock. Between the village
and the river were the water meadows liable to winter floods at
a lower level but providing some pasture for animals and now
used for hay crops. Somewhere near the first settlement would
be strips of land cleared from the scrub and ploughed. If the
land sloped too much the strips would usually be cultivated
across the slope, and the steady clearing of stones and ploughing would create terraces along the contours which are so
notable a feature of the Dales, particularly in the narrower
upper reaches. These lynchets, as they are known, go back to
Anglian times and formed the cultivation pattern down the
centuries. As families and villages grew new strips were added,
or fresh fields were opened up in similar strips. So one family
might own, after some time, a number of strips scattered over a
wide area.

This system changed only gradually down the years by the
exchange of strips between owners to consolidate their lands
and by a rotation of crops to encourage fertility, although
much was worked in common. Cattle and sheep roamed the
waste lands, their owners sharing the use of these in common.

After the Dissolution of the Monasteries this process speeded
up: by agreement, the strips were grouped into fields, each
under individual ownership; pastures were enclosed to keep the
cattle from straying and to improve the breeding of stock, and a
good deal of unused land recovered. From this grew the
enclosure movement of the eighteenth century. This had the

effect of legalising the procedure and hastening the disappearance of the old strip cultivation. Any group of landowners could promote a private Bill in Parliament to reallocate the lands of a township. Commissioners were appointed to approve or disapprove of each scheme.

Where such a Bill merely sanctioned agreed enclosures little dispute arose. It was where great areas of commons and moorland were involved that feeling ran high, not so much between farmers and landowners, for both gained by enclosure of unfenced land, but because the poorer village folk and labourers, who by ancient custom had fed their cows, sheep or goats on the commons and had gathered fuel and sometimes wild fruits and nuts for food from the land, were not consulted and were only meagrely provided for by charity plots. Many of these now landless families moved to the towns, where mills and factories were springing up, for as it was said with bitterness "where forty persons had their livings, now one man and his shepperd hath all".

Here and there in the Dales you will see 'intakes' high on the fellsides, where man has wrested a few more acres from the bents and untamed growth. Often he has been beaten by the land and the elements, so that all you can see are a few derelict stone walls and a few grey ruins of buildings. Here, unlike the plain we have crossed, the land offers no free bonus. Man has had to fight unendingly for his crops and his pasture.

From the Pennine backbone flow those rivers which have created the Dale country: in order from the north – Tees, Swale, Ure, Nidd, Wharfe and Aire. All of these except the Tees, which flows eastwards to enter the North Sea beyond Middlesbrough, flow in a generally south-easterly direction to make the Ouse, and so unto the Humber. Thus the frequently used simile of a hand of outstretched fingers. There are two exceptions. A little group of rivers in the far north-west rising in the fells which border Westmorland flow into the Lune; and the Ribble which rises in the Yorkshire fells but flows partly through Lancashire. Both end in the Irish Sea.

For long, topographical books about the Dale country have treated each of these rivers as separate entities each the subject of a special expedition. So they still remain for those who wish to explore their exquisite multitude of villages, waterfalls, old halls and ancient ways as well as the high 'tops' themselves, on foot or in a leisurely way. But in these days improved roads and motor travel have linked them as one unit not only for the visitor but the native, too. Where each dale was once an isolated community they are now so easily accessible that an event in one dale will bring participants and spectators who formerly were regarded as 'foreigners' from the next valley. A great area of them can be encompassed in a day's travel.

Dorothy Wordsworth and her companions took a whole day to travel from Leeming Lane, in the Plain of York, to Hawes, a journey which can be done comfortably today in a couple of hours. Walter White, whom we observed arriving at Hull by boat for his "month in Yorkshire", spent a great proportion of his time walking in the Dales. In all, he walked 375 miles and found "it is perfectly possible, while on foot, to travel for four -and-sixpence a day, sometimes even less".

Yet White, on foot, noticed a great deal of the essential Dale life which the modern motorist misses. At the top of Swaledale he observed that "with unlimited supplies of stone to draw on, the houses of Stonedale are as rough and solid as if built by Druids. Each door has a porch for protection against storms, and round each window a stripe of whitewash betrays the rudimentary ornamental art of the inmates." In the next dale "We had tea served after the Wensleydale manner – plain cakes and currant cakes, cakes hot and cold, and butter and cheese at discretion, with liberty to call for anything else that you like; and the more you eat and drink the more you will rise in the esteem of your hospitable entertainers." He retells the story of the Sabbatarian farmer who, on his way to chapel, noticed a fine calf in his neighbour's field, and when seated in his pew, was over-heard to ask the owner of the animal, "Tommy, supposin' it was Monday, what wad ye tak' for yer calf?" To which Tommy replied in an equally audible whisper, "Why, supposin' it was Monday, aw'd tak' two pun fifteen." "Supposin' it was Monday aw'll gie two pun ten." "Supposin' it was Monday, then ye shall hev't." And the next day the calf was delivered to the scrupulous purchaser.

Although Walter White's book ran through many editions (I have a copy of the fourth dated 1861 and of the fifth dated 1879) it has long been out of print. A copy might still be found on the shelves of a seller of old books. If so a visitor to the Dales – as, indeed, to the rest of Yorkshire – would find it enlightening reading.

He would discover, as did White, that each dale has its

distinctive character. Swaledale is wild and stern, with something still about it of what we imagine the Norsemen who settled it found attractive. It has many Scandinavian place-names – Keld, Gunnerside, Rogan's Seat. In parts it has an air of desolation which somehow links it with the old lead-miners who worked these hills. Reeth, known as the 'capital' of Swaledale, was once a mining centre, now it is a quiet almost forgotten little town standing on a hill looking down the dale.

Muker (pronounced 'Mewker'), at the head of the road through the dale, is the village where two famous naturalists, Richard and Cherry Kearton, went to school and where they began in a primitive way the art of nature photography now universal. Lower down is Grinton, with a stately parish church, the place to which the dead were brought for burial along the hillside 'Corpse Road', and there is a beautifully scenic road from here to Richmond and its huge Norman castle.

Wensleydale is longer, greener and softer in its landscape, with woods and many waterfalls, old halls and many side valleys. Between Hawes at its head and Leyburn at its foot there is a road running on either side of the dale with, at one side, Bolton Castle of the Scropes, where Mary, Queen of Scots, was imprisoned and at the other Middleham Castle of the Nevilles, associated with the notorious Richard III. This dale is the birthplace of Wensleydale cheese which is still produced there, although no longer from the milk of ewes, as the original monkish cheese-makers made it. Unlike the other dales it does not take its name from its river, but from the now small village of Wensley, which had a market as long ago as the thirteenth century but is now eclipsed by Leyburn.

Wharfedale is today a more sophisticated dale, accessible to the West Riding as a playground and holiday centre, still retaining the charm and colour which J. M. W. Turner, who stayed at Farnley Hall on its bank, found so attractive. It begins romantically in the fells, where its source is only a few yards from that of the Ribble, which flows in the opposite direction. Along its course you will find prehistoric remains, Norman churches, the old and once mighty Priory of Bolton, ancient villages like Kettlewell and Grassington, before you come to a Victorian spa at Ilkley, industrialism at Otley and a racecourse at Wetherby. What more could one ask of a dale?

Apart from a man-made reservoir at its upper end, a craggy section with underground caves and the strange, elevated, and tortuous-shaped rocks of Brimham, Nidderdale has become a dormitory dale, to which commuters come from Harrogate, Leeds and Bradford attracted by its gracious setting. Industry is creeping in, but is still dwarfed by the attractive hills on either side.

Finally, there is Airedale, which begins more mysteriously and more dramatically than all the rest amid the limestone crags and cliffs around Malham, and which ends more dismally than any other as a near approach to an industrial sewer. The mystery lies in its source, which is somewhere deep underground amid the fells. Its drama is in the massive limestone amphitheatres which surround its birthplace. Like a magnet this draws holidaymakers and other visitors in thousands to the upper dale which is a natural display piece of geology and natural history. The pollution which fouls its lower reaches is of comparatively recent origin. Cistercian monks who built Kirkstall Abbey on the river bank thirty miles away once fished its waters, and I have talked with elderly men in Leeds who remember bathing in the river as it flowed under Leeds Bridge. Yorkshire industry cares little for its river heritage.

Markets and Fairs

The character of Yorkshire folk is never seen to better advantage than on market day in any of the little country towns of the moors and dales. There is hearty goodwill about the buying and selling of sticks of celery, lace curtains, silk stockings, fish and potatoes in rural places which somehow seems lacking in an urban market. It begins early in the morning when the first stall-holders arrive to set up their displays with a good deal of lively jesting and the exchange of comments on how trade was at Settle yesterday, or Selby last week, or at Otley last Friday.

The stall-holders are part of a great army of nomads, moving from market to market every day of the week, with their fents and their jewellery, their fish and their vegetables and their literary fare bearing titles like *Her Last Chance, He Loved Too Well* and *Poppy's Romance*; and always the stall with the frieze of trousers hanging round its edge.

By mid-morning, when the buses start to come in bringing the women folk from the villages, things warm up.

"Here you are, Ma. Fine pair of slippers for your old man. Lovely they are. Make him happy for life!"

"Grand bananas, here. All C'naries. Cheap today!"

A growing crowd begins to press and heave and make little progress between the close-packed stalls. The square acquires a smell of peppermint and trodden vegetables, with occasional fishy gusts as the kipper man gets busy. But always, even on the wettest and coldest day, it is a cheerful place, full of household gossip, laughter and the bright chatter as of a family gathering. Often it ends on a cheerful note, too, as some rather merry soul removes his hat, performs a solo waltz in the market square, and then moves on a little sheepishly and unsteadily as he observes a policeman watching him with professional interest. Another hour and the market town returns to its ancient peace until the next week. In general it is a woman's day, as every homeward-bound bus bears evidence. The men have their own occasions at the cattle markets – which may or may not coincide with the orgy in the market square.

It is on these male occasions that you will find the answer to that old query of why farmers always carry a hooked stick when they go to market, for there you will see those sticks used for their right purpose – not to walk with but as the most effective instrument for handling sheep. With a dexterous hand at the end of the stick the most awkward of sheep can be hooked, examined, turned and penned in an instant. You can see the thing done to perfection at such markets all over Yorkshire. And you will see, too, something of the uncanny skill with which the sheep-buyer sums up the grade and worth of animals he is buying. With quick cunning hands he probes the fleece to assess the quality of the fatty tissues – and then will tell you the exact weight of the animal to within a pound. And he will calculate the weight of fifty as easily as of one.

I was once told the story of a sheep buyer who had imbibed a little too freely at the local tavern and who, passing some sheep, stumbled and fell, clutching their fleeces as he went down. He rose immediately with a look of determination.

"By gow, these are a grand lot o'sheep," he whispered to his partner, "we mun buy t'lot."

His clutching hands had discovered their worth even as he fell – and they proved a rare bargain.

The weekly cattle markets in our country towns are, like the housewives' market, the gathering grounds of real countryfolk, the true 'characters' of rural life. Despite the increasing present-day organisation of agriculture, cattle market day still holds its importance in farming life, though the marts are merely grading centres, and cars and tractors are more common than horses.

The old-time rural fair, at which our predecessors combined their shopping with their pleasure, has almost vanished in this part of the country, and even where it lingers it is only a shadow of its former self. There is an air of apology about it for even that frail existence.

"Nay, Ah doant't rightly know when there was last a fair 'ere. Mi owd father could remember it right enough, but it were afore my time. There's no fair 'ere nowadays."

It was an elderly farmer in a Craven village who spoke, perhaps a little sadly, as one who felt it right to regret something he had never known but around which tradition still lingered. I have listened to similar laments in a good many villages in recent years, and there has always been that wistful note of regret. From Hawes to Richmond, from Sedbergh to Pickering, the tale is the same. Only Hull, with its annual fair which has been held since its first charter in the thirteenth century, keeps up the old tradition, and even there you will be told, "Hull Fair is not what it was." They will probably be thinking of the great Bostock and Wombwell Menagerie which was said to occupy an acre of ground.

Not long ago I asked a well-known Hawes resident to give me the dates of cattle and sheep fairs which are held there. He brough down from a bookshelf an old history of the town and turned up a certain page. On it was printed a long and imposing list of the "Fairs and Markets held at Hawes". It seemed as though every week boasted a fair of some kind. But my informant pulled out a pencil.

"That's not held now," he said, striking out a date. "Nor that, nor that, nor that."

Before he had done, the list had shrunk to a poor half-dozen. "And I reckon some of those won't be held much longer," he added.

Skipton can tell a similar story. Less than two centuries ago there were nearly a dozen fairs held in the town each year, at which were sold cattle and horses, broad cloth and pedlars' goods. Only the annual horse fair in August lingered on as a reminder. Even small villages like Clapham and Ribblehead had their appointed fair days for sheep, cattle or other wares; the dates are now almost forgotten.

Long before there were commercial travellers, or 'representatives' as they are called in these times, the fair was almost essential as a means of trade in everything from horses to onions. These fairs and feasts in the rural areas were the counterpart of the miners' Gala Days in the industrial areas, in which merry-making was combined with political speeches and band-led processions. In the dales, roundabouts and swings appeared on village greens, gipsy caravans turned up in force, entertainers gave almost continuous shows, and exiles from the villages made it the occasion for a return to home territory to join the sports and attend the dances. Many exiles came from the textile towns of Lancashire where they had found work after the closure of the lead mines of Swaledale and Wensleydale. Conversely, when the textile towns closed mills and factories for their own feasts and holidays former dalesfolk would exchange work at the looms for a spell in the home hay fields "to keep their hands in" against a forlorn hope of sometime returning.

At one time Boroughbridge had five annual charter fairs, and its Barnaby Fair, which lasted three weeks at a time, was the liveliest in the North. Before the days of circular racecourses the town held an annual race meeting on a straight road over the common. This was abandoned when coach traffic got mixed up with the races and other towns began holding their race meetings on circular courses prepared for the purpose. Aysgarth in Wensleydale had its feast every October with a fox hunt as the big event, well supported in the village by amusements, sideshows and quoits matches; but all this died out in the Twenties and only the elderly remember its great days. Wherever 'horsey men' gathered, Lee Fair at West Ardsley was talked about, for hundreds of horses changed hands at "t'first Lee" and "t'later Lee" amid much galloping and showing off of paces, and a great deal of boisterous fun and occasionally riotous scenes.

A festival of a different sort was the ceremonial commemoration in February of Bishop Blaize, patron saint of the woollen industry and particularly of woolcombers. Every seven years until early last century Bradford's streets were paraded from ten in the morning to five in the afternoon by a great cavalcade of woolstaplers, spinners, merchants, woolsorters, combmakers, woolcombers, dyers and all their apprentices, with "a personage of very becoming gravity" as Bishop Blaize, attended by shepherds and shepherdesses, Jason "of the golden fleece", local actors as "the royal family", bands, flags and multitudes of small boys.

But why Bishop Blaize? And why woolcombers?

Thereby hangs a strange tale. The original Bishop Blaize lived in a cave in Armenia and cured many sufferers by prayer, such as a boy who had a fishbone stuck in his throat. Later St. Blaize was ordered to be scourged, and seven holy women anointed themselves with his blood. Whereupon their flesh was combed with iron combs, but their wounds ran nothing but milk and their flesh was whiter than snow; angels came and healed their wounds as fast as they were made. On this rather thin legend the Bishop was adopted by the industry and his effigy is carved at the entrance to the Bradford Wool Exchange.

Why Dewsbury, in the midst of the woollen district of the West Riding, should have an Onion Fair each October I can never discover, but it was a highly popular event for both mill-workers and youngsters who would declaim:

> Onion Fair! Onion Fair!
> If you don't give us a holiday
> We'll all run away.

They always got their holiday until the Onion Fair ceased to be, early this century.

Yarm, Topcliffe and Stokesley in the North Riding were all fair towns of importance. Yarm's has now declined from a three-day event to a two-day nuisance in the eyes of many residents. It still observes the ancient custom of 'Riding the Fair' at its opening, but the chairman of the parish council uses a motor-lorry instead of a gallant entry on horseback. Topcliffe-on-Swale's fair is chiefly a gipsy gathering at which some horses are sold. Stokesley Show and Fair still has something of the old-time glory, for many thousands of people from Durham and North Yorkshire pour into the town each September for the agricultural show and the fun of the fair which fills the main street with everything from a 'Flea Circus' to a 'Giant Speedway'. Kilburn continues to appoint a 'Lord Mayor' for its fair-day. This seemed a common custom in many areas, for Oswaldkirk, Bishopthorpe, Askrigg and other villages all took their 'mayors' in procession on this day. Bellerby, near Leyburn, went to the other extreme by carting a tarred and feathered victim round the village.

Curiously, even a century and more ago it was said that these fairs were "not what they were", and their early decease was foretold. Yet they continued for many years afterwards. It has been left to our more sophisticated age to witness if not their complete disappearance then their translation into something far removed from the days of home-brewed ale and cheese-cakes.

One traditional feature of North Country fairs now lost were the twice-yearly hirings – usually at Whitsuntide and Michaelmas – when men and girls wanting jobs lined up on the kerb in the square while prospective employers questioned them about their abilities. To indicate their skills those seeking employment often carried their 'trade marks' – grooms, a whip; stockmen, a cowband; farm maids, a scrubbing brush. The period for which they sought service was usually six months, at the end of which time they could come back for a change of job. Many, of course, stayed at one place for years – but they always came to the hiring fair, first to see how their friends had fared and then to have a good time at the stalls and shows and roundabouts.

No contracts were signed at these hirings. The employer gave the new employee a shilling – called a 'fastening penny' – shook hands, and that was an agreement rarely broken. It was all probably not half so romantic as history would suggest, for those were the days when maids were paid £4 for the half-year and farm hands about double that sum. But fair-day was at least a bright spot in their lives twice each year. Employment exchanges and appointments boards and 'situations vacant' have changed all this. 'Hirings' have gone. Will the rest of the fairs follow suit? Only on our weekly market days have we a link with a bit of rural life that goes back almost to the days when history began, a fragment of the old 'Merry England'.

Another 'merriment' we have lost was the old custom of 'beating the bounds'. Nowadays we have Boundary Commissions continually changing our lines of territory and Ordnance Maps to record them. Such methods are more efficient but far less picturesque than the centuries-old custom of solemn processions headed by the parish priest or beadle and local dignitaries and churchwardens perambulating the parish borders. Then small boys were bumped on hard boundary stones or whipped to impress upon them physically the extent of the territory. They were usually recompensed by cakes and sports, which were also presumably an aid to memory.

In some parts of the north these were also known as 'ganging days', because the village folk went out in gangs to make certain that common lands and boundaries had not been encroached upon, or any of the landmarks removed. Bounds beating, as such, became confused with the Rogation processions of the churches on the same day, with the result that peculiar ceremonies, half-religious and half-secular, were evolved. Thus in some places, as the procession went round the bounds with hymns, boys claimed the right of damming up the gutters and throwing water over passers-by until they were bought off.

The Derbyshire custom of decorating village homes, wells and springs, with flowers and tree boughs never seems to have attracted Yorkshire folk. At Tissington in Dovedale I have seen wells beautifully decorated with arches smothered with flowers stuck in the clay plastered over the wood, a custom which is still observed. The nearest approach to this – of which I know – was at Skipton where it was once the custom of boys at the Grammar School to gather flowers before they went to school on May morning. These they strewed on the steps of the master's house and the schoolroom floor. In return the master scattered coins for which the youngsters scrambled. I doubt whether staff or scholars would look favourably on such a custom today.

The most notable of all observances was, of course, that of maypole dancing. Dozens of Yorkshire villages from Redmire to Barwick and from Burnsall to Gawthorpe had their maypole on the green around which grown-ups and, later, children danced and plaited the ribbons round the traditional pole.

I can remember what was probably a lingering remnant of this when greasy poles were erected outside public houses in the Woodhouse district of Leeds, surmounted by a ham or a cheese or a copper kettle. He who climbed the pole – which was well covered in fat – claimed the prize. This later became a popular attraction at the time of Woodhouse Feast each autmun.

Curiously, chimney-sweeps and milkmaids made May Day their festival in some places in the north. A party of two or three sweeps would dress up in fantastic attire, carrying brushes and pans. With them was a Jack-in-the-green – a man

inside a framework of leaves and ribbons. They danced round the streets to the music of a drum and fife, possibly as a sort of 'harvest home' after a busy season of spring-cleaning. The milkmaids followed suit, except that their showpiece was a garlanded cow, and they carried a curious framework of wood decorated with borrowed silver ware.

You can find many women in our Yorkshire villages who remember how as young girls they went out into the fields on the first day of May to bathe their faces in the dew. It was believed to be a certain way to beauty. This faith in the magical cosmetic properties of the first May dew has a long history. Pepys, in his diary, notes how his wife went down to Woolwich to gather May dew, and the ritual was old then.

Music Makers

To come across a bandstand in a remote little valley with a waterfall in the background and sheep grazing nearby still puzzles many visitors to Hardraw in Wensleydale. True, the bandstand is unused and derelict, and the only way to both it and the waterfall is through the Green Dragon Inn, but it is worth a visit.

It recalls those days when dozens of Yorkshire towns and villages had their own brass or silver bands, their choirs, and their annual visits to Hardraw for contests. When an exile from these parts wrote to ask me recently if they still ran railway excursions to band contests and if they were still popular, I had to tell him sadly that there was now no railway to run trips, no crowds, and only a declining number of brass bands in the county. A few bands are occasionally broadcast, but they have to struggle to keep going.

The brass band movement is scarcely a century and a half old, and much of its early impetus came from the mining areas of Yorkshire. Blaina in Monmouthshire claims the formation of the first full brass band in 1832. A few years later a band was formed in Teesdale and the enthusiasm spread quickly. The typical mining village of Rothwell in the West Riding founded its band in 1838. "It was very natural that some of the villagers should try to find some pleasurable antidote to the tedious wear and tear of their life out of sight of the world of the pits wherein they gained their livelihood. This antidote was found in music." So said the *Military Brass Band Gazette* some fifty years later.

So many bands were formed that it was possible in 1845 for Sir Clifford Constable to hold the first recorded brass band contest at his home at Burton Constable, near Hull, and this event fired a young musician, Enderby Jackson, to throw his energies into the movement, and fifteen years later he could organise a contest at the Crystal Palace, the first ever held in the South of England, which lasted two days and attracted seventy two bands. And the first and second prizes went inevitably to Yorkshire bands. Meanwhile enthusiasm spread to Lancashire and the first of the long series of brass band contests was held in 1853 at Belle Vue Gardens, Manchester. This form of working-class music making spread to mills and factories all over the north as well as in Wales and elsewhere.

There were great struggles in those early days to raise money to buy instruments and landlords of village inns had often to dig deep into their pockets to help finance the band funds, probably not altogether through altruism as the local hostelry was often the band's headquarters and the playing of wind instruments was thirsty work. In the Dale country many bands were formed when moorland lead mines were at their prosperous peak, a "good blow wi't' band" being regarded as beneficial to health.

Some of the lead-mining companies supported the bands financially for this reason, and in the coal areas gifts to local bands were given by more enlightened mine-owners. Until quite recently there were bands in Muker, Reeth and other Swaledale villages. They played at the feasts, sports meetings, processions and choir outings. Wensleydale had its Brass Band Committee, and it was this body which organised contests at Hardraw and built the bandstand. At the village of Grassington in Wharfedale there were once two rival bands and, when they met, the band leaders would roar "Come on, lads! Let 'em have it," and they would play at full blast against each other.

Although as we shall see the moorland country of north-east Yorkshire had a strong liking for country dancing, sword dancing and Morris dancing, there was an Eskdale Tournament to encourage choral and instrumental music; and Loftus has a reputation for band performances, and also had a group of saxhorn players. On one occasion the drummer, who had quenched a keen thirst before the start, was so enthusiastic that he burst the drum. Rosedale had a band of twenty players, using wind, brass and stringed instruments once used in the church, and there was another at Farndale. Helmsley, in the Vale of Pickering, had at least two bands at various times, but none exists today. All these were popular as Christmas waits.

There are still bandrooms to be found in many villages in the industrial areas and even in some Dales villages. Here the musicians practised in the evenings or on Sunday mornings. I well remember joining a company of villagers outside the bandroom at Haworth in the Bronte country and listening to their comments and criticisms as the band played within. Sometimes a band would seek a field outside the village in rural areas, where they were free from adverse remarks and could blow to their hearts content. It is not easy to picture the old miners and weavers – often bewhiskered, to judge from their photographs – wrestling with the mysteries of harmony and counterpoint after long hours in the pit or at the looms. Traditions grew and were handed on from generation to generation.

Flockton United Band, one of the early starters, founded in a village near Wakefield, proudly claims to be the first brass band to play "Onward Christian Soldiers". The Rev. S. Baring-Gould, its author, was a curate at nearby Horbury Bridge. He composed it for a Whitsuntide Treat, and Flockton Band headed the procession – its conductor having written out his own band parts. Rothwell Old Band used a wagonette to transport it to contests, aided by a local named Old Jack, who carried some of the instruments in his pony and trap. Once in a huff he drove off in his trap with the instruments and all the music and had to be pursued by a small boy on a bicycle with instructions to bring back what he could carry. Many people who have listened to the Black Dyke Mills Band would be unable to say where it came from or even know that the mills from which it takes its name are at Queensbury between Bradford and Halifax.

Bramley's old Prize Band had a famous poem written about it in dialect of which four lines proudly declared:

> At Gala, Feast an' Flaar-Show,
> At Kirsmas an' May Day,
> At contests too, aar Band is sewer
> To carry t'prize away.

But the bandsmen for the most part have departed. Nowadays would-be musicians join dance bands and pop

SAINTS: *'St Wilfrid' in procession through Ripon*

AUSTWICK INCLOSURE.

I THOMAS BUTTLE, of *Kirkby Lonsdale*, in the County of *Westmorland*, Gentleman, the sole Commissioner appointed by an Act of Parliament, made and passed in the forty ninth Year of the Reign of his present Majesty, intituled, "An Act for inclosing and reducing "to a stint several Commons and Waste Grounds, with- "in the Township and Manor of *Austwick*, in the Parish "of *Clapham*, in the West Riding of the County of "*York*," in Pursuance of the said Act, and of another Act made and passed in the forty first Year of his present Majesty's Reign, intituled, "An Act for consolida- "ting in one Act certain Provisions usually inserted in "Acts of Inclosure, and for facilitating the mode of "proving the several Facts usually required on the pas- "sing of such Acts."

Do hereby give Notice,

That *On Saturday the Ninth Day of September, next*, at nine o'Clock in the Forenoon, it is my intention to enquire into, ascertain, set out, determine and fix the Boundaries of the said Commons and Waste Grounds, so to be inclosed and reduced to a Stint, by an actual Perambulation of the Boundaries of the said Commons and Waste Grounds, which Perambulation I intend to commence at *Oxenber Gate*, and proceed Northward to ascertain the said Boundaries, so far as the same respectively adjoin on the Manors, Townships, Hamlets or Districts, of *Lawkland, Feizor, Stainforth, Horton in Ribblesdale, Selside, Newby, Ingleton* and *Clapham*, or any of them in the Order before mentioned.

Given under my Hand the *Nineteenth* Day of *August*, 1809.

Tho. Buttle.

Commissioner.

A. FOSTER, PRINTER, KIRKBY LONSDALE.

groups, and the bandstands in our parks – and in the Dales – are deserted and forlorn.

Church and chapel choirs and a multitude of enthusiastic choral societies have had a longer life which has withstood the rivalry of radio and television. Their history goes back to the choral services of the cathedrals and monasteries and, later, to the congregational singing of the nonconformist chapels. The highlight of the year is, of course Handel's *Messiah*, which can still pack chapels with a critical audience aware of every note and nuance of the performance. It is almost regarded as a Yorkshire anthem. I once asked an elderly man sitting next to me as we awaited a performance in a West Riding chapel why *Messiah* always sounded better in these parts than if it were sung by a first-class choir in any other county. After all, there is nothing really 'Yorkshire' about the oratorio. His answer was forthright:

"The thing is that Yorkshire folk take *Messiah* for granted as the proper thing to sing at Christmas. It's as much a part of this season as Father Christmas himself. Other folk think of it as something special to be put on occasionally. Here we expect it and I know chaps who start humming it as soon as December arrives. Folk down south don't know it in the way that we do. They don't think of it as a right and proper 'chapel do' as in Yorkshire. They don't wait for notices to appear outside chapels and then discuss this year's principlals as football fans discuss new players, as we do in these parts.

"No" he concluded, "the singing of *Messiah* is a Christmas ritual up here as much as Christmas pudding or pulling crackers. And it stands to reason that we do it better than anybody else."

The work of the choirs is shared by those who listen to them, for it is the proper thing for their audiences to follow them with the score. Many well-thumbed copies of the worthy Handel have been fished out of drawers and shelves ready for the great occasion. And most chapel congregations enjoy having a sing themselves in a hymn before the *Messiah* starts and one afterwards if possible. You will notice that the closing hymn is always sung more lustily than the first, because they are trying to emulate the choir.

I believe Mr. J. B. Priestley has a story somewhere of a man who fell out with his friend because of a dispute about the rendering of a particular passage in an oratorio, and in those

RURAL YORKSHIRE: *1, An inclosure notice*

tortuous and winding passages for the basses and in those organ accompaniments there is much room for Yorkshire argument.

It is odd that this most popular of oratorios was written by Handel in a mere three weeks of concentrated effort. His concerts in this country had not been popular, and he was in a desperate financial plight when he received an invitation to conduct some concerts in Dublin. He was so pleased that he decided to give Ireland something new as a reward. And *Messiah* was the result. A year or so ago I stood by the now almost forgotten port of Parkgate on the Dee from which Handel is reputed to have sailed to Dublin with his oratorio in his pocket. It seemed a far cry from that mud-silted harbour to a hundred Yorkshire chapels at Christmas time.

Whether this communal music-making which has always been a part of our heritage has its reverse in the limited number of outstanding individual musicians and composers from the county is open to question. But the fact remains. Frederick Delius of Bradford stands head and shoulders above the rest. Yet there are lesser names which should not be forgotten. John Curwen, although coming from an old Cumberland family, was born in Heckmondwike in 1816 and gave us the tonic Sol-Fa system of music teaching. It grew out of his work of teaching Sunday-School children to sing and he published his first "instructor" in the system when he was 25. Later he went into publishing, and a Tonic Sol-Fa Association was formed to spread the system which was later adopted by some three-quarters of the elementary schools in Britain.

In a county noted for congregational singing it is not surprising that it should produce a musician to give it hymns to sing. The man was forthcoming in John Bacchus Dykes, a native of Hull, who for a short time was a curate at Malton, then later became a Minor Canon and Precentor at Durham Cathedral and eventually took the living of St. Oswalds, Durham. Today his name appears in our hymn books under such familiar hymns as "Nearer My God to Thee", "Eternal Father, Strong to Save", "Jesus, Lover of My Soul", and many others. He was a trained musician as well as a theologian. William Jackson, of Masham, the son of a member of the local Band was on the other hand almost entirely self-taught. The barrel-organ in Masham church, the self-acquired ability to play every instrument in the village band, appointment as part-time organist when a keyboard organ replaced the ancient church automaton – this constituted his musical education. Yet before he was 30 he had composed the well-known oratorio *The Deliverance of Israel from Babylon* and went on to compose others, as well as becoming conductor of the Bradford Festival Choral Society.

At Ilkley a quiet beauty spot known as Hebers Ghyll is a link with the Bishop Heber, whose name is for ever associated with the hymn "From Greenland's Icy Mountains"; and the familiar hymn-tune known as "Rimington" comes from a little village in Bowland and was the work of a local composer, Francis Duckworth. You can see the first line of the tune on his gravestone at Gisburn.

For so large and so musical a county it is not an outstanding heritage, and the reasons are not obvious. Lost in the midsts of time and anonymity is a great host of fiddlers, concertina players and other musicians who performed at village halls and inns for the dances and revelry which were so much a part of rural life in Yorkshire. There are stories still told of Kit and Dick and Jack who played at these homely functions and whose names were as familiar then as those of pop stars today. Here rather than in the halls of fame must our musical heritage be sought.

Digging up the Past
One day early last century a Settle man took his dog for a walk among the great limestone scars which overlook this old market town in Craven. It is a favourite walk of Settle residents even today, for once you have climbed on to the high fells there are magnificent views of a landscape which can have changed little over tens of thousands of years. Tracks through the greenest of grass bright with mountain pansies lead under the foot of the scars to Langcliffe and the Ribble valley or across the fells to Malham and the Aire valley.

Michael Horner had rounded the imposing Attermire Scar and wandered up a little valley when his dog disappeared into a hole in the valley side. He whistled after it and heard it bark inside a cliff. He climbed a slope of tumbled debris fallen from the limestone face, whistling as he went, and after some minutes the dog appeared, not through the hole in the rock into which it had vanished but from another crack nearby. From the hollowness of its bark it seemed certain there was a cave at the base of the cliff and a brief probing confirmed this, but close inspection was not easy because of the great bank of debris.

Apparently Michael Horner told some of his cronies in Settle of the dog's adventure but did not pursue the matter further, and there it might have rested had not a Settle tradesman, Joseph Jackson, with an interest in caves and knowing the story, decided some years later to investigate the holes in the cliff. So one day in the summer of 1838 which happened to be the day of Queen Victoria's coronation, he crawled through nettles and rubbish into the cave and dug in the mud inside. There he found some unmistakeable Roman remains as well as a number of bones. He promptly named the place Victoria Cave.

For some time he continued his solitary visits, even sleeping in the cave at nights, and gathered what Professor Boyd Dawkins, of Owen's College Manchester, described as "a remarkable series of ornaments and implements of bronze, iron and bone, along with pottery and broken remains of animals". There was Samian ware and other Roman pottery, coins of various periods from the Roman occupation, spear-heads, nails and daggers, rings and bracelets, and bones of deer and domestic animals. It was an unusual collection which Mr. Jackson used to adorn his home and showed to his friends and visitors.

Not for another thirty years however, was its significance fully realised. Then Professor McKenny Hughes, carrying out an official geological survey of the district, heard of the collection and inspected it. At once he realised its importance, and in 1870 a committee was formed to carry out a systematic exploration. Subscriptions were invited from notable scientists and local gentry, and the British Association contributed to the fund. Under the direction, first of Professor Boyd Dawkins, and later of R. H. Tiddeman, of the Geological Survey, and with the assistance of the now elderly Mr. Jackson, work was begun to probe the buried mysteries of the cave.

A collection of the reports of this committee covering the years to 1878 have come into my possession and they detail the remarkable discoveries of a persevering group of enthusiasts. The debris and screes which had made entrance difficult was removed layer by layer, revealing not only Roman remains, but Celtic ornaments and crude imitation Roman coins as well as the bones of Celtic shorthorn cattle. The Professor dated them back to the time of the evacuation of Britain by the Romans and added: "We can hardly doubt that the cave was used in those troublous times by unfortunate provincials, who fled from their homes, with some of their cattle and other property, and were compelled to exchange the luxuries of civilised life for a hard struggle for common necessaries." This was the first of a series of revelations which was to stir up many controversies.

Below the Romano-Celtic layer, some two feet thick, the archaeologists excavated again and removed some six feet of rock and soil which had fallen from the cliff face. Beneath this they came across a bone harpoon with double barbs and some flint flakes probably worked in Neolithic times when the first farming people arrived in this country from the Continent and the first steps were taken in our own civilisation. The explorers were now back into prehistory.

That, however, was not the end of the excavation or even the beginning of the history of this cave. Those Victorian enthusiasts went on with their digging – their financial accounts now begining to show "wages", paid presumably to local labour – and they came to a layer of laminated clay indicating glacial conditions. There were, too, glacial deposits with strange rocks brought down by sheets of ice through the nearby Ribble valley and deposited there when the ice retreated. By the sort of reasoning we are accustomed to in detective fiction, the scientists deduced that all this region was under a sheet of ice during those cold ages. Therefore any finds in or below these deposits must be evidence of the life which existed there before the glaciers were deposited. So when more bones were found in the lower layers, and these bones were marked by some sort of human tool, there was at once a great furore. Mr. Tiddeman recorded how the finds were made: "On the 10th of June 1875, when the Rev. Mr. Crosskey and I were at the cave, a small bone turned up bearing upon it marks which cannot be considered to have been made by other than human agency."

The marked bone was surrounded by other bones and the teeth of hyena, bear, elephant and rhinoceros, all of which pointed to their existence in a warm climate, all found in the lowest cave earth.

"Upon the whole, then, we have an assemblage of species which require, or could live in, a tolerably warm climate. Arctic species are entirely absent. . . . This state of things must have lasted a long time, but higher in the section the bones became more scarce, the more tropical animals are wanting." So wrote Mr. Tiddeman in his report, and he proceeds to describe how in the upper cave earth several antlers of reindeer were found, evidence that "reindeer lived in the district subsequently to the waning of the ice-sheet".

This theory was opposed by those who held that the Silurian rocks and boulders had not been left there by the ice-sheet but had fallen from the cliff subsequently. It was retorted that the cliff above the cave was quite free from boulders for a considerable distance and that as the boulders were so close to the cliff it was physically impossible for them to have fallen to their present position. They must therefore have been brought down by the ice and left when the glaciers retreated.

The greatest controversy raged over the discovery of a single bone which became a true bone of contention. It was found in the pre-glacial bed and was at first identified as part of a human fibula. This would, of course, have been strong if not conclusive evidence that man had existed here in pre-glacial times. It took the whole matter further than the problematical mark of a human tool on a bone. Later, doubts arose as to the authenticity of the bone as human. It might, instead, be that of one of the lower animals. As Professor Boyd Dawkins said at a meeting of the British Association in 1878, "the *fibula* had become a *fabula*". Yorkshiremen would have to cede the idea of tracing their pedigree back to a pre-glacial marrow-bone!

Perhaps we can let Mr. Tiddeman, of the Geological Survey, who began all this, sum up: "Even supposing we had never found traces of man in the Victoria Cave in the older pre-glacial beds, his great antiquity would be there fairly proved. A set of animals which are well-known to have existed with man elsewhere, is there shown to have lived before an age of great land glaciation, and to have had its remains swept from that country by it".

As there are, without doubt, many unexplored caves yet to be discovered among the limestone fells and scars of this western part of the county, there may yet be many secrets of Yorkshire's 100,000-year-old heritage still to be revealed. Meanwhile, although many of the Victoria Caves finds have unfortunately been scattered and lost, enough remain on view in a small museum in Settle to emphasise the importance of this century-old discovery. To look upon these fragments of life long ago brings a sense of gazing down a long tunnel of time through history into pre-history; all that has happened since seems of little account.

5

From Sheep to Cloth

'Black Country' – Drama in the Streets – Sporting Humours

When the writer of the Book of Job declared "My days are swifter than a weaver's shuttle," he found his imagery in an industry which by its close contact with everyday life has enriched our speech with a multitude of similes. You will still hear a Yorkshireman declare he has been "fleeced" – although in fact this must be a rare event, and he is probably "spinning a yarn". But most of us at some time have talked of "losing the thread" of an argument or becoming involved in "a tangled web" or lost in "a tangled skein" of thought or doubtful of "a fine-drawn" notion. The same industry has given us an abundance of personal surnames, like Webster (a weaver), Dyer, Taylor, Lister (another name for a dyer), Walker (a fuller who trampled the sodden wool) and Kempster (a woman woolcomber). Spinster, of course, is the feminine for spinner, and as an unmarried woman usually continued to work at the loom it became her accepted description. Indeed, after agriculture, no other single industry has so enriched our language as wool textiles.

The beginnings of the use of wool for clothing in Yorkshire go back into the mists of time, certainly as far back as the Bronze Age, and was probably always known as a domestic skill wherever there were sheep in the Pennine dales and among the moorland valleys. When, in historic times, Edward III brought Flemish workers to this country to teach us their skills some of them who came to Yorkshire can be regarded as the founders of the industry in these parts.

A feature of many towns and villages of the West Riding are the weavers' cottages. I am not referring to the rows of drab back-to-back houses built as part of the industrial revolution and which are now mercifully being swept away (often, alas, to be replaced by soaring blocks of flats which in time may substitute vertical slums for horizontal ones), but to the older weavers' cottages usually built in short rows of half a dozen or so, generally of stone, and which, close below the eaves, have rows of windows which do not appear to have a geometrical relationship with the windows below. They date from the seventeenth century onwards. In these well-lit upper storeys were the weaving rooms, fitted up with hand-looms, from which developed Yorkshire's textile industry. Little wonder that Dr. Nikolaus Pevsner regards them as "something rare and special".

To understand their importance and also their link with the cloth halls, which existed in Leeds, Wakefield, Halifax, Huddersfield and other towns, it is necessary to look briefly at the story of the woollen industry, once England's premier industry and described then as "the master wheel of trade".

It grew out of sheep. From Norse times sheep had been grazed on the farmsteads, and some of the stock may have been brought by the invaders. Later, with monastic encouragement sheep roamed the cleared fells and moors of Yorkshire where the largest flockmasters were monks. The Cistercians developed wool production with great efficiency and, for a time, much profit. The number of 'grange' place-names indicates the extent of their pastures on lands often far removed from the abbeys and in some cases – Fountains Abbey is an example – they built vast cellariums for the storage of wool collected from the sheep lands. As monastic houses are thicker on the ground in Yorkshire than anywhere else in Britain this was reflected by an immense wool output.

With such abundant supplies of wool available the making of this into cloth was an obvious next stage.

> No other industry [says Mr. E. Lipson] affords better material for studying the growth and decay of the various economic organisms which have taken root in English soil at one period or another – the 'gild' system where the worker owned both the material and the instruments of production; the 'domestic' system where he owned the instruments but not the material; and the 'factory' system where he owns neither the instruments nor the material.

And in no other county is this progress so evident.

Craft gilds of weavers, fullers, dyers and others existed at York, Beverley, Malton, Thirsk, Scarborough and elsewhere from about the twelfth century. Membership of the gilds was compulsory in the same way as trades union membership in industry today, and this was graded by skill and services into apprentices, journeymen and masters. No craftsman could set up in business on his own until he had served an arduous apprenticeship and proved his skill. Social life was fostered by the gilds and they took part in the mystery plays and feastings. In recent years, as we shall see, York has revived the performance of these plays in its streets as becomes a city famous for its crafts. Surprisingly the gilds included many women members long before the days when emancipation of women was discussed. This was almost inevitable, as the woollen industry has always been heavily dependent on women workers. In York at one time a quarter of the cloth produced was the work of women. The customs and liberties of the York Gild of Weavers were confirmed by Henry II, and they were granted the exclusive privilege of making cloths and tunics in Yorkshire for which they had to contribute £10 yearly to the exchequer.

This form of organisation gradually changed to the 'domestic' system as the demand for cloth grew, as new markets were found over wider areas, and as the great number of processes (estimated at fourteen) from raw wool to finished cloth called for a great number of specialists – spinners, weavers, fullers and shearmen and the like. At this point we first hear of 'clothiers' – who were not tailors but capitalist employers of the other craftsmen producing cloth. They owned the material and passed it round the skilled craftsmen who used their own tools, worked in their own houses and were paid by the piece.

I believe that more than in other parts of the country, the Yorkshire 'clothier' was an actual craftsman, himself taking part in the work of cloth making, rather than an outside employer. His enterprise was on a smaller scale than, for example, the West Country clothier, and more of a family business. He bought the wool and with his family, and others he employed, worked it up on his own equipment and on his own property, selling it at the end of the week to provide money to buy more wool for the following week. He also employed apprentices whom he trained.

How this apprenticeship system worked can be seen in the evidence given by a Mr. James Ellis, a clothier of Armley, now a suburb of Leeds, to a Committee on the Woollen Industry in 1806. His was only a small concern and he told the committee he worked with one apprentice, two hired journeymen and a boy, giving some work out. The committee then asked him to describe the different branches of trade which he had learnt and in which he instructed his apprentices.

"I learnt to be a spinner before I went apprentice; my apprentice was only eleven years old when I took him; when I went apprentice I was a strong boy, and I was put to weaving first. I never was employed in bobbin winding myself while I was apprentice. I had learned part of the business with my father-in-law before I went. I knew how to wind bobbins and to warp. After that I learned to weave. We had two apprentices and after I had been there a little while we used to spin and weave our wets; while one was spinning the other was weaving".

He was asked if he bought his own wool and replied:

"Yes. I had the prospect of being a master when I came out of my time, and therefore my master took care I should learn that. I kept an account all the time I was apprentice of the principal part of the colours we dyed and practiced the dyeing. . . . I was not kept constantly to weaving and spinning; my master fitted me rather for a master than a journeyman".

Finally he was asked if he instructed his apprentices in the same way. His reply notably sums up the soundness on which the industry was built.

"Yes, we think it a scandal when an apprentice is loose if he is not fit for his business; we take pride in their being fit for their business, and we teach them all they will take."

The industry remained 'domestic' for a long period, even when the demand for cloth increased the number of weavers beyond the capacity of the spinners to supply the yarn. The introduction of machinery – the spinning 'jenny', first turned by hand in the cottages, was transferred first to water power and then to steam; the power loom, invented by Cartwright in 1785, gradually replaced the hand-loom weavers by stream-powered mills and then moved to the factories – all of this transformed the industry to the industrial pattern we know today.

Although most of our links with this age-old woollen industry are now to be found in the larger towns of the West Riding, it is still possible to discover reminders of those early days in the rural Pennines which provided their background. Wander down many Pennine valleys and you will find derelict buildings which were originally corn mills supplying the local population. As they fell out of use when more corn was grown elsewhere they were taken over for preparing the wool and spinning and weaving it into cloth, and for preparing the finished material by 'fulling' – or walking – it, using the water power from the streams which had driven the old corn mills. The existence of such names as Mill Lane and Mill Gill is evidence of where they stood. On the fells above the valleys you will find the old pack-horse ways, now sometimes converted into motor roads, sometimes lost altogether, but some, fortunately, still traceable as the green tracks offering the most delightful walking in Britain.

These green ways followed the most practicable route linking one area of the country with another, going along valleys when they were not waterlogged, climbing hillsides when necessary, cutting round shoulders of the fells, crossing streams at fords (until bridges were built), and always arriving somewhere, not petering out in dead ends. For they were trodden out for a purpose. During many centuries such pack-horse tracks were our chief mode of transport, and in Yorkshire that transport linked the monasteries and their granges for the carrying of wool as well as for the supply of their own necessities. They made it possible to get wool to the ports (Fountains Abbey, for example, sent its wool by pack-horse to the Ouse at Clifton, near York, from which it went by river to Hull), and later they provided the means for the carriage of wool to the clothiers and the return of the finished cloth to the markets. An early writer describes how travelling merchants "go all over England with droves of pack-horses and to all the fairs and market towns over the whole island . . . it is ordinary for one of these men to carry a thousand pounds value of cloth with them at a time." The number of 'Woolpack' inns still standing is evidence of this traffic. A specialised trade of this kind was carried on by the 'broggers', who, by law, were allowed to travel to farms all over the north of England, buy small parcels of wool direct and carry it back for sale in the Halifax market. From this grew the middlemen of the industry who flourished by the purchase and sale of wool.

Defoe was one of many travellers who observed and recorded what took place in the public cloth markets at which the goods were sold. When he had recovered from his journey over Blackstone Edge, already referred to, he went on to describe a

visit to Leeds, where he saw cloth sold in Briggate, the street
which spanned the River Aire and is still today the main
shopping thoroughfare:

> The street is a large, broad, fair and well-built street, beginning at
> the bridge and ascending gently to the north. Early in the morning
> there are tressels placed in two rows in the street. Then there are
> boards laid across those tressels, so that the boards lie like long
> counters on either side from one end of the street to the other. The
> clothiers come early in the morning with cloth, and few clothiers bring
> more than one piece, the market being so frequent. At six or seven
> o'clock in the morning the market bell rings. . . .
> All the boards are covered with cloth, and behind every piece of
> cloth the clothier standing to sell it. As soonn as the bell has done
> ringing the merchants and factors and buyers of all sorts come down.
> When they see any cloths that suit their occasion they reach over to the
> clothier and whisper, and in the fewest words imaginable the price is
> stated; one asks, the other bids; and 'tis agree or not agree in a
> moment. . . . In little more than an hour all the business is done. Thus
> you see ten or twenty thousand pounds value in cloth, and sometimes
> much more, bought and sold in little more than an hour.

The same observant traveller, too, noted the close link
between the industry and agriculture for, after all, before the
clothier was a wool man he was probably a farmer, and in times
when trade was bad he would go back to his farming.

> Every clothier must necessarily keep one horse at least [said Defoe]
> to fetch home his wool and his provisions from the market, to carry his
> yarn to the spinners, his manufacture to the fulling-mill, and when
> finished, to the market to be sold, and the like, so every one generally
> keeps a cow or two for his family. By this means, the small pieces of
> inclosed land about each house are occupied, and, by being thus fed,
> are still farther improved from the dung of cattle. As for corn, they
> scarce sow enough to feed their poultry.

It was for the better handling of this trade that cloth halls
were built. One, known as the Piece Hall, opened in 1799, still
exists structurally at Halifax. It consists of a series of small
offices built on galleries round a large courtyard. Here the
'pieces' of goods or woven fabrics were brought from the houses
of the handloom weavers to be bought by dealers. It is now used
for other purposes. Leeds built its cloth halls when sales ceased
on the old Leeds Bridge. Ralph Thoresby, the Leeds topographer, refers to "the Moot Hall, in the front of the Middle
Row, on one side of which is one of the best-furnished
Flesh-Shambles in the North of England; on the other the
Wool-Market for Broad Cloth which is the All in All".

Bradford built its piece hall in 1773, where previously goods had been sold in Kirkgate, having been brought in on pack ponies or even on the backs of the weavers themselves. They would return home with fifty pounds of new wool to work up. 'Candle auctions' of wool were not unknown. When bales were on offer a candle was lighted with a pin inserted at a particular mark. The last bid received before the pin dropped out secured the bargain.

It was because sheep pastures were in close proximity to water and, later, coal power that the West Riding became the centre of the woollen industry, just as the Lancashire climate and the swift-flowing Pennine streams gave that county its supremacy in cotton. The plentiful supply of soft water as well as power from the rivers Aire, Wharfe and Calder brought the mechanised mills to the river banks. They marked the end of the old home craftsmanship, and substituted for it the modern factory system.

School history lessons reminded us of the violent opposition of the workers to this introduction by the new clothiers of their mills and machinery and the tragic riots which followed. Charlotte Bronte in *Shirley,* written not so very long after the event, describes one of the 'incidents' when the rioters attacked a mill:

> A crash-smash-shiver – stopped their whispers. A simultaneously-hurled volley of stones had saluted the broad front of the mill, with all its windows; and now every pane of every lattice lay in shattered and pounded fragments. A yell followed this demonstration – a rioter's yell – a North-of-England – a Yorkshire – a West-Riding – a West-Riding-clothing-district of Yorkshire rioter's yell. You never heard that sound, perhaps, reader? So much the better for your ears – perhaps for your heart.

Not only the operatives, as they were now called, objected. When mills moved to the towns residents opposed the building of factory chimneys because of their filthy smoke and the mills because of the noise of the machines. There came, too, revelations of the long hours worked by young children who had to be beaten regularly to keep them awake. One overseer boasted, "I am noted for being able to keep the children awake and going longer than any other man in the mill." Not until the first Factory Act was passed in 1833 was there any prohibition of the employment of children "under nine".

Miss Phyllis Bentley has pictured this coming to Yorkshire of the new textile age in a score of novels. It was a technological revolution – to use a now familiar phrase – which had far-reaching effects. Home-grown wool no longer met the needs of the developing industry. Other lands, including the colonies, which once bought English wool as one of our staple exports, now returned the compliment by selling us theirs. Other materials like alpaca and mohair came into use in the worsted trade. Shoddy, the re-use of old material, played a big part, and even the rival products of the cotton industry of Lancashire – which came upon the scene long after the start of the woollen industry – were used as warps in weaving to produce lighter fabrics.

Just as the West Riding had its woollen crafts so the North Riding had its own textile craft, the making of linen. But where the one flourished and became a mighty industry the other, so far as Yorkshire was concerned, dwindled and moved out of the county. For something like 200 years it flourished in the area around Northallerton, and it is only within the lifetime of older folk that the final decline came. A century and more ago it was a common sight to see rows of long white sheets of fabric stretched in the fields to bleach in the sun, and villages like Osmotherley and Brompton had more than a local reputation for their work. There are relics of the linen industry in other parts of Yorkshire, including the Washburn Valley, in Wharfedale, where, until 1870, a water mill stood at West End which once employed nearly 200 workers. Steam power brought about its decline, and the mill was acquired by Leeds Corporation, demolished, and the stones used in building the boundary wall of a reservoir.

A brief glimpse at the old records of industrial Yorkshire, especially as they concerned the textile industry in the days before the factory system came into being, reveals many of those homely and human touches lost in more formal histories. When hand-loom weavers worked in their own homes they preferred it because even though the conditions were bad and the hours were distressingly long, there was a sense of liberty and a freedom from restraint and supervision. Most of the family could be roped in to help, even cripples and old folk, which added to the meagre rewards. And there is some evidence that those brought up under this domestic system often lived to a ripe and hale old age.

Despite this liking for working at home, however, conditions in those crowded cottages must have been almost as bad as in the early factories which took their place. Look at some of those old cottages which still remain, and it is evident that they were low-built, ill-ventilated and even in their best days very damp. When work was done for fourteen or fifteen hours a day in the same room or one adjacent to where the family slept and lived, cooked its meals and ate them, when the wool and other materials used were frequently treated with evil-smelling oils and dyes, and where there was usually a constant state of overcrowding, conditions were far from salubrious.

> I have heard a patriarch tell [wrote a dalesman of a weaver of those days] how one week he had been unable to get half a stone of flour owing to lack of work, and how anxiously he looked forward to the following week for the accustomed luxury. On the Friday evening after he had paid up all the week's debts, he found he had exactly 4s. 2d. left, which was the price of half a stone. All the way down the village towards the grocer's shop he could hardly control his joy but when he arrived flour had risen to 4s. 6d. and he had to do without.

Yet I discovered that one worker, in 1806, declared, "certainly we prefer to work in our homes. . . . We can begin soon or late, and those of us who have families can train them up in some little thing." Perhaps that is what is meant by Yorkshire independence.

A few years ago Bradford's ornate stone-built Wool Exchange loomed large in the city's architecture. The woollen industry had increased its population from some 4,000 in 1780 to over 40,000 half a century later, and was rapidly bringing it towards the 400,000 mark by the end of this century. Automation has largely changed the very characters of the industry. Now the Wool Exchange is dwarfed by great sky-scrapers of office blocks and shops. The great mills and warehouses are being driven out of the city by, presumably, more profitable enterprises. The significant term 'man-made fibres' is heard almost as often as 'wool'. New synthetic materials are replacing the traditional forms of clothing. And what is happening in Bradford has its counterpart elsewhere in the West Riding. Is this the end of the story, or only the beginning of a new chapter?

'Black Country'

A standing grievance with Yorkshire folk is that their county of broad acres is so widely misrepresented as a black land of

pit-heads, belching mill chimneys, clanging steel works and grime-smothered houses. Unfortunately many of the modern 'ways in' have lent substance to this view. Because our railways were designed to serve industrial areas they entered where the murk was greatest. Because the roads from the south traversed the areas of coal and steel, the first impression of travellers was of blackness and noise. The traditional English way of entering a city through its backdoor of slums applies as much in the North as on the way into London. But you don't judge London by its backdoor! The blackness of a limited area of Yorkshire is, indeed, a comparatively recent development.

When Thomas Allen wrote his *Complete History of the County of York* in the 1830s he had little occasion to mention coalfields or the 'smog' of industry or the black landscape of south Yorkshire. He could refer to Doncaster as "one of the most convenient and beautiful towns in the empire". Rotherham, though condemned as "far from handsome", earned the epithet because "the streets are narrow and ir-regular and the houses, which are chiefly of stone, have in general a dull and dingy appearance". But no reference to smoke and permanent gloom. J. S. Fletcher, another Yorkshire historian and novelist, writing in the first decade of this century, is enthusiastic about the changes brought about in *The Making of Modern Yorkshire*. Doncaster, he writes, "up to fifteen years ago a purely agricultural town, is now the heart of a district in which the old, sleepy farming villages are being one by one transformed into something vastly different by the sinking and working of new pits". At Barnsley he notes that "the town itself and its whole neighbourhood are entirely devoted to coal-mining. Every village in the outskirts is a colliery village". And he becomes almost lyrical as he records that the "street, roads and lanes are for ever thronged with miners going to or from the various pits; the very skies seem to be in sympathy with the black earth underneath, the at-mosphere is charged with coal-dust". He summed up the capital value of it all in a succinct paragraph: "At the time of the Domesday Survey there was a wood in Sheffield Manor of four square miles in size; nowadays one square yard of Sheffield land is worth the four square miles of that wood."

This is the transformation which has given Yorkshire its 'black country'. Coal was occasionally mined in these parts as in many other parts of Yorkshire in very early times. There are

DALE COUNTRY: *1, Wharfedale from Simon's Seat*

the remains of simple pits and workings to be seen right across the county, although a search of the *Domesday Book*, detailed though the survey was, reveals no reference to coal or mines. An ancient track in Dentdale in the north-west is called the Coal Road. Outcrops were probably worked at Tan Hill near the Yorkshire-Westmorland boundary in· the thirteenth century. Near the old ridge-way of Rudland Rigg running up into Cleveland you can find nearly a hundred small pits spread over what must have been an extensive coal field. When wood for burning and for charcoal became scarce that coal was widely worked for local use.

When this first occurred is doubtful. Most of the early references are to "sea coal", which probably meant coal brought into Yorkshire ports by sea from Northumberland and Durham where it was mined much earlier. There are monastic references to coal mined on their lands by the Canons of Bolton Priory, by the Abbot of Jervaulx and by the monks of Kirkstall, indicating that besides being great sheep farmers the monasteries were also industrialists and had their own small forges and smithies. It is on record that the Dean of York was granted a licence in 1590 "to purify pit coal and free it from its offensive smell", which may have meant converting it into coke. By the fourteenth and fifteenth centuries there appears to have been a mining industry in south Yorkshire, usually worked from bell-pits, which were shallow shafts mined from the sides and frequently mistaken by early antiquaries for Iron Age pit dwellings. The addition of chimneys to large houses suggests that coal rather than wood was becoming a domestic fuel, as these would carry off the "offensive smell' which troubled the Dean of York.

Once the problem of obtaining a sufficiently powerful blast in furnaces was overcome, the use of coal for smelting was a natural consequence. This gave an impetus to coal production, first where seams outcropped on the hillsides and then in deeper pits. A long struggle followed to find means of disposing of the water which accumulated in the mines, and in this John Smeaton, of Austhorpe near Leeds, played a big part by adapting a Newcomen engine to a pumping mechanism, which after many trials and much error served its purpose.

Around Barnsley the seams were near the surface and were among the earliest to be worked, but as the search for more coal went on to the south and east it was discovered that the seams went deeper. Larger-scale operations were required, more machinery and bigger installations were called for, and this brought in the well-capitalised colliery companies. It also brought the grim days of female and child labour below ground, the toll of mining disasters, the pit spoil heaps, the conflicts of owners and men, the grime and all the mess that follows the getting of coal. Yorkshire's coalfields became famous, but at a price.

How primitive and dangerous were the efforts to fight the continuing problem of coal-gas in the mines, for example, is described in Kendall and Wroot's *Geology of Yorkshire*:

> To prevent accumulation of gas it was customary in some mines for a man to go every night through the workings exploding the gas which had gathered during the day. He was rolled in a cover of wool or leather; his face was protected by a mask and a hood resembling that of a monk, and he crawled along the earth to get as much respirable air as possible, for the fire-damp being lighter than air, rises to the highest part of the mine. For this reason he was provided with a lighted candle on the end of a stick, which it was his duty to poke into all likely corners where gas might have gathered.

Yet this did not prevent explosions costing many lives in a long series of disasters.

When child labour was taken for granted the pits of Yorkshire and Lancashire became notorious for their use of "children of tender age and young and adult women" in the performance of the same kind of underground work and for the same number of hours as men. A commission in 1842 reported that in great numbers of coal pits in the West Riding "the men work in a state of perfect nakedness, and are in this state assisted in their labour by females of all ages, from girls of six years old to women of twenty-one, these females being themselves quite naked down to the waist". The hours of work for children and young people were rarely less than eleven a day, more often twelve, and many told the commissioners they never saw the light of day for weeks together during the winter. Some – the youngest children – must have worked longer for, as 'trappers', who opened and shut the trap-doors along the underground pit ways as the trucks of coal went through, they had to be in the pit "as soon as the work of the day commences" and could not leave the pit "before the work of the day is at an end".

I have failed to discover which was the earliest pit-heading in

the county: that gaunt structure with its whirling wheels to lower and raise the cages, the engine room beside it, and the lamp-room nearby, all part of a landscape associated with Yorkshire and often regarded as its most dominant feature. For a long time a gin worked by two horses was used for raising baskets of coal and men. The horses walked round and round a drum linked with a pulley over the pit mouth. Ninety tons a day was considered a good output.

When mechanisation brought greater production it became necessary to dispose of the output more quickly. Horse or bullock haulage had been the accepted method of moving loads on land since Roman times, and probably long before. It was still so in early mining days. Up to the beginning of last century Middleton Collieries, a few miles from Leeds, had transported all the coal to the city, first by pack pony then by a railway on which waggons were pulled by horses. Then John Blenkinsop, a Northumberland man, devised his steam locomotive that worked on a rack-rail between the lines, and this was installed at Middleton. Thousands of people gathered to see this strange thing make its first journey and the trial was "crowned with complete success". Coal was taken to Leeds by a form of transport that "did the work of sixteen horses in twelve hours and cost £400".

In common with the rest of the mining country Yorkshire shared, and indeed led the way, in that rapid expansion by which, having so long a start, British coal exports dominated the world market until just before the First World War, when over a million workers produced some 287 million tons. Alas, that early development meant that the best seams of coal were soonest worked out. Mining had to be done at greater depths, in thinner seams and at greater cost. A grimmer cloud than coal dust hung over the industry.

Yet, in 1931, a century after Thomas Allen, and writing of the same area, J. B. Priestley in his *English Journey* could say:

> Along this road to Barnsley the sun flared hugely before finally setting. All the western edges of the slag-heaps were glittering. I saw in one place a great cloud of steam that had plumes of gold. In another, we passed under a vast aerial flight of coal trucks, slowly moving, in deep black silhouette, against the sunset.... When we looked down upon Barnsley, we saw it for a moment dimly ranged about an ebony pyramid of slag.

And, to complete the comparison, here is Sheffield: "We ran

under the murky canopy and were in Sheffield. The smoke was so thick that it made a foggy twilight in the descending streets, which appeared as if they would end in the steaming bowels of the earth." Three hundred years and more of industrial progress had submerged the great houses and parklands, the castles and abbeys, the bird-haunted valleys of a romantic stretch of Yorkshire into a black sprawl. Only in the last two decades has there grown up a new consciousness that the old Yorkshire adage of "wheer there's muck there's money" may not be universally true.

The spoil heaps are still there, but they are steadily being removed for 'filler' for our new motorways, or reduced to more manageable proportions, or converted into mounds of some beauty and less menace. There are new model pits, too, and wash-houses and institutes. There are pit closures and amalgamations and electrification and the growth of vast new power stations standing like monstrous cotton reels in the landscape. It is all cleaner and tidier and less polluting to the atmosphere. And as 'smokeless zones' spread in our industrial towns the epithet 'black' may no longer be applicable. 'Country parks' are being planned in what is left of the old countryside between Barnsley and Sheffield to provide 'lungs' for south Yorkshire – and certainly few areas need them more.

It is still possible to find unspoiled fields and woodlands, tractors and pea-pickers, birds and pleasant gardens not too far from the pit-heads and the steel works. Subsidence has marred the landscape in places. Pylons stalk across the countryside. There is an industrial smell in the air. But the old countryside of Thomas Allen's day struggles to come through, even if the great houses look a little forlorn and dingy and some of the fine and graceful churches bedraggled.

Away in the north-east corner of Yorkshire a similar transformation from green to black took place, but more recently and in a shorter time. I have an old map of the area which shows Stokesley, now a delightful little market town, as a place of some size and importance, the centre of a broad agricultural area. Not far away is a tiny hamlet of a few houses with a single road running through it. Its population was no more than two dozen. This was Middlesbrough, on the sylvan river Tees, a place of farmsteads, bird song and views of the Cleveland hills.

Few could have foreseen that within half-a-century of the printing of that map not only Middlesbrough but much of the riverside would have mushroomed into "the youngest child of England's enterprise", as Mr. Gladstone romantically called it. Blast-furnaces, 'puddling' plants, rolling mills, brickyards, shipyards and docks replaced the green fields. The noise of engines and the clang of metal ousted the birdsong. A pall of smoke obscured even the view across the new street of workers' houses.

Certainly such a transformation could not have been envisaged by the good Canons of Guisborough Priory, who, in the days before the Reformation, had found a source of income in the ironstone mines they opened up in the Cleveland Hills. In many quiet valleys between the Tees and Ryedale you can discover these old workings, now grass-grown and deserted. Later, alum was discovered in the same hills, as well as salt deposits. The way of life of any community is seldom divisible from what lies beneath its feet, as we have seen over the centuries in the coalfields, and as we are witnessing today in the new development of potash mining around Whitby. Farmlands give way to furnaces, pasture lands to mines. So it may be that the ancient fishing traditions and seaside holidays of Whitby may be transformed into a new industrial zone.

Middlesbrough and Teeside have paid a high price for the immense industrial progress since the famous partnership of two men, Henry Blockow and John Vaughan, began to exploit the iron mines on a big scale, linking them by rail with the blast-furnaces, and becoming great iron-masters. When the market changed from iron to steel the firm took the lead again by importing better ore from Swedish mines. So the docks and shipyards came, the workshops expanded, the population grew – and so did the slums. For miles the river banks are lined with sheds, cranes, steel yards and great mountains of metal. Still more recent developments have been oil and chemicals – which today includes plastics – and centres of this industry cease to be 'works' or 'factories' and instead are called 'complexes'. A far cry from a riverside village of some twenty people.

Over a longer period of time the wand of industry waved above the once-beautiful Don Valley and Sheffield, at the confluence of that river with the Derbyshire Sheaf (from which it takes its name), to make it as a century-old guidebook writer called it "the blackest, dirtiest, and least agreeable town in Yorkshire" – with the exception of Leeds. There was once a castle with village greens before it, and there is still a street called Castle Green. There were meadows and common pastures and moors. And there were the Hallamshire woods and a mythical Dragon of Wantley with a large appetite:

> House and churches
> were as geese and turkeys;
> He ate all and left none behind.

Out of those woods came occasionally the smoke of a charcoal-fed smithy. It was a portent of all that was to follow.

Chaucer in his fourteenth-century *Canterbury Tales* tells us that one of his company of pilgrims, the miller, had a "Shefeld thwitel (knife) in his hose", although whether there was a cutlery industry of any size there at that time is doubtful. Chaucer himself had previously visited the town and had probably brought back a "thwitel" as a souvenir. At some time in the next century an unknown pioneer looked at the streams running into the Don and mused upon wasted power. He remembered the fine-grained stones which had been occasionally quarried nearby and their value as tool-sharpeners. He knew there was iron-ore in the district, for this was used by the woodland smiths who had wood and charcoal available for its working. Perhaps he himself had some skill in cutlery. With the support of the lords of the manor the industry came into being.

Very early the cutlers devised their own private marks, which they registered in the lord's court. They enlarged their industry from knives to scythes and sickles and other tools, and they were joined by craftsmen from York who were irked by the strict regulation of the local gilds. The Civil War created a demand for arms which they could meet. And, most important of all, the industry bound itself together by the formation of the Company of Cutlers in Hallamshire with tight regulations regarding apprenticeship, the use of marks, and the insistence on fine products, including the compulsory use of steel for all cutting edges.

At this point the name of Benjamin Huntsman, a quiet Quaker of Dutch origin, born in Lincolnshire, comes into the story. He was at first a clockmaker in Doncaster, where he had a reputation for fine workmanship. Then, tradition says, he became dissatisfied with the steel watch springs of the time because of their uneven quality. He tried making finer steel himself, but ran up against the problem of finding a vessel which would stand up to the intense heat of the molten metal. He moved in 1740 to Handsworth, a small village near Sheffield, and using local fireclays made a crucible to his needs, and eventually the hard 'crucible steel' which the industry had long needed – and also, we hope, that which he needed for his watch springs.

A century later another name is heard, that of Henry Bessemer, this time of French origin, who sought a steel from which all impurities had been eliminated. He solved the problem by blowing cold air through the molten mass leaving only so much carbon as was needed for a high-quality steel. At first railway lines, then armour-plating for ships, were produced by the new rolling-mills. What began as the making of Chaucer's "thwitel" in a woodland smithy has become the vast heavy industry of today, in which the 'little masters' with their workshops of locally trained craftsmen skilled in the small wares of steel and silver have practically vanished.

We get a glimpse of the early days of the industry in the dialect poems of Abel Bywater, who, in the 1830s, published *The Shevvild Chap's Annual,* the first of the considerable number of dialect annuals and almanacs which appeared in the county during the following century and which enshrine much of our native writing. One of Bywater's poems was entitled "The Sheffield Cutler's Song":

Coom all you cutlin' heroes, where'ersome'er you be,
All you what works at flat-backs (knives), coom listen unto me;
A basketful for a shillin',
To mak 'em we are willin',
Or swap 'em for red herrin's, aar bellies to be fillin'.

The reward of labour was not apparently very high, but the craftsman took a pride in his work, as later lines reveal:

Ha! coom, an' tha's go wi' me, an' a sample I will gie thee,
It's one at I've just forged upon Geoffry's bran-new stiddy (anvil)
Look at it well, it does excel all t'flat-banks i' aar smithy.

Perhaps it was this pride in craftmanship which stirred John Ruskin to select Sheffield as one of the model communities of his Guild of St. George, in which working men were to show that by higher standards of work and a system of government based on the laws of fourteenth-century Florence the world could be both fruitful and beautiful. The experiment failed, like many more on similar lines, but it left Sheffield a legacy of art works, geological specimens, and Ruskin relics now cared for and exhibited by the Corporation. It is to the credit of this once small settlement now grown to a great city that in the post-war years it has largely rebuilt itself and, in so far as is compatible with the gigantic 'black' industry with which it is historically engrained, rid itself of much of the squalid darkness that was once synonymous with 'Sheffield'. Perhaps Ruskin's experiment was not wholly in vain.

Drama in the Streets

Yorkshire has a great richness of religious drama dating back to the fourteenth century, and linked with its industry. Its cycles or series of mystery or miracle plays which bear the names of Beverley, York and Wakefield provided scope for medieval dramatists and for local actors, the city gilds or trading companies being expected to provide actors, stage and properties.

Some of these early dramatic productions were revived nearly twenty years ago for the Festival of Britain, when the Mystery Play of York, originally acted on a series of two-decker waggons called pageants, formed part of the city's contribution to the festival, and, although the plays had been produced for circumstances far removed from the original idea, they yet retained to a remarkable degree the flavour of the early presentations. They were performed for the first time in 370 years, and have now become part of the city's annual festival.

The York Mystery Plays were written about 1350 and were performed each year by the craft guilds of the city on Corpus Christi day in the fourteenth, fifteenth and sixteenth centuries. The cycle deals with the story of the Creation and the Fall of Lucifer through the life of Jesus to the Last Judgement. The Biblical narrative is followed fairly closely with occasional deviations in which local humour and probably local satire had their place.

Each craft gild owned and decorated its own play. The fishmongers played "The Flood", the innkeepers "The Turning of Water into Wine", the bakers "The Last Supper", the goldsmiths "The Three Kings", the shipwrights "The Building of the Ark" and so on. The waggons were housed around Pageant Green, now the sight of the railway station, and on the great day each pageant in turn trundled round the city to twelve 'stations', at each of which the members of the gild

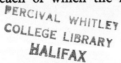

performed their one-act play. Thus a grimly determined spectator could stand at one of these street corners and see the whole cycle of Biblical plays between 4–30 a.m. and dusk!

A contemporary account says that once the stages were ready the procession started, "begynning to play fyrst at the gates of the pryory of the Holy Trinity in *Micklegate*, next at the door of *Robert Harpham*, next at the door of the late *John Gyseburn*, next at *Skelder-gate-head* and *North-strete-hend*," and so, as another writer says:

> to every streete; and so every streete had a pagiante playing before them, till all the pagiantes for the daye appointed were played, and when one pagiante was neere ended worde was broughte from streete to streete, soe the mighte come in place thereof, exceedinge orderlye, and all the streetes had their pagiante afore them, all at one time, playing together, to see which playes was great resorte, and also scafoldes, and stages made in the streetes, in those places wheare they determined to playe their pagiantes.

Thus the Play and Procession of Corpus Christi, in which those early Yorkshire players performed within sight of the old Minster of York the ancient dramas of Cain and Abel, the Slaughter of the Innocents, or the Deliverance of Souls from Hell.

The Mummers' Play, which was revived in the Craven district of Yorkshire in 1947 and is still occasionally performed in the county, has an even longer history. The Mummers are the lineal descendants of actors who performed in the temple and palace courtyards of Babylon, of Ur of the Chaldees, in the clearings of primaeval forest in many islands and continents.

There is some confusion in parts of the country between the Mummers' Play, the Pace Egg Play, and the many variants of the Fool Plough, and the confusion is occasionally added to by the incoming of elements of Morris Dances and Sword Dances. In Yorkshire it is generally true that the Mummers' Play and the Pace Egg Play are the same, only divided by being appropriated to different parts of the calendar. The Mummers usually perform at Old Year's Night, and the Pace Eggers at Easter, and no material change would be made beyond perhaps the elimination of Father Christmas as a character and a renaming to Old Time or some other non-seasonal name.

What are the essential elements of the Mummers' Play, this fragment of man's earliest dramatisation of his religious beliefs? There are nearly fifty versions in different parts of the country, but very commonly the play has a prologue spoken by a character who generally carries a mythological flavour – Father Christmas is perhaps the most popular. The speaker of the prologue usually introduces the characters as they appear in the action.

The two principal characters – summoned early – argue and quarrel. One of them is St. George to the folk of Yorkshire, King George in some other parts, and his opponent in argument is usually in the guise of a Turkish Knight, often having a black face. His name is sometimes represented as 'Slasher', but there are many variants. In Cumberland he is referred to as 'Farmer Dick'. During the course of sword play one of the principals falls down, either killed or disabled. Whether it is George or the Turkish Knight will depend on the part of the country in which the play is presented. Occasionally it is both who succumb. A novelty has been introduced in Yorkshire's Calderdale, where a performance is given each year by schoolboys. There a third character appears – Bold Hector by name – to extend the fight with the King and allow him a victory over three foes. But essentially it is the death of one champion which the play portrays, whoever he might be.

The other characters are not pleased when the champion falls. There is a loud and general lamentation, and from it emerges a claim by one of them, sometimes even the prologue speaker, that the dead or disabled man is his son. This has to be made quite clear to the audience. A doctor is brought to attend the fallen champion, but his skill is challenged and he vindicates it in a scurrilous rhyme. This doctor is a salesman at heart. He usually praises his special pills, and in some cases administers one. This is really only by-play. The point of the play is that the doctor produces some 'wonderful' drops or a 'bottle' and miraculously brings the dead man to life, well and vigorous again. There is general rejoicing and it is at this point that the play ends.

There was a good deal of symbolism about all this which I am afraid is lost in these modern days. Originally the Easter performance aimed to portray the triumph of summer over the darkness of winter and good over evil.

In the north-east corner of Yorkshire Goathland keeps alive from time to time what is known as the Plough Stots. According to tradition the performance should be given on 'Plough Monday' – the first Monday after Twelfth Night and the day on which farm hands return to the plough. The Stots – a dialect word for the bullocks who drew the plough – date back to Norse days. The performance is one of singing and dancing, identical as far as possible with the traditional entertainments of centuries ago.

The multi-coloured costumes used at Goathland are replicas of those used over many years, and some of the fiddle tunes are centuries old. Four boys in smocks – the junior Stots – drag the plough before the dancers. There are the Gentleman and Lady and t'Aud Man and t'Aud Woman who have their parts to play. The opening chorus goes to the tune of Auld Lang Syne, as follows:

> We're Gooadlan' Pleeauf Stots Com'd ageean,
> All dek't wi' ribbons fair,
> Seea noo we'll deea t'best we can,
> An' the best can deea neea mair.

Sword dancing enters into the play, and the Goathland team of long sword dancers is one of the few teams of its kind in the world. The late F. W. Dowson, who was largely responsible for the present-day revival of the custom wrote of it:

> There are many excellent sword-dance teams, of course, at the present time, e.g., Skelton, Lingdale, Kirkby Malzeard and Flamborough, but these are dance teams only nowadays. They have lost, or shed, whatever old pageantry or rude play they may once have possessed. The Goathland team, however, has been revived, and is now carried on almost exactly as it was more than a century ago. There are two distinct parts of the Plough Stots, viz., the 'Stots', or ploughboys headed by a 'Gentleman' and 'Lady', marching at the head of the procession and directing operations. These are accompanied by 'Toms', or collectors, and the rear of the procession is brought up by the Aud Man, 'Isaac', and Aud Woman, 'Betty'.
> All are in appropriate costumes. The sword-dancers (eight in number, and picturesquely clothed in pink and blue costumes, sashes, caps, ribbons, etc.), with their fiddler, form in reality a separate company under their own leader, or 'King'. With their graceful and intricate dance figures they take most of the picture nowadays. The team has a plough, which is, however, used for summer displays only, and is drawn by boys clad in smocks, and directed by a teamster with his 'gad', or whip.

There are other Yorkshire customs linked with Plough Monday – 6th January. After the Christmas holidays, which in other and less hasty times were more extensive and probably celebrated with more gusto than today, the men were not eager to return to the plough. So it became the rule on Plough

Monday for the men to get up early in the morning, clean and oil the ploughs, and then knock off for the rest of the day and have a final fling. Immediately after the midday meal the ploughs would be taken out, a procession would be formed, and the ploughs dragged through the village, while alms would be asked for, to provide a final feast and dance before settling down to work. There would be sword dancers and mummers in the procession and it was from all accounts a merry event.

In areas of Yorkshire where the plough is in regular use today – notably in the East Riding and the country round York – Plough Sunday is an occasion when the plough is dragged down the aisle of the church by representatives of the local farming community. So have Yorkshire farmers over long years sought official blessing on an implement signifying their craft.

Interesting recollections of his part in 'Plough Stotting' were given some years ago in a Yorkshire newspaper by an exile in Canada. He wrote:

> I never saw any script of the play; we simply learned by word of mouth from the older members of the cast; and, I suppose, being handed down from generation to generation, the original became somewhat changed, but there was always one thing you could be sure of – action.
>
> I remember many amusing incidents. The Fool was the first to appear on the stage, and he carried the handle from his mother's peggy (the cross-piece that she used to wash the clothes) and rapped on the front door to warn the inmates we were coming. It was also used as a weapon of defence against ambitious dogs, who, due to the strange costumes we were wearing, were interested, and willing, no doubt, to take a chance – once – on the calf of a boy's leg.
>
> We were a motley and awesome crew, being dressed in everything from the parlour curtain to father's Sunday trousers. I remember one little fellow (I forget his name) had filched his dad's trousers, and by the simple process of shearing them below the knees with an old razor, they were made to fit – that is as far as length was concerned – but there was a lot of 'seat' left, and he being of slim build the effect was rather grotesque. We were playing, I believe, at the White Horse, and one reveller perceiving that our King of Egypt had a lot of slack around the waist, pulled the slack towards him and dropped the house cat down the void. Needless to say there was great excitement, much wailing, and a budding Martin Harvey was very much discouraged and scratched.
>
> Another actor (Hector) had borrowed his sister's skirt, and after St. George had run him through with his sword, he found he could not fall to the floor wounded, as someone was 'unconsciously' standing on the hem of his skirt. Hector was suspended in mid-air until some bright

reveller pulled the string round his waist, when it was discovered that he had also borrowed his sister's red flannel lingerie. But – the show must go on. The cumbersome costumes of some of the troupers, helmet, sword, spear and shield, were rather a handicap if we got a hostile reception and the dog was turned loose.

Perhaps it was inevitable that from this historic seedbed of drama there should grow in later years a rich growth of acting ability displaying itself in chapel hall, village institute and through all the ascending scale of the 'little theatre' movement to achieve its most spectacular development in the Civic Theatres of Sheffield, Hull, Leeds, Bradford, and other Yorkshire cities and in the widespread popularity of the amateur, semi-professional or wholly professional repertory companies which existed in every town and in most rural areas until newer forms of entertainment on radio and television displaced them.

Days there were when the amateur relied upon a simple outfit of lights from the local plumber and rolls of printed paper prepared as 'The Oak Set', 'Ornamental Garden', or 'Autumn Woods' for 'scenery and effects'. In those days, too, there was a stereotyped selection of plays from which all amateurs made their choice. But largely through the educational work of the drama festivals and by the practical work of a number of inspired amateurs this era has gone, and even the local Women's Institute groups range from Restoration comedy to Eugene O'Neill and from the dialect plays of Yorkshire writers like J. R. Gregson, Austin Hyde, George Taylor and F. A. Carter to translations of Greek tragedy. City housewives have been heard reciting their lines from Shakespeare as they shook their morning mats, and it was no uncommon thing in a home-going bus to see half a dozen office workers 'swotting' their words for the evening rehearsal.

Not always was the Yorkshire amateur able to achieve his own ambitions, but at least it can be credited to him that he was ever willing to conquer new worlds. At a West Riding dramatic production I watched some years ago *Macbeth* was the play and local amateurs the players. To fit time and stage several scenes had been amalgamated, and Ross and Macduff were discussing the murder of Duncan actually over his dead body. Ross, played by a rural farm hand, reached the point at which he should have exclaimed:

"Is't known who did this more than bloody deed?"

But first-night nerves and a whole-hearted enthusiasm for
his part drove him to declare in roof-lifting voice:
    "Now 'oo the —— ——'s done this?"

Sporting Humours

In a world which 'follows the game' rather than plays it, and
which accepts its pleasures second hand in preference to
participation, home-made pastimes may appear to lack gloss
and glamour. Even cricket, which has for long been chief of
Yorkshire's sporting heritage, is played on fewer village greens
as it fills more television screens. Local football draws its
Saturday crowds to watch rather than play, and even the
traditional North Country interest in whippet racing and
pigeon flying has declined. Yet, curiously, one or two of the
Yorkshire games of great grandfather's time have enjoyed a
revival.

When I was a boy at a Yorkshire school it was a recognised
pastime to sharpen a short length of wood at each end, rather
like a cricket bail, place it on an even surface and then 'tip-it'
by striking one end sharply so that it rose into the air. The
'piggy', as we called it, was then struck as hard as possible with
a club as in a golf drive. One's opponent followed suit with
another 'piggy' and the longest drive, measured in strides, won.
It was dangerous but not unknown to play in a street with
breakable windows. A park or waste land offered a better
course, on which a series of drives was possible with less
opposition from irate householders. There were some memorable contests, and a well-balanced and well-seasoned 'piggy'
was as greatly prized as a well-tried 'conker' in the horse-
chestnut season.

This was my introduction to 'knurr and spell', played by
many generations of Yorkshiremen and declared by some
authorities to have been introduced by Norse invaders a 1000
years or more ago. The knurr was a sophisticated form of my
'piggy'. It was a small ball of very hard and tough pot, made
from clay, fired to a high temperature and weighing about
half-an-ounce. The spell was a device for throwing the ball into
the air – a wood or iron contraption with a spiked base for
driving into the ground and with a cupped spring on top to hold
the knurr. The striker tapped the trigger of the spring with his
club and hit the rising knurr, just as I hit my 'piggy'. Open
spaces on the outskirts of towns or near colliery pit-heads

provided the scene for Homeric contests in which red-faced, shirt-sleeved men would compete in matches of six, ten or twenty strokes each.

There was considerable variation down the years in the types of knurr, spell and club. In Strutt's *Games and Pastimes of England* the club was described as bat-shaped. In an illustration to Walker's *Costume of Yorkshire* it was depicted, 150 years ago, as a long straight stick with a flattened block of wood at the end, and in more recent times it was an ash stick with a head of hornbeam or other hard wood. All of which lends some colour to the suggestion that the game was a forerunner of both cricket and golf. Its name of 'Poor Man's Golf' was justified in that it could be played without course or green fees, often with home made equipment, and this commended it to the industrial areas of Yorkshire where it achieved its strongest hold. Devotees of 'knurr and spell' spread from the miners of Barnsley to the textile men of Halifax and to the towns and villages from Sheffield to Bradford, and in its heyday last century there were big 'gates' for the better known contests. Of late years the game has lost popularity despite attempts at revival, and its equipment has become a museum piece.

If you journey into the rural areas of Yorkshire the counterpart of 'knurr and spell' is quoits. This is still played by teams of men who compete in local leagues, although again there is some variation in the methods according to whether it is played in the north-east or north-west of the county. The game, which dates back to the days of Henry VIII, seems to have originated as a form of 'pitching horseshoes' on to a spike or hob set in the ground some distance away. The horseshoes have now become blacksmith-made rings of iron varying in weight from four pounds to nine pounds. The hob is often set in a box of clay or merely pressed into the ground. Standing some thirty feet away players cast their heavy quoits at the hob in turn, and I have seen a skilful player drop his quoit so heavily on that of his opponent so as to make it bounce right off the hob, and thus deprive him of a point. Around Whitby the game has long been popular on summer evenings, with considerable rivalry between villages, and I have watched it played at Kirkby Malzeard, near Ripon, and in the far west of the county around Bentham. The recognised prize in quoits competitions was a copper kettle, but money prizes or free pints at the 'local' were not unknown awards.

Wensleydale has its special game of 'Wallops', a form of

DALE COUNTRY: *2, Limestone 'clints' in Ribblesdale*

skittles played with nine sharpened pegs, the wallops, pushed into smooth ground – the roadway was the best site in the days before tarmac – at which thick throwing-sticks about two feet long were aimed from a distance of nine yards for men and six yards for women. Prizes were awarded for the most pegs knocked out of the ground in two throws. This game has long been a highlight of Redmire's annual feast.

In the Folk Museum at Hutton-le-Hole, near Kirkby Moorside, they will show you, and probably teach you to play, the game of 'Merrills', one of the oldest games in England. It is referred to by Shakespeare in *A Midsummer Night's Dream* as "Nine Men's Morris" and was probably played regularly by farm lads in Yorkshire, for it was comparatively easy to mark out a board or even cut it in the turf.

Twenty-four holes were cut or marked, joined by lines. Two players, using stones, or pegs, or buttons, each took turns to place nine of these (one at a time) in the holes in an attempt to get three in a row, while his opponent tried to prevent him by an intervening stone – but also trying to get his three in a line. A variation, in fact, of the children's game of 'noughts and crosses'. As each player has only nine pegs, there are then six spaces left. So the two players take it in turn to move one peg at a time to achieve the row of three. This then becomes a variation on 'draughts'.

I believe there are in Yorkshire remains of open-air 'boards' for playing this game dating back many years. It was once played at Goathland on the village green with children as the 'pegs'. There may well be old merrills boards stored away in attics because their use is forgotten.

On a little used road between Brandsby and Dalby in the North Riding is the 'board' of a game of which more is known about its history than how its was played. Protected now by low white wooden rails is an intricate 'maze' cut in the grass. It is too small to walk in, the path is only broad enough for one shoe at a time, and it would be impossible to be lost therein for the whole plan is visible at one glance. Yet it must presumably have been 'played' – or played in – at some far-off time, possibly by adults or more likely by children.

A nearby Tablet placed by the North Riding County Council explains all that is known:

This maze is the only surviving instance in the North Riding of an ancient game. Mazes pass under various names in different parts of

INDUSTRY: *1, Textile mills in the Calder Valley*
2, In a Bradford woollen mill

M

England such as 'Julian Bower', 'Robin Hood's Race', 'Shepherd's Ring', 'Walls of Troy' or 'City of Troy', the last mentioned being the name by which this example has always been known. . . . This shows the early association between Yorkshire and Scandinavia where Trojeborg (Troy Town) is the name given to similar mazes. The game and its origin are forgotten.

The tablet recalls that a reference to the game can be found in Shakespeare's *A Midsummer Night's Dream,* written in 1594.

I believe there are similar grass mazes in other places in England, and the suggestion has been made that the pious followed the twisting path on their knees in some religious observance. That would certainly not be possible in the Yorkshire maze, nor does any similar suggestion seem feasible. It must remain in Shakespeare's words, one of "the quaint mazes on the wanton green".

You cannot travel far in Yorkshire without encountering a 'bull-ring', either as a place name, or as an actual ring still exhibited in the market place indicating where bulls were tethered, to be baited by dogs as a public amusement. This form of pastime, like cock-fighting – which, too, has left its evidences – is one where the onlookers revelled in its goriness and measured its entertainment value by its cruelty. There was a financial element, too, in the betting on the result, but that the pleasure was in the fighting is shown by a custom observed at many old schools in the county whereby boys brought game-cocks to school on Shrove Tuesday to fight, a pursuit encouraged by masters. Even when this sport was made illegal, 'mains' were held on the moors or occasionally, as I have seen from evidence in old farmhouses, in attics or lofts away from the official eye.

It is surprising how recently cruel sports of this sort were prohibited. When a Bill was introduced into the House of Commons in 1802 for the suppression of bull-baiting it was thrown out as being "the first result of a conspiracy of the Jacobins and Methodists to render the people grave and serious, preparatory to obtaining their assistance in the furtherance of other anti-national schemes".

6

Three Novelists and A Diarist

Inseparable from any contemplation of Yorkshire's heritage is the thought of the men and women it has produced. It is not surprising that such a vast and varied, if stubborn, soil should blossom with a rich crop of characters. Some forty years ago G. C. Heseltine wrote *Great Yorkshiremen*, a collection of short biographies of sons of the county – he ignored the daughter – and limited himself to one "specimen" of each of a dozen callings. So he had a sailor (Captain Cook), a poet (Andrew Marvell), a plotter (Guy Fawkes), a philanthropist (William Wilberforce), a marvel (Blind Jack Metcalfe), a soldier (the third Lord Fairfax), a hermit (Richard Rolle), a chemist (Dr. Joseph Priestley), a reformer (John Wycliffe), a scholar (Dr. Richard Bentley), a bishop (Cardinal John Fisher) and an ancient (Henry Jenkins).

Every Yorkshireman who reads this will at once note its omissions. There are no physicians, no musicians, no engineers, no industrialists, no artists, no hymn-writers, no authors. Where is Chippendale, the furniture maker? Or Michael Faraday, the scientist? Or Scoresby, the explorer, or John Harrison, who invented the marine chronometer which made exploration possible?

More recently Marie Hartley and Joan Ingilby, as a change from their topographical books, compiled a gallery of *Yorkshire Portraits* more extensive in its coverage (nearly eighty celebrities are included) and ranging from the scholar-theologian Alcuin, who was born at York in the eighth century, to Sir Leonard Hutton, the cricketer of our own time. Yet they had to impose the arbitrary qualification of birth within the county to keep it within a reasonable compass, thus excluding some whose lifework was done within the county but had the misfortune to be born outside it. Even so, far more famous characters were omitted than were included.

The truth is that in a part of England where it is frequently claimed that every other man you meet is a 'character' the quality of greatness is not easily defined. It was once said that great men are the true men, the men in whom nature has succeeded. They are not extraordinary; they are in the true order. So while it would be possible to fill this and many other chapters with a catalogue of men and women of genius and talent who have come from the broad acres, it would still overlook those who in their own sphere can be defined as great but whom the world would term ordinary. The real character of Yorkshire folk can best be discovered in the dour stories of the Bronte sisters, in the historical novels of Phyllis Bentley, in Winifred Holtby's *South Riding* and in some of the writings of J. B. Priestley. In particular there are three tellers of Yorkshire stories who provide that rich and revealing background which makes them required reading for all who are curious about the variety of Yorkshire character.

A few years ago I stayed at a small guest house in a West Riding dale. It was really a farmhouse which in summer took guests who ranked a much lower degree of importance than the farm stock, but for all that fared considerably better than in many town hotels. After a 'high tea' of banquet proportions I smoked a meditative pipe in the tiny sitting room, which looked across a stream to a circle of high fells upon which, long ago, Norsemen had grazed their sheep, and over which more recently packmen, 'broggers' and travellers of all kinds had wandered. In the valley below a still earlier people, the Iron Age folk, had left stone circles of an unknown meaning, and at the end of the dale was a Norman church.

It was a romantic, stimulating landscape, and until the light faded and my hostess came in with an oil lamp there was enough to occupy both eye and mind in the view. Then I turned to the 'library' – a single shelf of much-thumbed books as varied as you could wish. There were a few recent novels left by previous guests, mainly paperbacks. An old and possibly valuable copy of Mrs. Beeton stood next to a book of sheep marks, a religious tome or two and then a batch of Yorkshire stories by William Riley and Halliwell Sutcliffe. Their titles – *Windyridge, Laycock of Lonedale, Ricroft of Withens, Shameless Wayne* – chimed with the landscape.

Yorkshire has not lacked authors and it has its literary shrines. Yet the most widespread popular recognition given to any author can be found on its garden gates and house nameplates. There are few urban suburbs in the north where 'Windyridge' does not appear as a house name. There are few rural houses which boast books at all that has not a Riley story on its shelves. It is a spontaneous tribute accorded to a novelist who in his life-time achieved affectionate following among Yorkshire folk at home and in exile. I have been told of a 'Windyridge' in Central Africa.

The curious story of this title deserves telling. William Riley was born nearly a century ago in Bradford, the son of a textile merchant. After schooldays ended he was impressed reluctantly into the family business but did not stay long. Wool trading held no fascination for him. A hobby of lecturing with the then primitive 'magic lantern' showing crude and inadequate pictures brought the idea of opening a shop for the making and sale of better photographic slides, hand-coloured, and using costumed models against scenery he painted, which would illustrate stories and lectures, religious and secular, then highly popular. The photography and colouring were done in an attic studio over the shop, and the business flourished, absorbing most of Riley's time until he was in his middle forties.

He might have continued as a successful business man, a career which he combined with much local preaching, had not a simple happening transformed his life and given Yorkshire a prolific novelist. A family living in the same Bradford suburb of Manningham was suddenly stricken by illness and death. Out of a family of five only two sisters remained. It was to fill the empty gap in their lives that one evening when Riley and his wife were sitting round the fire with the sisters, all in melancholy mood, that he suggested telling a story.

"I will write it down and read a chapter to you as I go along, week by week. It will keep us from brooding".

The story began as a sentimental one about a London girl who comes from the toil and rush of the big city to the quietness and homely ways of a moorland hamlet. It was written as if from the diary of the girl herself, and the setting was the little village of Hawksworth on a windswept ridge near Guiseley, at the fringe of the industrial West Riding. Hence the title. Week by week the instalments were written and read – without any pre-arranged plot, but developing a strong

Yorkshire background – with no thought of publication. It was only on the persuasion of his listeners that, after much hesitation, he agreed to send it to *one* publisher only. He typed out the manuscript himself – to avoid throwing away good Yorkshire money – and posted it. Within a fortnight he had received a favourable reply addressed to "Miss Riley".

Almost overnight it caught the public imagination. One reviewer compared it to *Cranford,* another to the then popular American novel, *Mrs. Wiggs of the Cabbage Patch.* Almost at once the craze for calling houses 'Windyridge' after the novel spread throughout Yorkshire. I believe that by now, for it still goes on selling, the total sales of the book have reached nearly half a million. The year of its publication was 1912 and, inevitably, it was followed by others from the author's facile pen. When, a few years later, the First World War brought the closing down of Riley's Optical Lantern Company and created a demand for wartime reading, he was launched as a popular novelist.

As I have said, the story of *Windyridge,* and indeed of the long stream of other romances which flowed almost unchecked until the 1950s, had no complicated plot. All the stories had simple but varied patterns, with a light and often humorous touch, and their characters were homely and real. As became a good Methodist, Riley avoided the sordid and scandalous, and although evil was necessary to his plots it was always vanquished by good. He preferred charitableness to ugliness, and kindness to vice. And if they are condemned for their sentimentality, it can be urged that there is a strong sentimental streak beneath the outer dourness of Yorkshire folk. They were true of the Dales countryside and its people.

An example is *Men of Mawm* ('Mawm' is the local pronunciation of Malham in Airedale) in which there is a fine portrait of a dalesman:

> Maniwel Drake (the greater number of his acquaintances did not know that his name figured as Emmanuel in the parish register, and he himself had almost forgotten it) was not to be numbered with the dullards. A man of the moors, whose ancestors on both sides for generations back had been moorland folk, the air of the uplands was to him the best of tonics, sweeping over his soul no less than his body, and containing what the old physiologist called 'a hidden food of life'. No gale, however wild, had ever been able to pierce the defences of his hardy frame and undermine his constitution, and he had long ago shaken off the ill-results of the accident which, by reason of the light

regard in which he had held it, had well-nigh cost him his life. With his one arm he could do more work than many could accomplish with two; but until now he had been content to lend a hand when and where it was needed, and his earnings had been precarious, which would have mattered more if his wants had not been few.

Opposed to him in the same book is Baldwin Briggs, the joiner, whose pride is that he has never changed his character. "Not I. I was for mysen then and I'm for mysen now." Trouble comes to him when a scheming employee ousts him from his own business and has him declared bankrupt, and the village shows its sympathy:

> Baldwin Briggs had been a fixture in the village, a piece of grit hewn out of the side of their own bleak hills and therefore naturally rough and unyielding – even coarse. Nobody had cared for him very much, for there had been in his nature none of that kindliness that either begets or responds to kindliness; yet there had been no marked aversion on the part of his neighbours, who were aware that all sorts of natures like all sorts of rock enter into the composition of the world . . . the villagers' sympathies warmed towards the man who was bone of their bone; for after all there is a vast difference between a devil and a poor devil.

Again, in *Windyridge,* there is an account of the Whitsun service in a moorland chapel, when the preacher in the afternoon is entertained to tea before the evening service: "The chapel people take the preachers according to an arranged plan with which they are all familiar. My old lady regards the privilege as in the nature of a heavenly endowment, and she has more than once reminded me that those who show hospitality to God's ministers sometimes entertain angels unawares. No doubt that is so, but the wings were very, very inconspicuous in the one who ate our buttered toast that Sunday".

The Riley novels had recognisable settings whose identification was not difficult to those who knew their West Riding. Some time before his death in 1961 – and at the age of 94 he produced his thirty-fifth and last book, *The Man and the Mountain* – William Riley gave me a list of the place-names he had invented, all of which had an actual setting. Thus, as "Windyridge" was Hawksworth; *Netherleigh,* his second novel, was Otley, not many miles away. Harrogate became "Spa", Castle Bolton, "Castle Scrope", Bolton Abbey, "Abbeyvale", and so on. He avoided too great a use of the dialect for, as he said, our West Riding form of speech "contains many words and expressions which are unintelligible to the ordinary York-

shire reader today. I just use enough to give my stories colour",
but his characters were recognisable for they came from life.

Still Yorkshire, but with a more romantic swagger about it,
are these opening sentences of *Pedlar's Quest*:

> The moor stretched desolate and wan, rise after endless rise, to the
> long ridge of Scummer Heights, and the sun was dipping fast behind a
> spur of rock and wind-swept heather. Scottie, the pedlar, seemed part
> of it all as he trudged forward, picking his way where the broken track
> lost itself at times between the green marshes and the bogs. His life had
> been spent in footing byways of the wilderness, and he seemed part of
> the moor itself, as a Brown Man might have been, sitting cross-legged
> on a boulder, or any other usual phantom. The man was thick-set and
> gnarled, like a weather-beaten thorn. But he was vigorous, alert with
> courage and resource. He knew every haunted corner of a heath rich in
> such grim ambushes, and whistled down the stealthy terror that
> waylaid him.... "It's all in the game," laughed the pedlar, and
> quickened his step in sheer defiance.

Of a different stamp altogether from William Riley – perhaps
even more soaked in the life and lore of the Pennine
Dales – was Halliwell Sutcliffe, whose *Pedlar's Quest* was one
of many 'thrillers' set in the North Country, and who in a space
of just under forty years from 1895 wrote nearly as many
novels, books of stories and some topographical volumes.
Where Riley's stories were in the main domestic – 'kitchen sink'
if you like, but with the sink kept spotless – Sutcliffe revelled in
vigorous historical romances which he based sometimes on fact,
sometimes on imagination, but always with the tang of the
heather, the clink of hooves and the din of rolling thunder in
them. None of his titles lent itself to a house-name, but had the
buccaneering ring of *Battling Keep*, *Shameless Wayne* and *The
Crimson Field*.

He began as a teacher and was for a time a schoolmaster at
Bingley Grammar School, where his father had earlier been
headmaster. He was born, like Riley, near Bradford, but in
later life claimed Lees, near Haworth, as his true birthplace as
it was there his family was residing. One feels that the claim
was strengthened in his own mind by the romantic tradition of
Haworth and the Brontes. Certainly he knew the Bronte
country almost as intimately as the writing sisters, and he
walked and cycled over the moors as he did over the hills round
his later home at Linton, in Wharfedale, which he romantically

christened 'White Abbey'. Throwing up his teaching, he made writing his profession, moving to London in the traditional way to establish himself.

The pull of the moors was too strong, however, and back he came to the North to absorb both its history and its atmosphere, and there began his long series of romances about gipsies and poachers, pedlars and squires, fair maidens and deep-dyed villains. He could tell a rattling good story and develop a murder mystery on the moors into a Crime Book Society novel. Always there was feel of the open air in his writing as befitted a man who knew the highways and the lesser-known paths so well as to become a much-loved supporter of ramblers' clubs and a popular speaker at their functions. And, like Riley, his topographical settings were accurate enough to be recognisable.

Which of these two West Riding novelists will continue to command an audience in a world where old-fashioned romance is out of favour is hard to foretell. As in my Dale guest house, there was a time when scarcely a Yorkshire home but had their stories at hand and where the characters in them, like Riley's 'Mother Hubbard', or Sutcliffe's 'Pam the Fiddler' were known by name almost as part of the family. Both pictured the folk of the dale country, in different lights and against different backgrounds, and if for no other reason they may well be treasured as delineations of a Yorkshire way of life that is now vanishing.

Away in the East Riding there was another Yorkshire novelist whose work may well be bracketed with Riley and Sutcliffe for its integrity and warm humanity. The flat lands of Holderness will always be associated with the name of E. C. Booth. He was one of three bachelor brothers who lived together at Scalby, near Scarborough. They were all men of talent. George and Bromley Booth were musicians. Edward C. Booth was a writer with an intense knowledge and love of the East Riding. In the early years of this century he began writing a series of novels set in this pastoral corner of Yorkshire, and the first of them, *The Cliff End*, appeared in 1908 when its author was 35. Once again it was an 'old-fashioned' novel in that it was rich in characters, in detailed settings, and had a somewhat sentimental plot – a period piece like a painting by W. P. Frith. Or, as Mr. J. B. Priestley said of it, "a piece of writing not unlike an interior by an old Dutch master doubly based on close observation and deep feeling, a scene filled with that rich humanity which is now being organised and bulldozed out of life and the arts".

Here is Booth's description of that sea-ravaged Yorkshire coast, of which I have written earlier in these pages:

Of foliage by the sea there is not a leaf, excepting mere divisional hedges. Fields in cultivation and out of it run to the very edge of the cliff – a sombre cliff of soft, dark earth, stained here and there to uprepossessing rusty red, with trickling chalybeate streams, and showing terrible toothmarks of the voracious sea that feeds its way inland on this part of the coast at the rate of a yard a year. Looking over the brink of it you can discern as many as half-a-dozen paths, in various stages of subsidence, that less than that number of years ago led people along the cliff top as the path you stand on leads them now. In other places you may see huge slices of grass land, descending like great steps downwards to the shore in their progress towards ultimate devourance.

And from that you can turn to this cameo of two East Riding farmers meeting:

"Noo then."

"Noo then" said Barclay in turn, showing his face and waving the reins at him with the right hand.

"Ye're not cuttin' out today, it seems?" Dixon inquired jocularly.

"Nay, Ah'm waitin' while it ripens a bit. Ah thought ye'd 'a been agate leadin' yours by noo."

"Ay," said Dixon. " 'Appen we may if rain dizzn't lift. We mud as well 'ave it damp as dry, ah think. 'Ow diz it suit ye noo, this tee-towtal weather?"

" Nay, it dizzn't fall to be no wuss nor it is. That's 'ow it suits me."

You can hear conversations like this, from *The Cliff End*, every day of the week in the East Riding today, old-fashioned or not.

For the next twenty years a steady stream of novels came from his hard-working pen, and Booth was a best-seller. Then suddenly the flow stopped, the stream dried up, and, except among a few perceptive readers, Edward was forgotten. The three brothers continued to live, almost unknown but contented, at their Scalby home. Bromley died and Edward Booth died at the age of 81 in 1954. It was an appreciation after his death of Edward's work by the Yorkshire editor of a London newspaper which led the surviving George to provide in his will for the republication of some of the novels, and four of them – *The Cliff End, Fondie, The Doctor's Lass*, and *The*

Tree of the Garden – reappeared as the 'Holderness Edition' in the 1950s to have a new lease of life.

I doubt if in an age which prefers nettles to roses in its fiction the novels of E. C. Booth will ever be restored to their old popularity, although public taste may not for ever relish the present school of fiction. But as a truthful picture of a way of life which existed and still exists in parts of rural Yorkshire these novels, as well as those of Riley and Sutcliffe, will be treasured.

A Diarist

Whether by coincidence or the outcome of a favourable mood of the time, it is curious that the same century which gave us the diaries of Samuel Pepys and John Evelyn also produced the outstanding diarist of the North of England, Ralph Thoresby. All three wrote their diaries not for publication but for the writer's own satisfaction, and all of them, in consequence, have a warmth and intimacy which endears them to us today. Pepys' and Evelyn's diaries are well-known, although, curiously, they remained in manuscript and unpublished for two centuries. Thoresby's diary is little known except by name, which is unfortunate for it gives a revealing picture of a provincial country gentleman, with all his interests and eccentricities. Where Evelyn's diary is a record of passing events noted at home and on his travels as seen by a wealthy cavalier and enthusiastic royalist, and Pepys' is a rare mixture of public occurrences and private confessions, Thoresby's diary, which covered fifty of his sixty-seven years, is the detailed jottings of a perpetually inquisitive topographer engaged in bringing back to life the past at his own doors. Someone said of him that he "takes a small familiar patch of land and repopulates it". It is in so doing that he reveals his engaging personality.

Ralph Thoresby was born in Kirkgate, Leeds, in August 1658, the year of Cromwell's death, the son of a cloth merchant who had fought in the parliamentary army under Lord Fairfax. His mother died when he was only 11 and he was left in the care of his father, a strong nonconformist. There is some doubt whether he attended a small private grammar school or the larger Leeds Grammar School, but his formal education was not extensive, and at 18 he was sent to London to live with a fervently religious family and learn the business of selling cloth. While there he saw many of the comings and goings of the Restoration: Charles II and his queen at the Lord Mayor's Show, soldiers training before the King in Hyde Park, fireworks on 5th November and other evidence of the gaiety which followed the new regime. It was during all these excitements of his London visit that he remembered his father's injunction:

"I would have you, in a little book which you may either buy, or make of two or three sheet of paper, take a little journal of anything remarkable every day." On Sunday 2nd September 1677 he began his diary.

His stay in London was short, and he was then sent to Holland to relatives who were also in the cloth trade, to enlarge his experience. When he was 21 his father died, and although he carried on the family business for some years it was against his inclinations. He confessed to his new diary that his love of books "doth draw my affection too much from more practical duties", and some years after he had abandoned cloth merchanting altogether he wrote on his birthday, "I was pensive for having misspent forty-eight years."

Yet he was no bookworm; he was more of a squirrel. He collected everything. Notes on sermons, epitaphs, his own experiences, stories of people and places, coins, curious events, any fragment of the past of his own town – all were gathered up into his notebooks or placed in his museum. And like all collectors, he gathered up much extraneous matter solely because it was unusual: a toothbrush from Mecca, the arm of the executed Earl of Montrose, birds' eggs, plants, all very much reminiscent of one's own boyhood hoard displayed in the attic.

One of the earliest entries in his diary described the storm which overtook the vessel on which he returned from Holland – a journey which lasted from early on Monday morning until very late on Thursday night:

The storm abated nothing all night, nor most of the next day, and the dreadful darkness continued till almost noon. Next day, at noon, we hoisted up sail, and saw land, and, which infinitely more affected me, the Ram in the Bush – I mean a delicate large ship, in this very tempestuous storm, dashed in pieces upon that very sand which we supposed had been our death-bed all the night. The goods were floating upon the sea, two of the masts broken down by the tempest, a third standing for us to look upon as a monument of God's distinguishing mercy to us. The poor comfortless creatures held out a flag for help, but alas! I was told that without manifest hazard, or rather certain ruin, we could not do them any good.

The death of his father affected him greatly, but within a few days he was at Batley Church copying an epitaph. He called upon a Pontefract physician, Dr. Johnston, who "as a physician prescribed for his health and, as an antiquary, for his studies". Soon he set out upon his travels "observing stately buildings and curious libraries". He journeyed to London and returned on horseback, having some tremors as he "passed safely the great common where Sir Ralph Wharton slew the highwayman and Stone-gate Hole, a notorious robbing place". But his spirits were restored at Newark when "in the ruins of the old castle, I saw the place where my grandfather was kept prisoner". The danger of highwaymen working in collusion with landlords was nevertheless always present on his travels. There was a disturbing incident when on a journey from Leeds into Scotland he and a friend, Mr. Hickson, rode first to Boroughbridge and Topcliffe:

> Where, supposing we would not stay long, left my charged pistols in the bags, which at my mounting again, being gone, caused a great jealousy of some design against us; and the rather because Mr. H. and his debtor had come to high words, and the landlord took the debtor's part and denied to send for the ostler till, upon some brisk compliments, we were just for riding to depose upon oath before Sir M. Robinson, and then in the very same straw we had carefully sought before, they were found, and one of them where the horse could not get to; which more fully manifested the knavery as also their leaving, for a pretence, the red bags in the holster; but we got very well, though late, to Northallerton that night.

Nothing was too lowly or apparently insignificant to interest Thoresby, even his own apprehensions. When he made his first coach journey instead of riding on horseback as usual he wrote: "Up pretty timely, preparing for a journey, and somewhat concerned about company, fearful of being confined to a coach for so many days with unsuitable persons, and not one that I know of."

This sentiment is not unknown today, although the dangers of travel, (for the traveller at least) in our own age is not such that before making a journey we request the vicar of the parish to offer prayers for our safety, then a not uncommon procedure. Thoresby took this precaution and was laughed at for it by two fellow townsmen. He noted the fact in his diary and added, "how piteous a case are we in, who, being exposed to continual dangers, and have so many instances of such as never return home, one merchant of this town lately cast away . . . and yet

cannot desire the prayers for the merciful protection of God".
The perils of travel were so often in mind, perhaps because
at times he had a morbid taste for public hangings and local
horrors. He could turn from taking the waters at Harrogate, a
place, he found, "very unfit for serious thought", to showing
notable visitors his coins and museum, and then visit an
exhibition by a street mountebank:

> Went to see a man (one Sam Fry of Dorsetshire) eat brimstone, lead,
> bees-wax, sealing-wax, pitch, rosin, blazing hot: he dropped brimstone
> in a blaze upon his tongue; and so wax, and made thereon the impression
> of a seal, which I have; and (which I went most to see), he walked upon a
> red-hot bar of iron, which I fancied to be somewhat like the way of
> ordeal, much in use among the Saxons, to try persons' innocency by,
> who possibly might come off victors, though never so culpable, if they
> had money enough to purchase such a secret from the monks.

Yet a few days later Thoresby found himself "partly in the
same predicament as the Quakers". He received a summons to
appear at the Sessions for attending a "factious and seditious
conventicle" at Hunslet, on the outskirts of Leeds, and penned
in his diary "Lord, direct me what to say in that hour!"

As a nonconformist for a long period of his life, he was
involved in much religious controversy; he lived through the
period of the Restoration, the Popish Plot, and wars with
France, yet his chief concern was the price of paper, the delay
in publishing his topographical book *Ducatus Leodiensis* and a
fire in his home which burnt his children's clothes. In general
he had little interest in great events, in trade, or even in the
government of his local town. He did, however, undertake the
revision of the West Riding section of Camden's *Britannia*,
"which I am as unwilling as unfit for, yet urged by friends to do
what I can", and he lent the editors of that work coins from his
collection, some of which they appear to have lost.

When he was approaching 40 he was elected a fellow of the
Royal Society. Of the occasion Thoresby wrote: "Dean Gale,
without giving me the least notice of it, proposed me to the
Royal Society who, upon his recommendation (who had entertained too great and favourable opinion of me) admitted me
Fellow." This enlarged his growing circle of learned friends
with whom he could communicate about Roman coffins found
in York, an earthquake in Yorkshire, the odd behaviour of a
girl at Rawden near Leeds, thunderstorm damage at Went-
worth Woodhouse and a thousand other things. As we read his

diary we smile and nod with him as he exhibits one discovery after another and works towards his great ambition, his topography of Leeds. *Ducatus Leodiensis* was published in 1715 and proved to be a sort of extension of his museum on to paper, a record of his town discoveries, family trees, genealogical studies and speculations with, at the end, a catalogue of the actual treasures in his museum in Kirkgate. He displays his treasures and conceits like a lively schoolboy, probably with that smirk of satisfaction you see on his portrait. And perhaps that is the clue to his character. Like the schoolboy collector in most of us with our attic hoards, he gathered his treasures but he never grew up. He was never a trained scientist or antiquarian, he was not a profound thinker. But he enjoyed the gathering and the probing. And this gave him a human appeal which holds us when reading his diary.

There is rather a sad footnote to the life of this enthusiastic collector. His health began to fail in 1723, although he still read and visited – calling on Lady Elizabeth Hastings at Ledston Hall among others – and was still alert enough to record on his return "safe to Leeds'and found my family well: the harness broke but the horse and charioteer performed well. There had been a fire at Mr. T.'s the confectioner's, that burned down three rooms, but was suppressed by the engine without further damage." Almost the last entry in his diary notes a visit he received from "the noted poet, Mr. Wesley" (the father of John Wesley.) And finally, on 13th September, he records that his eldest son preached in the parish church from the text "Be ye angry, but sin not." A month later Ralph Thoresby died. Alas, his collection of treasures, which he bequeathed to his clerical son, no doubt in the hope that it would be preserved, was within the year sold by auction to a London broker, and against many items in the auctioneer's catalogue can be read grim notes: "All these things were thrown away to clear the room." "Eggs – all broken." "Plants – all rotten and thrown on the dunghill." "Serpents – these thrown away."

Fortunately his diary remains, though long out of print. My own copy of *Ralph Thoresby, The Topographer, his Town and Times*, published in 1885, is numbered "350" out of a limited edition of "five hundred copies only". Perhaps if it was brought back into circulation it would achieve a minor degree of the fame accorded to the diaries of Pepys and Evelyn.

7

A Postscript and some Books

In one of his historical studies of Yorkshire Mr. Harry Speight recalls that he asked a man in the North Riding how long a certain family had lived at the Hall. "Hoo lang?" said the man. "Why, sure eneuf they've bin here ivver sin' t' time o' Noah's Flood." "Come", said his questioner. "You don't mean to say they have been here since the creation of the world?" "Aye, Ah do. Some folk says they've bin here sin t'time o' Adam."

When you live day by day against a background of a long historic or even prehistoric past like that old Yorkshireman you take that history for granted. As we saw at Victoria Cave there were people living here some 6,000 years before Christ. On the coast at Bridlington and in Upper Nidderdale have been found implements which may take us back another 10,000 years to Palaeolithic times – the Old Stone Age of the glacial and inter-glacial periods. Excavations at Starr Carr, near Scarborough, have revealed settlements built on rafts by a post-glacial lake where primitive people lived by hunting and fishing, and on the moors above are the long barrows where they buried their dead.

You cannot travel far in Yorkshire without encountering tangible evidence of this past. In the museums are the flints and stone axes and food vessels of those early days. Spread over the countryside are the stone circles and monoliths erected for a purpose now only vaguely guessed at. In a walk in the Dales country you may come across the foundation stones of hutments and walls of long-forgotten communities. At York are the excavated walls of a Roman fortress erected on the clay ramparts first thrown up by the Governor Petilius Cerealis about AD 71, and at Aldborough, not far away, is the civic town on the Ure, now only marked by the remains of a 'town

INDUSTRY: 3, *In a South Yorkshire mine*
             4, *Furnacemen in a West Riding foundry*

hall', the tesselated floors of villas and many homely sculptures.

Gazing upon some of these evidences of early man in Yorkshire I have often tried to picture those early forerunners of ours who wandered among the limestone hills of the west and over the windswept tracks of the east or who excavated their burial places on the Wolds. They were, to judge from their remains, a smaller people than today, with a liking for personal adornments of armlets and metal collars even in early times. Their garments were sheep skins – perhaps with the wool still upon them – or those of other animals. Tools for making them and for other work were primitive but presumably effective.

Imagination brings to life one of those early men at work at his cave entrance or by his primitive rock shelter, his matted hair falling over his eyes, alert to any sound or movement, chipping and flaking the stones and flints which were his essential tools. His most sophisticated implements then were arrow heads or stone axes or fish hooks. They became sharpened scrapers for cutting and cleaning the hides he wore. Occasionally he made ornaments for his wife, who moulded the wet clay which when dried or baked became the food vessels for the family. Such a picture takes us back to the earliest of our Yorkshire ancestors – "t' time o' Adam".

Later, as he became more skilful, he made vehicles like chariots and harness for his horse and querns for the oats he was learning to grow. Much, much later he produces some form of coinage which means he can move from barter to real trading. His work is all manual in the real sense of that term, for it will be long before his tools are sophisticated enough to transmit other than muscular energy.

Frank Elgee describes the burial barrow on the Wolds of one who must have been a man of importance in his time:

> In the happily-named King's barrow there was the skeleton of an old man lying on his back in a large circular grave. Near his head were the skulls of two pigs and on each side the iron tire of a chariot wheel nearly three feet in diameter, and its nave hoop of iron coated with bronze. Under each wheel lay the skeleton of a small horse. There were also two linch-pins, two bits of bronze-coated iron, two larger and two smaller rings of the same material.

As we have seen, the place-names of the county tell the story of the Scandinavian incomers after the Roman left, and it is tempting to think that another of their legacies was the increased stature of succeeding Yorkshire folk. As we have

AUTHORS: 1, *William Riley* 2, *Halliwell Sutcliffe*
3, *Edward C. Booth* 4, *Ralph Thoresby*

seen, too, the Norman castles, the monasteries, the village churches, the farms and manor houses and mansions continue the tale. These are more than monuments or even attractive ornaments in our countryside. They are the background to and indeed part of the substance of our heritage.

This long record of human life in these parts has many byways. The farm folk in my Dales village – like the workers in the age-old textile crafts, like the trawlermen at Hull and elsewhere on the coast, and like the miners and the iron and steel workers of the Black Country – all owe something to that history from those far days when the Brigantes stood against the invading power of Rome; when the strange wild men from across the North Sea made their homes here; when the marauding Scots raiders came deep into the country; when civil and religious strife tore the new English nation to pieces and repatched it and gave it its present form.

The task of interpreting a county with so rich a past as Yorkshire presents both opportunities and difficulties. One has to eliminate much to keep a sense of proportion yet to seek such completeness as to give the true essence of its heritage. Is one nearer that essence in a Dales market-place or on a high fell top? Listening to the clatter of machinery amid the pervading acrid smell of a woollen mill or wandering along the lonely bank of a great river draining half the county? Hearing Evensong in a noble minster or watching a lost chapter of history being dug up stone by stone in some long-forgotten village?

Surely the true heritage must be discovered in the lives of those to whom Yorkshire is home, from the earliest cave-dwellers and the Stone Age peoples whose burial mounds are on the moors to the nobility and gentry whose once emparked and reticent houses are now holiday showplaces for the curious. Every city, town and village, every house and highway has its ghosts which may not walk at high noon but which can be summoned up in a thousand shapes to anyone with a seeing eye and a mind tuned to their times.

As the ghosts come and go I think we can obtain a glimmering of that North Country character which is so distinct from that of the South, and which is more marked in Yorkshire than elsewhere. Down the centuries there has been an intense struggle to survive, from the days of the caveman in a new and raw environment to the historical struggles against outside enemies whether they were invading Normans, marauding Scots or contending armies battling across the broad acres. With industrial development that struggle became more intense and more personal. It required toughness of an unusual order to survive those early days in mines and factories. Similarly over a large area of rural Yorkshire there was an unending battle against the elements as against the very land itself until a pattern of agriculture emerged. In the process the countryman and the townsman alike developed that tough realistic outlook which gives him a reputation for brusque hardness and makes him judge his fellows on his own terms: "It's not what a chap says but what he does that matters." And "what he does" is measured not as a gloss of manners or good form but as a practical action to a practical end.

In setting down this notebook of our heritage I have been continually aware of two sages looking over my shoulder. Says one: "You see, in all that story there is nothing new under the sun. Can you show that the Yorkshireman of today is fundamentally different from that ancient man chipping flints at his cave entrance?" To which the other retorts: "All things are incessantly changing. What is there in common between the flint-chipping Stone Age man and the technological worker at those Teeside chemical plants?"

The truth lies somewhere between these opposing principles of change and continuity. Anyone looking at the long story of Yorkshire will at first sight be most aware of the changes. They stand out like signposts on the road of history, indicating so many turns in the way, marking the main lines of progress, pointing down the by-passes, sometimes leading to *cul-de-sacs*. It is only after a closer scrutiny of this or that aspect of Yorkshire life which I have endeavoured to make in this notebook of our heritage that the element of continuity is perceived. The traveller finds that though the road has a new look it is the same in its essential character. A sudden turn may seem to break the continuity, but it leads back to the old road, even though at a different point. As I listen to the daily crash and rumble of demolition and change and read the gloomy predictions of councillors and planners of progress and see the old order changing, bringing strange new sights into remote country villages no less than into great cities, and to ancient highways as to previously untroubled vistas of moorland, I am sometimes tempted to despair. Yet I prefer to detect in it all just one more prank of that sprite which moulds our history into new forms and unexpected patterns but yet cannot change the vital living character of those who live in its broad acres. At some time in the future, maybe, another hand will record these present changes in a notebook of our history – but the basic story will still continue.

Perhaps this is the best reason of all for adding yet one more to the many books on Yorkshire; that each year there is less and less remaining to recall our ancient heritage, that before long the Old Curiosity Shop of Yorkshire may have "Closed" in its window, that the ghosts will no longer be conjured up when their familiar haunts have vanished, that the performance must come to an end when the last of the existing dissolving views of the past has no meaning. But by that time there will be new ghosts, new curiosities and new views, and they will be of our own age and way of life.

Some Books

Few counties of England outside London have called forth so much writing in prose and verse as Yorkshire. The broad acres and their people have been dissected, described, analysed, praised or condemned from the days of the Domesday Survey. One of my rarer treasures is a volume published just a hundred years ago entitled *The Yorkshire Library,* compiled by William Boyne F.S.A. and containing over 300 tightly packed pages listing the works then known of more than 250 authors on some aspect of the county. A similar-sized volume would probably be required to record the contributions of the last century.

Clearly anyone who writes of the county today must have regard to much which has already been written and recorded and will be particularly indebted to many of these volumes, as well as to the many travellers who passed this way and set down their thoughts and impressions in their journals, to the poets who sang of the shire in verse and to the novelists who found their stories and their backgrounds here. There is no space in these pages for another *Yorkshire Library,* but a note of some of the books I have found particularly valuable may be of use to others who would like to know the territory better.

One of the earliest commentators was John Leland, who visited these parts in the middle of the sixteenth century and who wrote an *Itinerary* of his travels. He noted many natural features including "a well of a wonderful nature called Dropping Well" near Knaresborough, which 400 years later still draws its visitors. Michael Drayton, a few years after, devoted one of his songs in *Poly-Olbion* to "the most renowned of Shires" and was incidentally one of the earliest notable visitors to enter the county by way of Blackstone Edge. William Camden, too, came about the same time and included an account of Yorkshire in his *Britannia,* written in Latin prose.

The other travellers I have followed in their journeys have been Richard Brathwaite ('Drunken Barnaby'), whose lively journals have been published under many titles and can be obtained from most antiquarian booksellers; Daniel Defoe, the author of *Robinson Crusoe* of our childhood, whose *Tour Thro' the Whole Island of Great Britain by a Gentleman* first appeared in 1727, and can be obtained in Dent's Everyman series; Thomas Gray, of the "Elegy", whose *Letters* are available in most libraries, as is Charles Dibdin's *Musical Tour of England,* now very scarce.

The Diary of John Evelyn has been frequently reprinted and is obtainable in six volumes or condensed into one, published by Oxford University Press or in a shorter form in an Everyman edition. John Byng (Lord Torrington) wrote twenty-four volumes in *Diary* form covering his extensive travels. These writings were widely dispersed and were only gathered up into an edited form published by Eyre and Spottiswode just before the last war. It is the third of these volumes which deals with his Yorkshire journeys. Lastly, among the travel books, comes *The Journeys of Celia Fiennes.* My much-read copy was published in 1949 by Cresset Press and covers her three major journeys in the South of England, in Yorkshire and the North, and then to the Lake District, the Border country and to Cornwall and London.

A great many other observant travellers came into these parts and left notes of their discoveries and impressions according to their interests. It is part of the pleasure of probing into Yorkshire's heritage to discover how differing aspects of it called forth comment from those who encountered what they regarded as unknown territory, almost as man today regards the moon.

Novelists who took Yorkshire for their scene are thick upon the ground, although many of their writings are, alas, out of print. Of the three of whom I have made special mention, all William Riley's stories were published by Herbert Jenkins, but only three or four are still available. Halliwell Sutcliffe was published by T. Fisher Unwin, but most of his romances are now only obtainable second-hand. Four of Edward Booth's novels were republished in 1956 by Putnams. J. S. Fletcher I will refer to in a moment as a topographical writer, but he too wrote many Yorkshire novels, which, to his mortification, appeared unappreciated in the county. The name of Cutcliffe Hyne is now almost forgotten, although he was an outstanding personality in the Dales, with a lively pen, but his fame was built around a vigorous *Captain Kettle* who could claim few Yorkshire associations.

On the wider stage of literature the parsonage figured prominently. Laurence Sterne, Vicar in turn of Sutton-in-the-Forest, Stillington and Coxwold, gave us *Tristram Shandy* and *The Sentimental Journey*, wherein Yorkshire figured but slightly, save perhaps as inspiration, but away in the West Riding at Haworth the gifted daughters of the Rev. Patrick Bronte gave us in *Wuthering Heights, Jane Eyre* and *Shirley*, brilliant studies of Yorkshire life last century, essential to any understanding of the county. At Foston-le-Clay, between York and Malton, another parsonage was inhabited by the witty Sydney Smith – who unfortunately left little written work about the county but found it congenial ground for his pungent jests.

Charles Dickens, as befitted one who had served his time as a newspaper reporter, made good use of his Yorkshire visits in *Nicholas Nickleby*, in part of *The Lazy Tour of Two Idle Apprentices* (which he wrote with Wilkie Collins) and as the inspiration for *Master Humphrey's Clock* and probably much else besides, transmuted into the familiar characters of his fiction. Tobias Smollett had already, in *Humphrey Clinker*, noted the seaside holiday and its rituals at Scarborough and had been more than a little scornful of Yorkshire hospitality: "I think I can dine better, and for less expense, at the Star and Garter, in Pall-Mall, than at our cousin's castle in Yorkshire."

Sir Walter Scott wrote much verse about the Tees and the Greta, some of which I have quoted, and William Wordsworth, as a considerable traveller in Yorkshire, was moved by its legends and scenery to compose poems on "The White Doe of Rylstone", "Malham Cove" and the "Hart Leap Well", between Askrigg and Richmond, while his sister, Dorothy, might well be included among our distinguished travellers, so graphic are the accounts in her *Diary* of journeys in the county. Rudyard Kipling wrote a love story, *On Greenhow Hill*, and John Ruskin, among many incidental notes on the county, describes a view from Ingleborough and also "a Yorkshire breeze" which was so strong that he had "a vague sense of wonder" as he watched "Ingleborough stand without rocking".

In our own time a galaxy of novelists have made Yorkshire the setting for their stories. Some I have already mentioned as we travelled through the county, but there are still J. B. Priestley (West Riding), Phyllis Bentley (with her wool textile saga which began with *Inheritance*), Storm Jameson (Whitby and the coast), Lettice Cooper (who has written a study of the West Riding as well as many novels) and J. Fairfax-Blakeborough (with his *Lizzie Leckonby* stories). A more modern trend has been the recent discovery of the county as a desirable setting by local writers of crime novels.

Richly endowed as we are with this considerable library of travel and fiction, it is when one looks at the topographical shelves that one is overwhelmed by the wealth of knowledge enshrined in everything from massive tomes on the whole county to slim booklets on a single region, a village, or even its church. I can but pick out a few at random which I could not be without, yet am aware of so many others one dips into for this or that fact or reminiscence or particular study, whether of history or craft or ways of life.

As always one turns to the volumes of the *Victoria County History* (still not completely covering the whole of Yorkshire); the remarkably detailed series of regional histories by the late Harry Speight (who wrote some of his earlier studies under the nom-de-plume of Johnnie Gray); J. S. Fletcher's *Picturesque Yorkshire*, the English Place Names Society's ten volumes covering everything in the three Ridings from towns and villages to field names; the *White Rose Garland* published by the Yorkshire Dialect Society; the long series of volumes (dating back to 1868) of *Transactions of the Yorkshire Archaeological Society*, and the fine run of *Old Yorkshire*, edited by William Smith, as well as the writings of Dr. Whitaker, Walter White (*A Month in Yorkshire*) and J. H. Dixon (*Chronicles and Stories of the Craven Dales*).

All this richness has been supplemented in our own day by the books of Gordon Home, Arthur Norway, Frank Elgee, A. J. Brown, Dr. Arthur Raistrick, Bernard Wood, and the delightful studies of Dales life by Marie Hartley, Ella Pontefract and Joan Ingilby.

The spate continues even as I write, so great is the expanse of Yorkshire, the fascination of its history, the diversity of its interests and its people, the beauty and range of its landscape. Those who live in these parts believe that Drayton was justified in his description of the county as "the most renowned of Shires", and this long roll of its scribes is evidence that its renown is still undimmed.

Index